# The Search
# for God
# at Harvard

# The Search
# for God
# at Harvard

HARVARD UNIVERSITY
## THE DIVINITY SCHOOL
ANDOVER HALL
ROCKEFELLER HALL→

# Ari L. Goldman

TIMES ⓣ BOOKS

RANDOM HOUSE

The Hasidic tales that begin the chapters were taken from *The Hasidic Anthology* by Louis I. Newman.

GRATEFUL ACKNOWLEDGMENT IS MADE TO THE FOLLOWING FOR PERMISSION TO REPRINT PREVIOUSLY PUBLISHED MATERIAL:

*JASON ARONSON, INC.:* EXCERPTS FROM *THE HASIDIC ANTHOLOGY* BY LOUIS I. NEWMAN (FIRST JASON ARONSON HARDCOVER EDITION, 1987). COPYRIGHT 1934 BY CHARLES SCRIBNER'S SONS AND COPYRIGHT © 1963 BY SCHOCKEN BOOKS, INC. REPRINTED BY PERMISSION OF JASON ARONSON, INC.

*TOM LEHRER:* EXCERPT FROM "NATIONAL BROTHERHOOD WEEK" BY TOM LEHRER. COPYRIGHT © 1964 BY TOM LEHRER. REPRINTED BY PERMISSION.

*NAVAJIVAN TRUST:* EXCERPTS FROM *ALL RELIGIONS ARE TRUE* BY MAHATMA GANDHI. REPRINTED BY PERMISSION OF THE NAVAJIVAN TRUST.

LIBRARY OF CONGRESS CATALOGING-IN-PUBLICATION DATA
GOLDMAN, ARI L.
    THE SEARCH FOR GOD AT HARVARD/BY ARI L. GOLDMAN.
        P.      CM.
    ISBN 0-8129-1653-0
        1. JUDAISM—UNITED STATES.    2. JUDAISM—20TH CENTURY.
3. UNITED STATES—RELIGION—20TH CENTURY.
4. GOLDMAN, ARI L.—RELIGION.
5. HARVARD DIVINITY SCHOOL.    I. TITLE.
BM205.G55    1991
291'.0973—DC20                              90-49162

DESIGN BY LEVAVI & LEVAVI, INC.
MANUFACTURED IN THE UNITED STATES OF AMERICA

9  8  7  6  5  4  3  2

FIRST EDITION

To Shira,
Who makes it sing

# Acknowledgments

My parents gave me a love for Judaism and the freedom to pursue a career in journalism; Abe Rosenthal gave me the opportunities. Abe took me on as a reporter at *The New York Times* in 1975 and, ten years later, gave me a sabbatical to study religion at Harvard.

It was at Abe's paper—and for nearly twenty years *The New York Times* was unquestionably Abe's paper—that I learned how to write. I am forever indebted to my colleagues there who helped me, especially the five metropolitan editors for whom I worked, Arthur Gelb, Mitchel Levitas, Sydney Schanberg, Peter Millones and John Darnton.

Several friends read the manuscript of this book at different stages and made generous suggestions that improved the final work. I wish to thank my brothers, Shalom Goldman and Dov Goldman, as well as Irving Wiesen, Peter Steinfels, Richard Shepard, Kenneth Briggs, Nessa Rapoport, Samuel Freedman, David Margolick and Joseph Telushkin.

There were also many who never read a word of the

manuscript but whose support, guidance and friendship helped me make it through. I wish to thank Heinrich Joachim, Arnold Douglas, Dena Kleiman, Sam Howe Verhovek, Dennis Stern, Michael Shapiro, George Vecsey, Edward Kessler, Yehudah Cohn, Josh Barbanel, Jack Nelson, Piva Spinelli and Judy Wilner and the technology office of *The New York Times.*

Three beloved friends—Paul Cowan, Rabbi Eli Chaim Carlebach and Rabbi Wolfe Kelman—passed away in the course of the five years I worked on this book. Each, in his own unique way, continues to have a profound effect on my life, my faith and my work.

My researcher at Harvard, Julia Lieblich, was enthusiastic and thorough, as was the Divinity School's Stephanie Hunt, who helped me track down graduates all over the country. I also wish to acknowledge the many Harvard students who opened up to me about their personal and spiritual lives. In retelling their stories in these pages I have sometimes changed identifying details and used pseudonyms; the stories, however, are those of real people and not composites.

My agent, Bob Markel, was my tireless one-man cheering squad. My editor, Sandee Brawarsky, understood what I needed to say, sometimes even better than I did; she had vision, intelligence and patience and forever challenged me to do better. When the time came, Paul Golob enthusiastically carried the book through its final stages, and Peter Osnos generously shared advice and good counsel. I also wish to thank Susan Horn, Susan M. S. Brown, and Nancy Inglis, who helped with the words; and Naomi Osnos and Nancy Buirski, who helped with the pictures.

Nobody lived with the making of this book more than my wife, Shira. I constantly tried out parts on her at odd hours of the day and night, and she read the manuscript in each of its incarnations. Shira pushed me to write when I didn't think I had the energy or the inspiration. She gave me both, and took on the extra joys and burdens of parenting so that I could find time to write.

My children, Adam and Emma, didn't always understand why Daddy had to disappear to work at the word processor. At the age of six, Adam is a dedicated fan of Batman, and Emma, two, is enamored with Puff, the Magic Dragon. I suspect it will be some time before they can understand what I have written. But, ultimately, I have written for them. I want them to know that while religion can comfort and enrich, it is too important to be taken for granted. Judaism must be probed, studied, questioned and challenged, for, in the struggle, it comes to life.

Ari L. Goldman
New Rochelle, NY
February 1991

# Contents

# The Search
# for God
# at Harvard

# Introduction

F our went down to the orchard. One fell gravely ill and died, one became a heretic, one went mad and one, Rabbi Akiba, emerged whole. I thought of this story from the pages of the Talmud often when, at the age of thirty-five, I moved to Massachusetts with my wife and our infant son to enroll as a graduate student at Harvard Divinity School.

The Talmudic story of the rabbis and the orchard had thrilled me ever since I first heard it as a youngster. These were clearly no ordinary rabbis. The ones I usually learned about in Jewish day school were the type who stayed in the study hall morning to night, learning the holy books and answering the queries of the faithful. Rabbis were not the type who took chances. But this tale provided another model, four adventurers going off like so many early-day versions of Indiana Jones, their black fedoras cocked at rakish angles, heading for the orchard . . . and trouble. But where were they going? This obviously was no simple orchard of dates and apples. What trouble were the rabbis courting? And why the ominous three-to-one odds? One survivor. One heretic. One madman. One dead.

There are several interpretations of this Talmudic tale, which dates to the first century. The explanation that has always made the most sense to me is that the adventurers were embarking on a perilous interfaith journey. Rome beckoned, with its philosophy, art, science and letters. So did Christianity, with its message of love in an era when rabbinic Judaism was being set into law with the Mishna, the legal code that often appeared to emphasize Judaism's rules over its compassion. Alternatives to Judaism were there, gleaming and shining and easily within reach, like fruits on a tree in an orchard. As God had once told Adam and Eve, the Talmudic story had an implicit warning about these tempting fruits: "Don't touch."

I was born nearly two thousand years later and two continents away, in 1949 in Hartford, Connecticut. Still, the story of the rabbis and the orchard resonated. Well into my adulthood, the threat of the pagan and Christian worlds loomed large for me. The "Don't touch" signs still hung beside the trees.

Now, in 1985, as an adult, I was enrolling as a student at Harvard Divinity School, the result of an unusual leave of absence from my job as a reporter for *The New York Times.* I was going to Harvard for a year to study comparative religion—and all I could see were forbidden fruits. What could I expect from my encounter with Harvard Divinity School? Would I emerge whole, like Rabbi Akiba, or suffer the fate of Elisha Ben Avuya, the brilliant young Jewish scholar who emerged the heretic? Or worse, would I go mad or simply expire?

These might seem like strange and powerful fears for someone who had been exposed to just about every human and municipal failure as a reporter working for ten years in New York City. Before going to Harvard, I had written about—and rubbed shoulders with—corruption, murder, drug addiction, disease, crime, the subways, City Hall and the Statehouse. The study of the development of religious thought would seem tame, almost pure, to most people. But my apprehensions, complete with the Talmudic parables dancing in my head, were far more emotional—and even mystical—than they were rational.

Maybe it was the words of my great-aunt Minnie, a regal woman in her nineties who blended religious piety with a strong streak of superstition. It was Aunt Minnie who had helped raise me after my parents were divorced when I was six years old. Now, three decades later, Aunt Minnie was very much opposed to my going to study religion at Harvard. "You have one of the best schools for religious studies right here in New York—Yeshiva University," she told me. But when she realized that I was going to Cambridge despite her entreaties, she gave me her blessing. "Remember," she whispered in my ear at a family gathering shortly before I left for Cambridge. "You can study all the religions, but Judaism is the best."

In my family, Judaism meant only one thing: Orthodoxy. I come from an unusual American Orthodox family. The most unusual thing about it is that it is still Orthodox. There is an ugly adage about American Jewry that I was brought up on, although not until years later did I realize it was not only ugly but false. The adage goes like this: The first generation is Orthodox, the second is Conservative, the third is Reform and the fourth is Christian. I am a third-generation American-born Orthodox Jew. All four of my grandparents were born in the United States, all of them, in fact, on the Lower East Side of Manhattan, the sons and daughters of the migration in the late 1800s of Russian and Polish Jews. For over a century, we kept "authentic Judaism," as we saw it, and that burden of family history weighed heavily on my shoulders.

Enrolling at Harvard University was yet another step in the sometimes reluctant worldly education of an Orthodox yeshiva boy who was not always sure it was worthwhile to be worldly. I was brought up in a warm cocoon of Orthodox observance, and when I cautiously ventured forth, propelled by a curiosity and a hunger to experience the world, I often felt it was a mistake. Maybe I should have stayed home.

The story of my religious exploration is different from that of some of my friends who were brought up in assimilated Jewish homes and then spent their adulthoods looking for their Jewish roots and the meaning of religion in their lives. Anne Roiphe and the late Paul Cowan spoke eloquently for these searchers in their respective books *Generation Without Memory* and *An Orphan in History*. As Paul put it, he was looking inside himself for Saul Cohen, the descendant of rabbis in Germany and Lithuania.

I never had to search. My parents gave me the Hebrew name Ari, which means "lion," then backed it up with the somewhat redundant middle name Lionel, just in case I needed or chose to avail myself of a Christian name. (As it has turned out, I've never used Lionel.) If anything, over the generations, my family—which found refuge in America from the persecutions and economic hardships of Eastern Europe—was becoming more and more confident of its religious place in the world. While in another family the name Saul Cohen was evolving into Paul Cowan, in my family, the name of my namesake, my great-grandfather Louis Goldmann, was becoming Ari Goldman.

For me, the challenge was not Judaism, but the non-Jewish world. First, as a reporter for *The New York Times* on a variety of subjects, I encountered the secular world, taking in its pleasures with mixed emotions. Later, as a religion writer for *The Times*, I was plunged into New York's diversity of churches, synagogues, mosques, temples and other, more private, forms of religious expression. Through it all, I remained the outsider, knowledgeable enough about my subject to write about it, but detached enough not to feel it. Not feeling it, in fact, is supposed to make you a better reporter, truer to the journalistic god of objectivity. If for the sports reporter there is no cheering in the press box, then for the religion writer there are no "Amens" after the sermon and no humming along with the church choir.

After a year of writing about religion with the detachment that had always served me well as a reporter, I approached my editors with a request for a one-year leave of absence. The idea was that I would go to Harvard—the most prestigious of American divinity schools—for a dispassionate encounter with Christianity and the religions of the East, then return to *The Times* to write about religion with greater knowledge and authority.

Much to my surprise, I found that Harvard Divinity School was in the throes of its own administrative and philosophical nightmares, troubles that in many ways were a metaphor for a broader crisis of religious faith in America. Mainline Protestant religion, which the Divinity School had once come to exemplify, had lost its way in the 1980s. Nonetheless, the obstinate spirit that for more than a century had propelled Harvard Divinity managed to shine through. At Harvard Divinity, I learned that there is little dispassionate about the study of religion. From my first day at the Div School, as it was known on campus, I was emotionally engaged and spiritually challenged.

At first I tried to resist. In those opening days of school, I carried a small reporter's notebook wherever I went, ostensibly as a way to record the experience. It was one of those lean spiral books that fit neatly in one hand, just right for jotting down the sounds and sights of a train wreck. The notebook has also served another purpose; it has long been my shield against getting involved. In church, it assured me I was not a Christian; in the hospital, it said I wasn't sick; in the police station, it said I wasn't in trouble; at the gay rights parade, it said I was straight.

My shield seemed to work fine for the reporter on the street, but it was wrong for the student of religion. I had to come to terms with the fact that the incessant scribbling was a way of hearing but not feeling. After several days at school, I put the notebook down and allowed myself to enter the worlds I had so feared. Cautiously, I let myself experience Buddhist meditation, Christian hymns, Muslim poetry.

No, I did not convert. My deeply nurtured Jewish identity never seriously came under siege. But what did happen was an extraordinary dialogue, one between the religious ideas that I encountered and the Jewish ideas within myself. The dialogue continued every day in the classroom, in the words of the New Testament, the Koran, the Upanishads and in fellowship at my own Sabbath table, around which I assembled people of various faiths. As a result of these encounters, I learned how others experience their faith. But more important, I developed a richer and fuller understanding of myself and my own Judaism.

In many ways, the year at Harvard helped knit together the many diverse facets of my life, my stormy childhood, my disordered education, my passion for journalism and the powerful, mystical pull faith continues to have on me. And I hope that many of these themes, while intensely personal, will resound for others who are struggling to understand their own lives and their own religious traditions.

Every pollster will tell you that there is a renewed interest in religion today among Americans of all faiths. The problem is that the interest of most people ends at the doors of their own churches or synagogues or mosques. By and large, Christians are interested in Christianity, Muslims care about Islam and Jews want to know about Judaism. It is a phenomenon that goes back to the first century, when the Talmud fretted over the four searchers who went down to the orchard.

This is a memoir about what happened to me when I went down to the twentieth-century version of the Talmudic orchard. To say that it changed me forever is only the beginning of my story.

# Orientation

Who is a wise man? He who learns from all men.

— Simeon ben Zoma,
in *Ethics of the Fathers*

I t began with a funeral. I bounded up the gray stone steps leading to the cathedral-like Divinity School building in the northern reaches of the Harvard campus with excitement and an extra measure of the normal fears that accompany any new enterprise. It was a sunny and crisp fall day, the kind that New England is famous for. The leaves on the tall patrician trees on Francis Avenue had already put on their autumnal colors and made a blazing canopy for my arrival. I reached the great oak doors of Divinity Hall, put my hand on the heavy brass door latch and then I spotted the sign: "Due to the Funeral Mass of George MacRae, HDS Orientation Has Been Cancelled for the Morning."

Five days before orientation was to begin, the Reverend George W. MacRae, the acting dean of Harvard Divinity School, collapsed and died while leading a spiritual retreat at a Catholic seminary in nearby Brighton. He was fifty-seven years old. MacRae was a Jesuit, a member of that intellectual and progressive order of Catholic clergy that spawned the peace activist Daniel Berrigan and Father Robert Drinan, the liberal member of Congress who gave up his congressional seat at the insistence of the Vatican. MacRae, a New Testament scholar and member of a committee preparing a new Protestant translation of the Bible, seemed like an appropriate person to be the first Catholic to head Harvard's very Protestant divinity school. He had received the appointment less than two months before his death.

Disoriented by the death of a man I never knew, I followed a solemn line of students and faculty across Harvard Yard and into St. Paul's Roman Catholic Church for the funeral mass. I took my seat among the mourners as the organ played sad and robust melodies. A procession of white-robed priests, led by Bernard Cardinal Law of Boston, entered, followed by deacons and an assortment of altar boys. An all-boys choir sang.

I shifted uncomfortably in my seat. No matter how many times I have been in church—and, as a reporter, I often find myself in one—I never feel right. One of the Orthodox rabbis of my youth, a Rabbi Siegel, always seems to catch up with me there, waving his finger in my face even before he starts talking. "A church? What are you doing in a church? Didn't you study Jewish history? Don't you know what they did to our people in the name of that cross? Didn't I tell you that it is forbidden to step into a church? No. No excuses. I don't care who died. I don't care if there is a storm outside. I don't care if the whole world is on fire and this is the only escape. Out of the church. Out. Out. Out."

I took my spiral reporter's notebook out of my pocket and impulsively began jotting down words from the eulogies. Most of them, including Cardinal Law's, were pretty prosaic. ("His ministry continues in the lives of us all.") But I was struck by the words of MacRae's nephew, Gordon MacRae, like his uncle a Roman Catholic priest. "The most profound search of my uncle's life was not for wisdom or knowledge, but for peace," the young MacRae said. What a fine tribute to a man who, after all, was a scholar. The nephew looked out into the church, which was crowded with MacRae's colleagues and students, and said, "My family shared George's blood, but you have shared his soul." A cut above, I thought. I was able to see the profound influence George MacRae had had on this young priest and understood why he had chosen to follow in his uncle's footsteps; maybe he was the son that MacRae could never have as a celibate Catholic priest. For a moment, I mourned George MacRae, or maybe I mourned that I would never be touched by him.

Cardinal Law, a strappingly handsome Harvard graduate with a full head of white hair, celebrated the funeral mass. I had never seen him before, although I was familiar with the American church leader he was then most often linked with, John Cardinal O'Connor, the archbishop of New York. I came to Harvard after covering O'Connor during the 1984 presidential election, when he was taunting Geraldine Ferraro, the Democratic vice presidential nominee, for her stand on abortion. Ferraro, a Catholic who supported the right of women to choose whether or not to have an abortion, once signed a letter that said there was a "diversity of Catholic opinion" on abortion. O'Connor said there was no such diversity, rather there was only one Catholic position on abortion—that it is not permitted.

Joining in the O'Connor attack from Boston was Bernard Cardinal Law. Law and O'Connor (sometimes jokingly referred to as Law and Order) are both very polished, very personable and very conservative. Both had been appointed by Pope John Paul II to key posts in the American Catholic hierarchy the year before the 1984 election. The appointments were an important element in the Pope's plan to bring the American Catholic church in line with orthodox doctrine.

Law stood at the altar surrounded by a dozen priests, who looked at him in what seemed like genuine awe as he lifted the communion wafer above his head and recounted the words of Jesus, words that in the Catholic belief would transform the wafer into the body of their Lord. "He broke the bread, gave it to his disciples and said: 'Take this, all of you, and eat it. This is my body, which will be given up for you.' " I noticed the assembled priests silently mouth the words of Jesus along with the cardinal.

Law put down the broken wafer and lifted the cup. "When supper was ended, he took the cup. Again he gave thanks and praise, gave the cup to his disciples, and said: 'Take this, all of you, and drink from it.' " Again I saw the lips of the assisting priests move in unison. " 'This is the cup of my blood, the blood of the new and everlasting covenant. It will be shed for you and for all, so that sins may be forgiven. Do this in memory of me.' "

I've always admired the Catholic Mass as it moves from this moment of consecration to the sharing of communion with all members of the church. It is so much more dignified than the Jewish *kiddush*, the collation of sweet red wine and sponge cake that follows the Sabbath service. After the synagogue prayers on Saturday morning, the crowd descends to the social hall and stands chattering around the tables of food while waiting for the rabbi to say the *b'racha*, the blessing, on the wine so that everyone can begin. I grew up with these b'rachas, an essential part of the everyday life of an Orthodox youngster. *"Baruch atah Adonai Eloheynu Melech Ha'olam hamotzi lechem min ha'aretz,"* one says before eating bread. "Blessed are you, God, King of the Universe, who brings forth bread from the ground." There is another b'racha for vegetables (". . .who brings forth the produce of the ground") and another for pastries (". . .who created different kinds of cakes"). And then there is a whole different category—b'rachas that you say when you see lightning or a rainbow, b'rachas after recovering from an illness and, most routinely, a long laundry list of b'rachas in the daily prayers—giving thanks for waking up, for freedom, for new clothes, for the ability to study Torah—there is even one, recited by boys and men, thanking God for not

making us women, and another, recited by males and fe-
males, praising God for not making us Gentiles. Upon leaving the bathroom, we make a b'racha thanking God for our
internal plumbing system. In yeshiva, our rebbe taught us
that "a good Jew" has to say one hundred b'rachas a day.

My mother spent my childhood years on b'racha patrol,
making sure that nothing would pass my lips without thanks
to the Almighty properly expressed. After she gave me a
cookie, she would watch closely for the mumble. Saying
b'rachas is a habit that never left me, and it still sometimes
looks like I am talking to my food before I pop it in my
mouth. It is an involuntary act and, on those rare occasions
when I think about what it is that I'm doing, I kind of like
it. In the great scheme of things, it seems only right to give
thanks.

Still, with all this reflexive Jewish background and a thousand b'rachas on my tongue, I feel irresistibly drawn to
Communion, the high point of the Catholic Mass. Unlike
the kiddush after the synagogue service, at Communion
there is no need to reach across the table and secure a piece
of sponge cake and a shot glass of wine. For the Catholic, it
is total submission. Open your mouth and the wafer is
placed there. Open your mouth and the cup is placed on
your lips, "so that sins may be forgiven." There is no work
involved. Just give yourself over to Jesus and you will be
saved. It is entirely different from the Jewish approach; the
Jew must work for his redemption, whether at the kiddush
table, in the study hall or in the marketplace.

I am sitting in church at George MacRae's funeral and
imagine myself lifted from my pew. In my daydream, I join
the line of Catholics—good, confessed and fasting Catholics
—leading up to the cardinal, who stands at the altar in his
white robe and embroidered stole. A gold cross dangles from
a chain around his neck. Some open their mouths reverently
and the cardinal places the wafer on their tongues; others,
in accord with the reforms of Vatican II, hold out their
hands, accept the wafer and put it in their mouths them-

selves. I am now standing face to face with the cardinal, and I hear him whisper the words "Body of Christ" as he directs the wafer to my mouth. I say my b'racha, thanking the Almighty for the bread of the earth. I open my mouth and I eat His flesh.

It was ironic that my first Harvard experience should be a Catholic one. Harvard is deeply rooted in the American Protestant tradition, having been founded in 1636 by the General Court of the Massachusetts Bay Colony as a training ground for Puritan ministers. Two years later, the school took the name of a major benefactor, John Harvard, himself a Boston preacher. The colonial legislators and John Harvard no more expected Catholics to be in his school than they expected Jews or blacks to be there.

Div School administrators love to remind the rest of Harvard of the university's original purpose. The Div School catalog, in fact, is the only one at Harvard to include the following quotation from an early document about the founding of the school:

> After God had carried us safe to New England and we had builded our houses, provided necessaries for our livelihood, rear'd convenient places for God's worship, and settled the civil government: One of the next things we longed for and looked after was to advance learning and perpetuate it to posterity; dreading to leave an illiterate ministry to the churches, when our present ministers shall lie in the dust.

Religion was so much a part of everyday learning in the early days of Harvard that for nearly two centuries no one thought of setting up a separate Divinity School. In the college, students gathered daily for prayer and readings from the Scripture. Hebrew as well as Greek were required subjects, because an educated person was expected to be able to read the Bible in the original tongues. Those graduates who aspired to the ministry "tarried in Cambridge or its environs to read on their own in the College Library, or with the

President, or with some established minister," according to the school's official history. "For the 17th and 18th Century divine, there was no professional degree," the history notes.

But in the early nineteenth century, the first graduate program in "ministerial studies" was organized. When that program accepted its first class in 1816, the Divinity School was born. The Div School became the second professional school of the university. (Harvard Medical School was founded in 1782.)

For most of Harvard, the religious roots of the university —like the religious curriculum—had long been forgotten by the time I enrolled. The Div School went from being the centerpiece of the university to being an awkward stepchild. There was even talk in the 1950s of closing it down. What was the place of religion at a modern—and therefore fully secular—university?

During the nineteenth century, Harvard Divinity was for all purposes an arm of the Unitarian church and served as a principal training ground for its ministers and church leaders. In the early 1900s, the school severed its denominational ties and began training ministers for all Protestant churches. The Div School does not ordain anyone, however. It trains students in Scripture and theology, then sends them back to their denominations to be ordained. In recent years, the school, operating with a vision that Christianity cannot be studied in isolation, has developed a strong department for the study of world religions. All candidates for the Christian ministry must take at least one course in world religions in each of their three years of study. Today, the Div School faculty is as well known for its Islamicists and Hindu scholars as for its Christian theologians.

Much of this background can be gleaned from the school's catalog. The image it conjures is of a devout and sober, if not celibate, student body, determined to shape the future of the American Protestant church. That, at least, is what my wife, Shira, and I thought when we arrived at the Harvard Divinity School Orientation Dance.

The event sounded serious, even if it was billed as a dance, so we fished out of our trunk some preppy-looking khakis and tweeds. Anticipating an evening of hymns and mulled cider, we told the baby-sitter we'd be home early. The party was being held at the Div School Refectory—from the Latin *refectus*, "to make again, renew, restore"—so how much of this could we really endure?

As we approached, music was blaring from the Refectory, and lights were flashing on and off. We checked the invitation to be sure we were at the right place on the right night. What we encountered inside was spiked hair, fishnet stockings, short skirts and couples, both heterosexual and homosexual, dancing to U2, Michael Jackson and Duran Duran.

We called the baby-sitter and told her we'd be late.

With that night, I began to get to know my fellow students and their stories. There was Ann—the one with the fishnet stockings—who had given up her job as a buyer at Lord & Taylor to train to become a Unitarian minister. And there was Justin, a twenty-three-year-old midwesterner from a family of ten children, a Roman Catholic with a girlfriend, who flirted with the idea of becoming a celibate priest.

There was Lynda, a forty-one-year-old mother of three who happened on the religion listings in a Harvard catalog and pursued them with a passion she never knew she had. And there was Robert, a middle-aged banker who decided to devote his life to God after he saw his bank go under and his wife deteriorate into alcoholism. (Robert did not abandon all earthly pleasures, however; his dark blue Mercedes stood out in the Div School parking area, which usually had the look of a used-car lot.) There was Diane, an apple-cheeked all-American kid from suburban Detroit who was the leader of the school's Gay and Lesbian Caucus. And there was Soho, a Buddhist monk from Japan who brought his search for nirvana to the Harvard campus.

The students were enrolled in one of two basic master's degree courses. One is known as the M.Div., or master of divinity, the degree for those aspiring to the ministry. It is a three-year program that enables the student to go to his or her Protestant denomination to be ordained.

The second basic degree is the M.T.S., the master of theological studies. One administrator described this to me as "the most popular and most useless of our programs." The reasonable assumption was that those with the M.T.S. would become educators or go on to pursue higher degrees, such as a doctorate in theological studies, also offered at the Div School. I soon found out, however, that the most unwelcome question one could ask students in the M.T.S. program was what they planned to do after graduation. Most of them, it seemed, hadn't the foggiest idea.

In this sense, I found the Divinity School very refreshing. In an age when most students on college and university campuses were increasingly oriented toward landing good jobs and making oodles of money, here I was surrounded by those who wanted to pursue the ministry (one of the worst-paying professions) or simply pass the time until they knew what to do with their lives. In many ways, it was a school that belonged to a different era, the sixties perhaps, a time when questions like "What are you going to do for society?" and "What are you doing tonight?" seemed so much more pressing than "How are you going to make a living?" At Harvard Divinity, the hair was worn a little longer than at the other schools of Harvard and the jeans tended to be torn and faded rather than designer.

I felt taken back to my college days. From 1967 to 1971, I attended Yeshiva College in Manhattan, the undergraduate school of Yeshiva University. The rebellion, excitement and turmoil of the times did not escape my largely Orthodox Jewish college. After all, we were only a few subway stops away from Columbia, the epicenter of student rebellion in 1968. We felt the shock waves and the sense of liberation that the students there helped spread. Finding myself back as an adult, it was good to be in a school that in many ways was a throwback to my earlier student days, even if I had made the transition from a Jewish to a Christian school.

In my first days at the Div School, I was still somewhat pleased with myself that I had been admitted to Harvard. But after talking with some of my fellow students, I was brought down a few notches. I learned that the Div School is the second easiest school at Harvard to get into. (The easiest is the School of Education.) Divinity accepts 60 to 70 percent of applicants. And that is a piece of cake when compared with Harvard College, which accepts fewer than 20 percent, or the Law School, which takes only 10 percent of those who have the confidence to apply. With about 450 students—just over half of them women—the Div School is the second smallest of Harvard's graduate schools, just a tad bigger than the School of Public Health.

The Div School is also one of the cheapest—$6,640 the year I was there. Not only is it far less expensive than the other schools (the Law School was a third more expensive and the Med School twice as much), but a full 85 percent of Div School students attend on some form of scholarship. I was one of the tiny minority who were paying full fare, and that was only because my newspaper was footing the bill.

Aside from the tuition, *The Times* continued to pay my full salary, picked up the cost of moving my family to Massachusetts and subsidized the rent on our Somerville apartment. It was like winning the lottery. And for weeks after arriving I still couldn't believe our good fortune.

It had all been very unexpected. I had been writing about religion for a year when I had a routine lunch with my boss, the metropolitan editor, Peter Millones. "What I really need to do this job right," I told Millones, "is a year studying comparative religion. It's a shame Abe doesn't allow leaves." Abe was A. M. Rosenthal, who as executive editor made every important decision at *The New York Times* and was rarely contradicted by his subordinates.

"I think it is a mistake," Millones said.

"What?" I said, not quite believing my ears. Millones was about as loyal to Rosenthal as they came.

"I think it is a mistake that Abe doesn't allow leaves of

absence, especially for something worthwhile like you mentioned. Ari, why don't you write up a proposal about taking a year to study religion, and I'll give it to Abe."

The next day Millones had a proposal on his desk with my three options for study—Union Theological Seminary in New York, the Divinity School at the University of Chicago and Harvard Divinity School. Within a few days, the proposal came back to me with Union and Chicago crossed out. No one ever explained the decision to me, but I assumed it was the Harvard name that carried the day; in academic circles, however, Chicago was considered a superior school. I didn't really care. I was blissfully on my way to Harvard.

On my last day in the office before going off to Harvard, Elizabeth Eller, the enterprising Metro Desk office manager, called and said that John Vinocur, who had just arrived from Paris to be the deputy metropolitan editor, wanted to see me right away. When I got to his desk, there were a half dozen bottles of champagne and a stack of plastic cups. Soon corks were popping, and everyone—from copyboy to editor—was shaking my hand and wishing me well. Peter Millones was out of the office, so the usually irascible Vinocur raised his cup in a good-natured toast. "Ari, I don't know you very well. But I know I am speaking for everyone here when I say, 'I am as jealous as all hell.' "

One of the reasons I was thrilled about going to Harvard was the reputation of the outstanding faculty at the Div School, but another one of the lessons of orientation was that most of the prominent faculty members had either left the school or were themselves on leaves of absence. The names of those who had left the Div School in recent years were far more illustrious than those who had stayed. George Rupp, the former dean who had reorganized the curriculum, had left to become president of Rice University. Henri Nouwen, a popular Catholic lecturer, had left for a monastery in France, but not before blasting the Divinity School for lacking in Christian spirituality. Krister Stendahl, a former dean and pioneer in Jewish-Christian relations, had left to become the Lutheran bishop of Stockholm. And Harvey Cox, the faculty member who was launched into fame by his 1965 best-seller *The Secular City*, was on one of his frequent sabbaticals the year I attended. In addition, the List Chair of Jewish Studies had remained unfilled since it had been endowed three years earlier. Add to this the death of George MacRae, who, in addition to being acting dean, was the Charles Chauncey Stillman Professor of Roman Catholic Theological Studies. The Harvard faculty looked pretty much decimated.

One of the first faculty members I met was Rusty Martin, a genial, redheaded Quaker in his forties who is an expert in post-Reformation English church history. He taught one course a year and spent the rest of the time, with the title associate dean, ballyhooing the Div School's virtues as its principal fund-raiser. With me, however, Martin was very candid about the school's shortcomings. In part, this reflected a certain openness, but it also was an outgrowth of the turmoil and unhappiness many on the faculty felt. Martin, I was to learn, was only one of many who were looking for jobs elsewhere. "We're running on our reputation," Martin confided to me at one orientation function. With a name like Harvard, though, it seemed the school could run with mediocrity for quite a while before too many people would notice.

I got to meet the remaining Div School faculty members over the next few days of orientation in tea-and-cookie receptions that were supposed to be informal but made almost everyone uncomfortable. At some point, the chairman of a department would genteelly bang a spoon against a glass to quiet the room. Then we were introduced to the faculty.

"Aren't they embarrassed?" I wrote in my little notebook. "Harvard professors are standing up like snake-oil hucksters trying to convince us to take their courses." The sales pitches took place during three orientation sessions that introduced us to the school's principal areas of study:

Scripture, Christianity and World Religions. One by one, the professors stood up before this audience of incoming students and told what their courses would be like. "A few are electrifying," I wrote of the lecturers, "but most I feel sorry for."

While the sessions provided glimpses into what different faculty members were like, they gave a false impression of accessibility. It soon became obvious that the faculty made their presentations because they had to. To my amazement (if not disappointment), most then disappeared for the year into their classrooms or offices hidden among the library stacks.

The four days of orientation also gave me an introduction to the numerous interest groups on campus. I began to perceive a decided left-wing tilt. Everyone, it seemed, had organized a caucus. There was the Black Caucus, the Women's Caucus, the Roman Catholic Caucus, the Gay and Lesbian Caucus, even the Jewish Caucus.

I was among about a dozen students who showed up for the Jewish meeting in a tiny dining alcove off the Refectory. It was there that I learned the dangers of asking what people planned to do with their degrees. None of the Jewish students was there to become a rabbi; only Christian denominations accept the Div School training for their clergy. All the Jewish branches require rabbinical school. So what were the Jewish students doing here? They all spoke in generalities about the joys of studying comparative religion and then quickly changed the subject when I asked of what practical value this would be after they graduated. All but one of the Jewish students were candidates for the M.T.S. degree. The one who was pursuing the M.Div. degree—the course of study for Christian ministers—was really at a loss to explain her intentions. She was a kinetic young woman named Sally, who went on excitedly about making a Friday-night dinner at the beginning of the Sabbath and inviting the Christian faculty to a "Jewish experience." From the way she spoke, I knew it would never happen.

As I left the Jewish student meeting, I stopped to look in at the Gay and Lesbian Caucus Tea, which was in full swing with scores of participants in the Braun Room, the stately reception room of the school, which had a gallery of portraits of Divinity School deans in full academic garb going back nearly one hundred years. The gay and lesbian students were talking animatedly in what looked more like a party without music than a student planning meeting. From the wood-paneled walls, I thought I saw the faces of the former deans stare down with fascination.

# CHAPTER 2

# First Days

A man expressed the wish in the presence of the Belzer Rabbi to die like a good Jew. The Rabbi commented: "Such a wish is wrong. Desire rather that you may live like a good Jew, and it will follow as a consequence that you will die like a good Jew."

"My first real class in twelve years," I wrote in my reporter's notebook. I was sitting in the Div School's main lecture hall, the Sperry Room, recording my impressions as my classmates were writing down what the professor was saying. "Not since I graduated Journalism School have I been in a situation like this. And that wasn't really school—that was job training. But this—a course in contemporary theology at Harvard—this is school. Probably more school per inch in this lecture hall than I have experienced at any time in my life. It's at once scary and exhilarating."

The hall, named for Willard Sperry, dean of the Div School in the 1930s and 1940s, had 135 seats covered in red fabric and tiered upward from a well where the instructor stood. The room, complete with an arched ceiling, exposed wooden beams and leaded-glass windows, was right out of one of those old movies on late-night TV about Freud in Vienna. But instead of Dr. Freud defending his theories on psychoanalysis, Dr. Sharon Welch was introducing us to the ideas of Tillich, Rahner, Barth and Bultmann. The names were, of course, different from those I had studied in Jewish schools, but more than that, the language being used was different. In my sixteen years of yeshiva education—a stint that began with first grade and took me through college—I never studied theology in the real sense of the word. I studied religion.

Theology is, simply put, the study of God and of God's relationship to the universe. The word comes from the Greek words *theo,* meaning "God," and *logos,* meaning "discourse." God-talk is much more of a Christian concern than a Jewish one. From the earliest centuries of Christianity, there were debates—they called them councils, held in places like Nicaea and Chalcedon—about the relationship of man to God and of God the Father to God the Son. Augustine puzzled about the Godly realm and the earthly sphere, and Martin Luther about salvation. The debates about the nature of God continued right up to our own time, when in the 1960s Christian theologians began to ask the question "Is God dead?"

The Orthodox Judaism I was brought up with never bothered itself with God-talk. Instead, Judaism was focused on doing, what we call *mitzvahs,* good deeds which we were told made us better Jews. In this system, understanding the nature of God is not important. Doing mitzvahs is all that matters. There are 613 mitzvahs in the Torah and thousands more added by the rabbis in the Talmud and the legal codes that followed. They apply to daily personal and religious life, two realms which became almost indistinguishable.

Mitzvahs shape the life. Upon waking, immediately wash your hands. Then thank God for "restoring my soul" after the night's sleep. After using the toilet, thank God "who with wisdom fashioned the human body, creating openings, arteries, glands and organs, marvelous in structure, intricate in design." Put your right shoe on first, then your left shoe; but tie the left one first, and then the right. Prayer, either individual or communal, comes before breakfast. Put on your prayer shawl and bind the tefillin—black leather straps and boxes containing verses of Scripture—on your left arm and forehead. Breakfast is, of course, kosher. No ham and eggs here. If you are having bread, ritually wash your hands. After eating, say grace. And don't forget to wear your yarmulke.

And mitzvahs don't end there. Being honest in business, telling the truth, sharing with a friend, honoring one's parents, visiting the sick, giving charity to the poor, all these are mitzvahs too. When my mother wasn't pushing b'rachas, she was making sure I would do my mitzvahs. "Ari, honey, do a mitzvah," she would implore in all seriousness, "take out the garbage." God is, of course, somewhere in this system of mitzvahs, but the practitioner is usually too busy to notice. Rather than theology, this is a system of religion in the purest sense of the word. Religion, from the Latin *religare*, "to bind back."

Each of the mitzvahs binds a Jew back to history. Sabbath, for example, commemorates Creation. Passover, the redemption of the Exodus. Shavuoth, the giving of the Torah. Hanukkah, the rededication of the Temple. The modern Jewish holidays do the same. Yom Hashoah commemorates the Holocaust. Yom Ha'atzmaut, Israel's independence.

So studying Christian theology conflicted with studying Jewish religion in a dualism that has been called Christian creed versus Jewish deed. At the same time, there was another, related dualism, involved for me in this academic exercise. Couched in philosophic terms, it was the struggle between learning and experience. More simply put, I was afraid of school.

I had always gone with experience. School never interested me, and, as a result, I was a lousy student. I have always attributed my poor academic performance to my street-smart intelligence, stemming from an early awareness that what was really important in life was going on outside the classroom. Growing up in the late 1950s and

early 1960s, I knew I was ahead of my time. It wasn't until
the late 1960s that it seemed the rest of the country caught
up with me. School, the counterculture declared, was irrelevant.

But there was another reason for my poor student performance: my parents' divorce. The divorce came when I was
about to enter the first grade and made the whole notion of
a supportive home environment for traditional learning a
preposterous dream. Truly, what was going on in my personal life outside the classroom was far more compelling
than the ABC's. To be sure, experience was much more
important than learning.

So I accepted, almost as a fact of life, that I was a poor
student. Despite this—or maybe because of this—I was a
popular kid. I put my energies into what I enjoyed most—
writing, singing, clowning about for my classmates, all the
while never forgetting to do my share of mitzvahs.

So my baggage to Harvard was heavy. Aside from my
antitheological bent, I arrived with a deep-rooted antipathy
to the academic world. Still, despite myself, I was determined that, for once in my life, I would make school the
centerpiece, a kind of penance for the missed classes and lost
learning, for the years of clowning and excessive doing.

At breakfast the first morning of school, Shira noticed. I
sat silently mixing my cereal.

"Nervous?" she asked.

I said nothing.

"Listen, relax. When you were a kid, you were from a
broken home. Now, you are from a happy home."

She looked at our one-year-old son, Adam, happily mas-
saging oatmeal into his curly blond hair. The floor was spat-
tered with the rest of his meal—apple slices, Cheerios and
gobs of yogurt. "Dirty, maybe. But happy."

The first few days of the Harvard semester alone provided
ample opportunity to forgive many past academic sins.
Following the four days of orientation came the next pre-
paratory phase: "the shopping period." With my new

excitement about academic learning, I viewed this as the transformation of Harvard into the midway of a giant amusement park. For me, the campus was filled with a thousand carnival booths, each brimming with delectable opportunities. Some were games of chance, unknown courses with titillating titles ("Magic, Science, Religion, and the Question of Rationality" or "Religious Healing"), and others were a sure thing, like cotton candy ("American Religious History" or "The Cultural Legacy of the Ancient Near East"). Students walked quickly through the halls with open catalogs, zipping in and out of classrooms, collecting syllabi and impressions.

I was the boy on the midway with a dollar bill who wanted to taste everything, not caring that a stomachache awaited him the next morning. There were the two hundred courses offered by the Divinity School alone, but also, through a cooperative effort called the Boston Theological Institute, scores more available from the catalogs of eight other Boston-area divinity schools, encompassing Jesuit, Greek Orthodox and Evangelical Christianity. Add to this all the courses in Harvard's undergraduate and graduate Arts and Sciences offerings. There were no restrictions, few requirements. The possibilities were limitless.

I was walking down the hallway of the Div School, on my way to sample a class called "Constructing the Concept of God," taught by the Christian theologian Gordon Kaufman. From the corner of my eye I thought I saw my rebbe, Rabbi Siegel, standing in a doorway dressed as a clown. His mouth was circled by big red lips painted sloppily over his black beard. His voice sounded like the canned laughter pouring out of the carnival fun house. "Look at this, look at this," he said, rocking back and forth, waving the Divinity School catalog in the air. "Constructing the Concept of God," he read, holding the catalog up to his nose. "The intention is to encourage students to examine critically their own thinking about God with a view to reconstructing it appropriately for contemporary life."

When he pulled the catalog from his face, the smile and clown outfit were gone. Rabbi Siegel stood there sternly before me in his black suit. "Reconstructing God!" he boomed. "You want to know who God is? God created heaven and earth. God split the Red Sea. God made water flow from the rock. God saved your parents from the flames of Auschwitz! But He didn't do it so that you could come here, to this unholy place, to *reconstruct the image of God!*"

I turned and ran down the hall.

After the first week, I narrowed my choices to nine courses, five more than I could take. Even with my specific goals—I wanted to understand why and how people practice religion so that I could be a better journalist—I had trouble paring down my list. In the end, a mix of lecturing styles, hunches and maybe even the ghosts of some old rabbis helped me make my decisions. Unlike most students making such choices, I, somewhat naively, did not consider require-ments, such as term papers, reading lists and final examina-tions. These, I thought, I could handle without any problem. After all, I was a professional writer, accustomed to turning out thousand-word news stories in an hour and catchy fea-tures in an afternoon. Academic papers and exams would be a cinch.

A good reporter can cover anything—a fire one day, a mob indictment the next day, a murder, Mets game or obit-uary the next. When I became a religion writer one year before entering Harvard, I figured that it would be an easy beat. Not only was I a quick study, I reasoned, but I had an edge. After all, I knew what it was like to go to synagogue, so I figured I knew what a Christian felt in church or a Muslim felt in a mosque or a Buddhist felt in a temple. If you know one religion, I reasoned, you know them all.

Nonetheless, religion writing proved difficult. I could cover the routine press conference at the National Council of Churches or a sermon at St. Patrick's, but I had trouble with theological language and history. I didn't really know a Presbyterian from a Methodist, a Shi'a from a Sunni or a Fundamentalist from an Evangelical. My ignorance was one of the things that drove me to ask for the year at Harvard Divinity School. And, on the first day of classes at the Div School, I learned that my basic assumption was wrong.

The class was called "World Religions: Dialogue and Diversity," and it was a survey of the five great faiths—Hinduism, Buddhism, Judaism, Christianity and Islam. On the first day of classes, the professor, Diana Eck, looked out at the sea of faces and declared: "If you know one religion . . . you don't know any."

Now *there* was some cold water in my face. If you came here with any preconceptions, she was saying, toss them out. It is unfair and unwise to try to understand one religion by the yardstick of another. Each religion is unique.

She backed up this idea with a reading list of ten weighty books that looked at each faith from within. These books, she said, would help us "walk in the shoes of people whose lives we do not lead." The books included *What the Buddha Taught* by Walpola Rahula, *Ideals and Realities of Islam* by Seyyed Hossein Nasr, *A Hindu View of Life* by S. Radhakrishnan, *Between Time and Eternity* by Jacob Neusner and *Honest to God* by John A. T. Robinson. But maybe the book on the list that summed up the course best was by Mahatma Gandhi. It was called *All Religions Are True.*

Eck tried to banish other preconceptions by writing the name of each faith on the blackboard and, like the barker at my imaginary carnival, asked us to fill in the percentage it represents of world population.

"Hindus, what do I hear for Hindus?" she called out. "Five percent," said one voice. "No. No. Just think of all those people in India. Thirty percent," said another.

"Jews, what do I hear for Jews?" "Ten percent," called out one student. "No, too high," responded another. "It's more like three percent."

It went on like this for a while, with Professor Eck at the blackboard recording the guesses. Then she put down the real numbers, which surprised more than a few people, including myself.

| | |
|---|---|
| *Christian* | *32.4 percent* |
| *Muslim* | *17.1* |
| *Hindu* | *13.5* |
| *Buddhist* | *6.2* |
| *Jewish* | *0.4* |

Her course in world religions was offered jointly by the Divinity School and Harvard College, and college people outnumbered Divinity types two to one. The course, offered in a turn-of-the-century building called Emerson in Harvard Yard (complete with a statue of Ralph Waldo in the lobby), was enormously popular. During the shopping period, people were sitting in the aisles. The group thinned out a bit after the requirements were spelled out (midterm, final, term paper and the ten-book reading list), but still, with 151 registered students, you had to get to class early for a good seat.

Diana Eck, who held a joint appointment at the Div School and the college, was an enchanting teacher. Her lectures were meticulously constructed (she admitted to staying up into the wee hours of the morning polishing them) and included the comical and the studious. She was in her early forties, unmarried and pretty. She had the habit of pulling her blond hair behind her ears so that her simple gold earrings would show. In the winter, she favored turtleneck sweaters and oversize sport jackets.

She was also enigmatic. She came across very warmly, almost seductively, from the lectern, but many students reported that Diana Eck was standoffish and remote when they approached her after class. Early in the semester, Shira good-naturedly, but only half in jest, accused me of having a crush on this professor of world religions.

Another teacher whom I met in the first few days of the fall semester I undoubtedly had a crush on. He was Louis

Jacobs, a scholar from England who was at Harvard Divinity for the year as a visiting List Professor of Jewish Studies. Jacobs was short and stout and had a white goatee and oversize bags under his eyes that made him look perpetually tired. But when this man opened his mouth in class, the room came alive. There was wisdom, animation, stories, insight and laughter.

Jacobs, who was educated at the Orthodox Jewish seminary in Manchester, England, fast became one of the most popular professors at this elitist Protestant divinity school. Quickly he became known as "the rabbi," as in "Have you heard the rabbi?" "You must sit in on the rabbi's class." "The rabbi is a storyteller."

The administration, not quite knowing what to make of the rabbi, assigned to him a small seminar room for his classes. All the chairs around the table were quickly filled. Latecomers would steal chairs from less popular neighboring classes or simply sit on the floor. For everyone else, Louis Jacobs was a window into Judaism; for me, an insider, he parted the curtains and let the sun shine in.

The Orthodox Judaism I grew up with was warm and embracing. I learned quickly that it was filled with inconsistencies and contradictions, but I followed the lead of the Talmud, which either fashions fanciful explanations or falls back on faith. "Tay-ku." It sounds like the name of a Japanese restaurant, but it is the Talmudic formula for questions that have no answers. Tay-ku essentially means "have faith, some day the Messiah will come and answer the unanswerable."

I grew up accepting the law, primarily Sabbath observance and keeping kosher, knowing that the original reasons I was taught—God rested on the seventh day and animals shouldn't suffer—are hopelessly outdated and make little sense in modern society. Though I believed differently as a child, today I have no illusions that the chickens I pick up at the local kosher meat market suffer any less than Frank Perdue's poor birds in the supermarket freezer.

Being a believer in experience over knowledge (deed over

creed), I have been primarily interested in living Judaism and not necessarily understanding it. I believe there is virtue in the life-style, in the tradition. In a more cosmic sense, I believe there is a Supreme Being who delights in my efforts to live as a traditional Jew.

All of this is not to imply that I was brought up with an anti-intellectual approach to Judaism. In all those years in yeshiva, I studied the history, philosophy, literature and, most of all, the laws of my people. I also delved into hundreds of pages of Talmud and can still recite a few key passages by heart. But in so doing, I always drew a line. I did not subject my Jewish learning to an unbridled intellectual inquiry, but judged it on its own terms. I did not step over the line because I felt that to do so would be to endanger my personal faith and ultimately to destroy it. I could live with a few tay-kus in my life; not everything had to have an answer.

Louis Jacobs was the first pious Jew I met who really wanted answers. And when he sought them, some of the old shibboleths fell, but to my amazement they did not break. Because of his faith, Judaism emerged alive and well and even fortified.

An example. *Torah MiSinai* is the belief that God gave the Law word for word to the Jewish people on Mount Sinai. I believe it as a doctrine of faith even though it goes against rational thinking and historic fact. In the opening lecture in his class on Jewish law, Jacobs spoke matter-of-factly of the widely accepted four-author breakdown for the Five Books of Moses: First there is J, so called because he (or, according to Harold Bloom, she) refers to God as JHWH. Then comes E, who calls God by the plural word *Elohim*, and later P, a priestly contributor who adds Leviticus, and D, who completes the Pentateuch with Deuteronomy. Four different authors writing Scripture in different times.

The theory is derived from the words, idioms and tones used in the various parts of the Bible as well as from downright contradictions. Even something as basic as the Ten Commandments changes from its first appearance in Exodus to its reiteration in Deuteronomy: "Remember the Sabbath Day and keep it holy" is the account given in Exodus 20:8. But, when the commandments are repeated in Deuteronomy 5:12, it says, "Observe the Sabbath Day and keep it holy." Biblical scholars attribute the change—in the account of the same event on Mount Sinai—to different concerns of different authors writing at different times. One was stressing memory, the other observance.

The Talmud, holding fast to the idea that the Bible was dictated by God to Moses, could not entertain the idea of different authors. Instead, it invented an explanation for the inconsistency in language. "Remember and Observe were uttered in one sound." That is, God, in His own supernatural way, uttered the two words as one. One word was spoken, but two were heard. Exodus records one utterance, and Deuteronomy the other. Therefore, the Talmud asserts, there is no contradiction between the texts, they are merely recording different aspects of the same event.

For the theologian, this is a sleight of hand unworthy of serious consideration. But for the religious person, it is the perfect escape from the horns of a dilemma. Since the religious purpose is to bind back with the past, the Sabbath can be enhanced with two supporting imperatives—observance and memory. The explanation, complete with its little lesson, is comforting to one who accepts the Torah as the word of God. And, besides, it is easier to accept than a crisis of faith.

After class, I walked Jacobs home and told him what troubled me. "Once you show that the Torah is flawed, that it is not really God-given, what happens to your faith? What is your Judaism? What compels you to lead a religious life? What is its binding force?"

Jacobs listened to me patiently and then pointed to a stately oak ablaze with fall colors. "Do you know how that tree began?" he asked. He bent down and picked up an acorn and rolled it in his fingers. "Just because you know how it began doesn't mean you cannot enjoy the tree."

I relaxed in its shade and gave it all some thought. Is the

Torah divine? An affirmative answer is easy if you know one religion. But if you know many, the questions multiply and chase each other in a wild circle. Is the New Testament divine? Is the Koran? And if they are, what about the Torah? Or is it possible that none of the holy books is God-given? Maybe they simply represent man's striving to understand and ultimately reach the divine. And if I accept this argument, can I still be an observant Jew? Do such insights destroy my faith or give it new depth and understanding?

Ahhh. To live like this, I thought.

I had been at the Div School just a few days when I decided that I would never leave. My life had so radically changed for the good that I could not imagine ever turning back. I had left behind the subways, the soot, the deadlines and the cramped quarters of Manhattan for Cambridge. I walked through Harvard Yard on my way to class as if I were walking on the moon. The sensation was entirely new to me. I felt lighter, brighter and totally unencumbered by any worries. The challenges of my day were delightful: finding the right book in the library, getting to class before the bell of Memorial Church finished striking the hour, discovering a new café in which to savor a cup of cappuccino.

My family was thriving. Shira's free-lance writing career was taking off nicely. She was getting assignments from national magazines, and the Boston bureau of *The New York Times* was beginning to use her as a free-lancer. As for our son, Adam, who was just past his first birthday, we found a terrific, nurturing and loving day-care center. It was called Children's Village, and it lived up to its name. The first thing we saw when visiting it was the center's sprawling, child-filled yard, with youngsters on tricycles, swings, slides and monkey bars. Adults were there as well, but they were so caught up in the motion and laughter that they too seemed like children.

I made it a habit to run over to Children's Village a few days a week after class to play with the children in the toddler room, where Adam spent the day with eleven other tykes. Adam would initially be excited to see me but soon get absorbed in mixing clay, dismantling a puzzle or playing fireman with a friend. I would take a children's book off the shelf, sit down on the floor and begin to read. Within minutes I would have a child on my lap, and then another and soon a half dozen, giggling and jockeying for a piece of my lap that also afforded a view of the book.

What a nice life, the interior life of nurturing, sharing and gaining knowledge. Can anything compete?

Shira, Adam and I lived on a lovely tree-lined street in Somerville, just over the border from Cambridge. We sublet the second floor of a house from a Ph.D. student in French foreign policy and his wife, who were off to study at the Sorbonne for a year. Their apartment, with arched doorways and bay windows in every room, could have been on the Left Bank.

The house was on Chester Street, a street that had its very own real, if unofficial, mayor. He had the unlikely sounding but very real name of Bill Doe, and he knew everybody on Chester Street. Bill, a retired career army man who lived alone, spent a good part of his day smoking cigars and swapping stories in front of the small apartment building that was his home. He came over and introduced himself the day we moved in. I told him that I was Ari Goldman from New York and that I was attending Harvard Divinity School.

A few days later, as I was walking home from school, Bill, engaged in a conversation with another neighbor, waved and called in a booming voice, "Hello, Rabbi." I crossed the street to explain that I was not a rabbi, just a student of religion, but Bill was already introducing me. "Rabbi, I would like you to meet the Judge." The Judge, long retired from the bench, was a small man who lived on the corner and also smoked cigars.

I smiled politely, shook hands and excused myself, thinking, I guess there isn't much harm in him thinking I am a rabbi. Besides, I thought, maybe that is what I should do with my life—finish this year and then enroll in a rabbinical school, maybe find my true calling.

Without knowing it, Bill had planted a seed that was to continue to grow throughout my year at Harvard.

# CHAPTER 3

# Spirituality

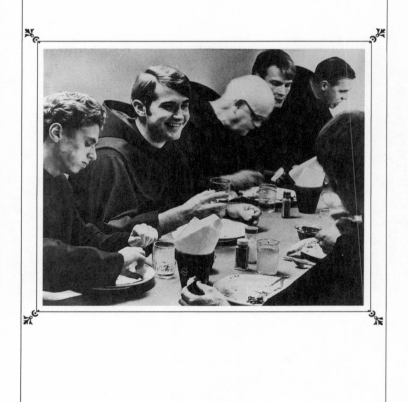

The Kobriner Rabbi said: "Once I chanced to visit an inn, and the time for the afternoon prayers arrived. It was a Catholic holiday, and the inn was filled with noisy merrymakers and dancing couples. Still I prayed there with complete devotion, thinking to myself: 'If so much enthusiasm is given to physical enjoyments, why cannot I be even more enthusiastic in matters of the spirit.' "

The most elusive experience for me in my early days at the Div School was, to my great surprise, the Christian experience. Everybody, it seemed, was trying so hard not to offend the wide diversity of people that were gathered there that Christian spirituality did not emerge.

If, for example, there was a mention in class of the divinity of Jesus, the lecturer would offer an apology to the non-Christians in the room. If there was a Christian prayer offered at a convocation, you could be sure that some Buddhist meditation would follow for balance. Religious truth did not seem to exist at the Div School, only religious relativism. My expectation of finding old-time Christian piety had been merrily shattered at the Div School Dance, but I continued to search for a clue to what these Christians really felt.

I made sure to attend the regular Noon Worship in the imposing Gothic chapel on the second floor of the Div

School, but found it used mostly as a forum for discussing political issues, such as the Sandinista revolution in Nicaragua, prison reform, gay rights, homelessness and abortion rights. The concerns were, in large measure, a reflection of the liberal agenda of the mainline Protestant churches and their umbrella organization, the National Council of Churches, once the most powerful religious organization in the United States. In the 1980s, however, with a conservative tide sweeping the country and Ronald Reagan in the White House, the mainline churches and their agenda had become marginalized. The more fervent Evangelicals and the dogmatic Roman Catholics dominated.

The Div School took little notice. The Noon Worship, organized and led by students, would include some tepid hymns, an inoffensive reading from Scripture and a short sermon, usually on the liberal political topic of the day. The sermons that I grew up with in synagogue exhorted the gathered faithful to change themselves; here in the Div School chapel the plea for change was directed outside, well beyond the church walls.

Despite its stained-glass windows over the altar, dark wood pews and stately pipe organ, the chapel felt cold to me. There wasn't even a cross in the room, only the wooden likeness of an eagle with outstretched wings under the pulpit. I often passed the chapel when I was on my way to and from classes. Occasionally, I would see someone sitting there meditating, but in my entire year at Harvard, I never saw anyone on his or her knees.

To my mind, kneeling is the ultimate expression of Christian supplication. It is something so Christian that, as a boy, I was taught never to fall down on both knees, even while playing in the park or retrieving some toy from under the sofa. "Always keep one knee up," my counselor said at Camp Kol-Re-Na, an Orthodox all-boys summer sleep-away camp in the Catskills. "Jews don't kneel."

At the Rabbi Jacob Joseph School on the Lower East Side of Manhattan, my sixth-grade math teacher used to do arithmetic problems on the blackboard using an uppercase T as a plus sign. "What if someone walked into this room and saw me drawing crosses all over the board?" he asked.

I learned early on that Jewish signs and symbols are different. And so is Jewish spirituality. The Judaism I was taught was more mitzvah-centered than God-centered. But that did not mean it was without transcendence. Spirituality for me is the sum total of all the acts of my day, waking with a prayer, eating kosher, sharing with my friends, even, in my mother's constellation, taking out the garbage. Judaism makes everything holy, ties me back to history and connects me with the spirit of God. When God breathed life into the world, He not only made a piece of clay come to life but he also enabled that piece of clay to transcend life. That is my spirituality.

But where was the spirituality at Harvard Divinity School? I asked my Anglican friend Lynda, the one from Canada with three kids and lots of savvy. "It's here," she reassured me, "but it's hidden under a real thick layer of intellectualism and politics."

Where do you find it? "I don't think spirituality happens in the morning prayer or in the noon prayer," she told me one day over lunch. "It happens in the connections between people."

She said that she found an especially strong spiritual connection among older women at the Div School who, like her, had returned to study after raising a family. Each, in her separate way, had gone through so much to be there; they savored every moment and each other.

The school did not provide you with a spiritual community any more than the "real world" does, Lynda said. "Out there, you've got to build it, and that's what you've got to do here." The Div School gave you the tools. Lynda was taking Gordon Kaufman's "Constructing the Concept of God."

Lynda's own concept appeared to be evolving. She addressed me firmly but with respect—as a Jew and as a man.

"The fixed image we inherited from you guys—God as the puppeteer pulling the strings—just doesn't work anymore today." Ossified images like that, she said, inhibit spirituality. People make it flourish.

Lynda had landed at the Div School pretty much by accident. She grew up in Montreal and Toronto and embarked on a career as a nurse. Husband and children put an end to that, something Lynda never regretted. The family settled in a comfortable colonial home in one of the historic suburbs outside Boston. They had a nice backyard and a big, fuzzy butterball of a dog named Oscar.

With her husband caught up in the world of corporate finance and her three boys in grade school, Lynda sent for the catalog of the Harvard Extension School, which offers adult education courses in Harvard Yard after the Harvard students clear out in the late afternoons. "I didn't know what I wanted to do when I grew up," Lynda said, as she recalled leafing through the catalog page by page. "I wanted to take Psychology, but there was nothing that interested me. After *P* came *Q*. Nothing there. But then came *R*, and I began to look at Religion. I decided to take a course in Second Isaiah with Paul Hanson."

She was hooked. "I couldn't wait for Thursday afternoons. The two hours went like ten minutes." The course was offered in the Yard, but Lynda began to do her research and studying at the Div School library. "People were helpful, friendly. Everywhere I looked, it said, 'This Is the Place You Belong.' "

One day in class, Professor Hanson, a Lutheran scholar of the Old Testament, said that if anyone felt "over their heads," they should come and see him. Lynda beat him back to his office. She may have been insecure, but she wasn't shy. "Professor Hanson, I'm your token housewife," she began.

He cut her off. "Now wait a minute," he said. "I'm married to one of those, and she's the most challenging person in my life."

The next year Lynda enrolled at the Div School. There, for the first time, she read feminist theologians, like Rosemary Ruether, who believes in opening up the Catholic church to women, and Mary Daly, the self-proclaimed "post-Christian" who exhorts women to reject the church as hopelessly sexist. There, for the first time, Lynda began to think about what is known in church circles as "inclusive language"—effort to revise the liturgy and hymns to include women, by changing phrases like "God the Father" to "God the Mother." When they sang the old Methodist hymn "Good Christian Men, Rejoice" at the Div School, it went like this: "Good Christian Friends, Rejoice."

Lynda was adjusting with alacrity. "I feel pretty sure that there are militant feminist women here who look at me and see a middle-aged woman who is probably pretty traditional," Lynda said. "And in a lot of ways I am." Lynda still runs the house and takes care of the four males who have come to depend on her. But she takes her religion studies very seriously, considers herself a feminist and draws her spiritual sustenance from the women like herself at the Div School.

For my Unitarian friend Ann, spirituality at the Div School was even more subtle. Ann, who majored in linguistics at the University of Chicago, said that her source of religious inspiration was words.

Ann was twenty-four; she was quick to laugh and moved with rapid, breezy strokes, like a young gazelle on an open meadow. She was the one wearing the fishnet stockings and the miniskirt at the Orientation Dance. In class she favored black stretch pants and loose-fitting gray sweatshirts. The feminists didn't like her.

"For me, language is a spiritual process," she explained. "Parsing a sentence doesn't feel like a prayer, but the discipline is the same. When I heard Mary Daly talking about God as a verb, I really understood what she was saying. Seeing God as a verb was really helpful for me.

"You've got to remember John 1:1. 'In the beginning was

the Word, and the Word was with God, and the Word was God.' Everything starts from language. That is very fundamental to my spirituality.

"When I studied Russian, I copied everything out like a medieval monk. I used different-colored inks for my declensions and conjugations. I'm taking German now, and my study has the same kind of medieval feeling. In some ways, working with words substitutes for a prayer life. When I do *The New York Times* crossword puzzle, for example, I feel an emptying of my conscious thought, free associations. It leaves me in a better place.

"I see religion as being the search for context and meaning for all these words, and finding words for the meanings we have that we can't articulate. Still, there are those experiences that are wordless, but it helps to try."

Isn't this brand of spirituality a very lonely pursuit?

"On the contrary," she said. "You may feel like you're alone, but words bring you into community. We find community through the spoken word. Language fosters community, enables community. You can't have community without language.

"I see God in language, as well as in being. As a Unitarian, I believe that God is in every person. We participate in God's creative process through language. And language is an end in itself."

Ann grew up in a solid, churchgoing Unitarian family outside of Boston. The Unitarian church is the most liberal of the faiths in the Christian tradition, teaching that Jesus was a great teacher but not a deity. Still, Ann's family was very liberal yet very committed to religion. When she was young, her parents, who own an electrical components business, took family vacations on Star Island, a religious retreat center off the coast of New Hampshire.

When Ann was twelve, her congregation hired a female minister. "Unitarians had been ordaining women for a hundred years before I was born," Ann said, but seeing one in her pulpit made a lasting impression on the girl. She knew she wanted to be a minister, but first she had to get some other aspirations "out of my system." So, after college, Ann moved to New York City. "I had this idea I was going to be an actress, but I never even got my pictures taken," she said. "I got an apartment and a waitress job in the East Village." Then she moved on to Lord & Taylor, where she spent six months as a dress buyer.

A year in New York was enough to convince her to revive her earlier ambition. She moved back home and found a nearby Unitarian minister who was willing to be her mentor as she helped out in his church while applying for admission to the Div School.

From the beginning, Ann found that she had trouble fitting in, especially in the Carriage House, one of the Div School residence halls. "On my first day, my roommate put on the fridge a list of things we were to boycott," she said. "Now, I can understand grapes and lettuce, but she also listed Campbell's soup and Pepperidge Farm cookies!

"They're not only left-wing," she said of her fellow Div School students, "but they assume that you're not and they're ready to argue with you. They looked at my skirts and said, 'Are you a feminist?' "

Aside from finding spirituality in words, Ann said that she found it in her relationship with the other Unitarian students at the Div School, who gathered once a week for their own worship service. "For that alone, I am glad I didn't just stay with my books but got involved in the larger community."

For my friend Robert, the businessman turned theology student, spirituality at the Div School was no problem. He found it "everywhere," he told me—in the classroom, in the library, in the chapel, in the faculty and in his fellow students. "I cannot ever recall feeling more at home in a place.

"I think it helps being forty-seven years old. I'm at a time in my life when I don't have to impress anyone or find a job. I am here for myself and for God. I am so happy to be here, I could go out and hug a corner of the building."

For Robert, the Div School was a refuge from crisis. Only a few years earlier Robert had been a successful developer, the CEO of a $32 million business in the Boston area. In the early eighties, however, the business collapsed, and he was plunged into bankruptcy.

"I had a wonderful firm with fifty people," he told me as we lunched at a downtown Boston business club, a hangout from his corporate days. "We financed human service projects with the use of federal funds. And then, one by one, Reagan canceled every program we financed."

Robert, his hair turning gray, wore a tweed sport jacket and a bow tie that was unevenly, yet fashionably, tied. "In three years, I lost the business, my father died, my father-in-law died, my wife became an alcoholic and my eldest child was committed for a year to a hospital.

"One day I was on my way home and could barely drive the car. I got out of the car and got down on my knees and prayed for help. I had hit bottom. I admitted absolute and total defeat. I prayed for help not believing that anybody could help me. But when I got up, I knew something extraordinary had happened. For the first time, there was a clarity, a lightness, a sense of peace.

"And then, almost by accident, I met the members of a monastic order. I had not been in church for many years, but I began to go to their church every morning at seven. I read the Scriptures, mostly the Psalms, and found they had a meaning I never saw before. When I went into the church the first time, I read Psalm 30. 'In my prosperity, I said, "I shall never be moved." ' I realized that I had suffered from the sin of overconfidence."

Overconfident no more, Robert enrolled in the Div School and threw himself into the study of Scripture, early Judaism and Christian theology.

Robert, who had fallen away from the Episcopal church as he climbed the ladder to financial success, was now firmly back in the church. He dreamed of someday becoming an Episcopal priest.

# CHAPTER 4

# Original Sin

For I hate divorce, says the Lord the God of
Israel.

— Malachi 2:16

My classmates at the Div School, I was
soon to find, were different from
those at the other professional schools at Harvard. While
there were many bright and thoughtful students at the Law
School or the Business School, there were few for whom the
law or business was at the core of their lives. These were
disciplines they did and did well, but the disciplines didn't
define them. The more I got to know my fellow Div School
students, the more I found that, for them, religion was at
the center. My encounter with my classmates drew me to
examine my own life and try to find just where religion fit.

More than any other event in my life, my parents' divorce
in 1955, when I was six years old, shaped me into the person
I am, professionally, emotionally and religiously.

My earliest memories center on the place where, before
the divorce, we briefly called ourselves a family, a three-
story house on Westbourne Parkway in Hartford. Our family—my mother, father, older brother, Shalom, and

younger brother, Dov—lived on the top floor, and to get there we would walk up an open wooden staircase in the rear that took us through the toy-strewn porches of our downstairs neighbors. We had a clothesline that stretched from our porch across the backyard to another three-family house.

My favorite diversion was hunting in the backyard for bugs and worms and, after a rain, maybe a frog, and playing with them on the back porch. In those days, dry-cleaning stores and drugstores used to run promotions giving away goldfish, turtles and salamanders. These became my greatest treasures. And once my father brought home a baby chick whose feathers had been dyed kelly green—a St. Patrick's Day promotion. The chick ran wildly around the house until my mother shooed it out the back door and it lived out its brief, green life in a shoe box on my porch.

The St. Patrick's Day chick incident might sound like an amusing vignette out of *I Love Lucy*, but in our house it was the trigger for a fight between my parents. Loud verbal confrontations in the house were often followed by a door slammed in anger and an eerie, tension-laden silence.

I loved that back porch. It was my playground, my menagerie, my stage, my tree house and my refuge from family turbulence. My mother said that she knew I was back from nursery school when she heard me singing as I climbed up the back stairs to the porch.

There was another element of that life that I loved. Friday night. It was a time when, by the magic of the Sabbath candles, we were transformed into a happy, picture-book family. The recriminations and bickering would cease and the music would begin. Dov was just a baby at the time, but Shalom and I would sit at the gleaming white table in our "Shabbat outfits," dark blue pants and white cotton shirts open at the collar. Our hair was still wet from our pre-Sabbath baths, and it was combed neatly across our foreheads. Yarmulkes were bobby-pinned to our heads. My mother waved her hands over the lighted candles and covered her eyes as she stood in a silent moment of meditation. Afterwards, she took us into her arms and kissed us, lingering an extra moment to drink in our freshness. She told us that we looked like the two angels that tradition says accompany the men home from the Friday-night synagogue service.

When, a little while later, my father returned from the synagogue, we lined up in front of him for the Sabbath blessing, the eldest, Shalom, first and then me. "May God make you like Ephraim and Menashe," he said invoking the two grandsons of Jacob who, as Joseph's children, were especially beloved. Bending down to reach us, my father cradled our heads between his strong hands as he recited the blessing. "May He bless you and keep you . . . and give you peace."

My father, who worked hard all week managing and selling real estate, became our rabbi and cantor on Friday night. He took us through the meal singing the joyous melodies of the Hasidim and the resolute songs of the Chalutzim, the Israeli pioneers who, we were told, were singing the same songs as they worked to turn the desert green. My mother, a confirmed "listener" rather than singer, hummed along with a smile of contentment on her face.

On one such Friday night, I sensed the perfect opportunity. "I want a dog," I announced between songs.

"Not again," my mother said. "Sweetheart, I already told you, no dogs. Anyway, I think you're allergic to dogs."

"Judy," my father interrupted. "You don't know that for sure and besides, I don't see the harm—"

"Marvin." Her voice was rising. "Don't contradict me in front of the children." And that was the end of the singing. The music stopped and the candles went out.

No long after, my parents were divorced. The fight over the dog, of course, had nothing to do with it. It was just another in a series and, no doubt, one of the more benign of their tortured nine-year marriage. But try telling that to a five-year-old boy.

All sons and daughters of divorce blame themselves. In their minds, the only way to expiate the guilt is to re-create what was lost. That is why each of us harbors a dream, the dream of bringing our parents back together again. On a subconscious level, this becomes our life's work. For me, the mission was to re-create the serenity and harmony of the Sabbath table. That was all I needed to do to restore our fall from Paradise.

Strictly speaking, there are no Jewish prohibitions against divorce. This is sometimes hard for Catholics to understand. My Catholic friend Hugh recently asked me, "If your parents were so Orthodox, how come they got divorced?" The question was a good illustration of Professor Eck's axiom, "If you know one religion, you don't know any." Seen from the Catholic perspective, authentic Judaism should be as much opposed to divorce as is authentic Catholicism. But seen through Jewish eyes, the issue is quite different.

From the perspective of traditional Jewish law, there is nothing wrong with divorce as long as you follow the rabbinic procedures. The Torah says that if a marriage isn't working, end it. Or rather, the man should end it: "When a man takes a wife, and marries her, then it comes to pass, if she finds no favor in his eyes, because he has found some unseemly thing in her, that he writes her a bill of divorcement, and places it in her hand, and sends her out of his house" (Deuteronomy 24:1).

The authors of the Talmud say that such an event is regrettable, but it is certainly doable. To help ensure that divorce is not taken lightly, the rabbis made the procedure a complicated one. The divorce document, known as the *get*, is written by a scribe with a quill pen on parchment in a solemn ceremony before two witnesses. But once it's sealed and delivered, the marriage is over and both parties are permitted to remarry. (The man may remarry the very next day and the woman three months later. The woman has to wait just in case she is pregnant so that there is no question about the paternity of the offspring.)

Jewish law, as is often its tendency, gets excessively mired in the legal details of divorce and makes little provision for those who most suffer the consequences: the children. There is an entire volume of the Talmud that deals with divorce, a volume called Gittin. It is one of the largest and most complex tractates, dealing with every detail, from the ink used in the divorce document to the distribution of household goods. Only on its very last page does the Talmud offer any judgment on the whole process when it says: "The very altar weeps for one who divorces the wife of his youth." Still, nowhere in the tractate's 180 pages is there a substantive discussion of the custody of the children. Children get lost in the shuffle of papers and legalisms. Thus, the most serious—and most moral—issue of divorce is sorely ignored.

To my mind, divorce is a deplorable breach of contract, and I say without humor that children should be allowed to sue. Consider the facts: Two people agree to create a human being and promise to give it love, a home, security and happiness. They take this step with the best of intentions, to be sure, but then something goes awry. They find they really hate each other or for some other reason cannot live together. But in separating, they put themselves first and forget about the contract they have with their child. I do not believe, as you often hear soon-to-be divorced parents say, that the separation will be "best for the child." My experience has taught me better.

But didn't my parents spare me an unhappy home where fighting and angry confrontation were the mode of communication? I believe not. I believe that they—as incompatible as they were and remain today—could have learned to stop shouting or slamming doors. At least they could have learned all that more easily than I learned to be a child of divorce.

With divorce so common these days, mine is not a popular

position. Some—usually divorced people with children—
accuse me of being selfish. But it's not just me. Someday
they will hear it from their own children. A lost childhood
cannot be recaptured.

For a move so fraught with consequences, the act ending
my parents' marriage was a starkly simple one. One morning after my father left for work, my mother gathered up
the three of us and boarded a New York–bound train. From
Grand Central Station, we took a taxi to Jackson Heights, a
working-class neighborhood in New York's borough of
Queens where my mother's twin sister, Jean, lived with her
husband, Herb, a doctor. With a young family of their own,
they lived in an apartment on the ground floor of a private
house, using the front of the apartment for Herb's medical
practice and the rear as their living quarters. My mother,
Shalom, Dov and I moved in. Shalom and I slept on couches
in Herb's waiting room and had to clear our bedclothes out
of the way before the first patients arrived in the morning.
After a few months, my mother found a place of our own, a
cramped one-bedroom apartment a few blocks away.

Despite the turmoil, however, there was one constant in
my life that proved critical—the practice of Orthodox Judaism. Whether I was in my mother's apartment in Jackson
Heights or in the Hartford home of my father, I knew that
on Friday night we would gather around a table covered in
white. For twenty-five hours, from sundown Friday until
the stars came out Saturday night, we observed a kind of
limbo time, where, in effect, everyday life came to a halt.
The same set of rules in both homes: no watching television,
no turning on electric lights, no talking on the telephone, no
riding in cars and no writing anything down, not even
homework assignments. The Sabbath was instead a time for
attending synagogue, reading a novel, taking a leisurely
walk to the park or reflecting on the week past.

To someone not brought up with these rules, all the Sabbath restrictions might sound onerous. But, for me, the

faithful practice of Orthodox Judaism proved to be the one comfort in my childhood, the one act that was filled with the possibility of redemption. I clung—and I continue to cling —to it like a raft in a turbulent sea.

Am I devoted to Orthodox observance then for the wrong reasons? Am I still mired in a juvenile fantasy that the Sabbath table will bring my parents together? Do I still need so desperately to find a common bond between my two very different parents?

One of the lessons of Div School was that there are no wrong reasons. When, in our conversation after class, Rabbi Jacobs picked up the acorn, he was saying that origins aren't everything. There is the tree, and the tree exists in and of itself. Enjoy the tree. Knowing that it was once an acorn doesn't make it any less sturdy or any less shady. Likewise, in the observance of Judaism, the origins of the laws— whether made by God or fabricated by man—are not the factors that determine validity. Neither is the Sabbath diminished because it sustains me with a comfort that my parents could not.

As wrenching as divorce was, and continues to be, for me, it did provide great job training. What better place, after all, to learn to be a journalist? Divorce made me a specialist in entertaining different points of view without having to make judgments about them. Take a simple thing like packing clothes for a weekend trip, something I did often while shuttling between my mother in New York and my father in Connecticut. Since I would always be attending synagogue when I visited my father, I had to pack a sport jacket. My mother believed that in packing jackets, the buttons should be fastened and the arms folded back, like a shirt from the laundry. My father, however, insisted on turning the jacket inside out, punching in the shoulder pads and folding it inside out into the suitcase. So, when I headed north to Hartford, my jacket was packed Mom's way; when I headed south, it was packed Dad's way.

After the divorce, my father, then in his early thirties, moved back to the home of his parents. By today's standards, it seems like an odd move, but then it made perfect sense, especially since his mother, Grandma Nettie, was there to help take care of "Marvin's boys" on our frequent visits. Grandpa Sam, recently retired from the clothing business after the city built a highway through his store, was the world's greatest devotee of newspapers. Each morning after breakfast—as Grandma cleaned up the kitchen and geared up for lunch—Grandpa would sit in a big high-backed, embroidered chair near the front door and read the morning paper, *The Hartford Courant*. When he finished, he would begin on the Yiddish paper, *The Tag-Morning Journal* (which he read with fluency, despite the fact that he, like all my grandparents, was American-born). Then he moved on to the *Connecticut Jewish Ledger*. The smell of one of Grandma's soups would soon fill the house, and Grandpa would yell, "Nettie, I'm getting hungry." After lunch, Grandpa would sit in his chair by the door waiting for the afternoon paper, the *Hartford Times,* to drop.

He was a simple man, this lover of newspapers. I never saw him read a book, except for a prayer book, which he followed without passion every Saturday morning in the synagogue. At home, he was stern and impatient and would peer over his paper to mete out verbal discipline when we got too noisy or into fights. And he played favorites. My brothers and I, the products of divorce (in his mind, the products of failure), were something of an embarrassment. What he took pride in were his other grandchildren, the offspring of his son-in-law the rabbi, the one who'd married his eldest daughter, Ruth, and led the big Orthodox synagogue in the Bronx. When friends came over, Grandpa would put down his newspaper and proudly talk about "Ruth and the Rabbi"—out of deference, he wouldn't even use his first name—and their kids. It made no difference to my grandfather that "Marvin's boys" were playing in the next room.

My father was my refuge, especially on Saturday mornings. He insisted on being among the first men in the synagogue, and I eagerly joined him because I loved our walks together. The streets were quiet; we had them all to ourselves. I put my hand in his, and we began to sing. I must have been seven or eight years old, but already we were preparing for my bar mitzvah. We sang the traditional songs of the synagogue and sometimes improvised by putting the words to more modern Israeli and Hasidic melodies. Everyone told me I had a good voice, a sweet voice, a voice so high that it could touch the heavens. In the synagogue, I sang the solos that could be performed before one reaches the age of maturity, and I looked forward eagerly to my bar mitzvah.

The bar mitzvah service was held in 1962 at the Orthodox synagogue near my mother's house in Jackson Heights. My father and several of his relatives, who, like us, do not drive on the Sabbath, stayed in a motel about a mile away on Queens Boulevard. Using the traditional singsong chant, I read the Torah portion of the week. It was B'raishis, In the Beginning, and took in the first five and a half chapters of Genesis, the Creation, the Fall of Man and the birth of Noah. I read it from the Torah scroll, but I knew every word and detail without looking. The earth was emptiness and void and from it God fashioned the world. He created the sun and the moon, light and darkness, oceans and streams, and all manner of vegetation. God made the creatures that crawl on the earth and that fly in the heavens. And finally, in His crowning act, God breathed life into a pile of clay and created Adam. But Adam was unhappy, so God caused a heavy sleep to come upon him and He took Adam's rib and created from it a "helpmate" for Adam. Adam was pleased and called her Eve, "because she is the mother of all living things."

The happiness of creation was only to be followed by the tragedy of the first sin and the banishment of Adam and Eve —Mother and Father—from the Garden of Eden. For Chris-

tians the story of the first sin—Original Sin—is replete
with meaning. It represents the Fall of Man, a fall that could
be redeemed only through the coming of Jesus. For Jews,
however, there is no belief that a Savior is necessary for
redemption; instead, the individual has the power to redeem
himself or herself through good works and repentance.

Long before I knew of the Christian approach, the Fall of
Man had a special meaning in my own life. The story harked
back to a time when my parents were together, gathered
with their children around the Sabbath table, a state of grace
that was to be only short-lived. At my bar mitzvah, the fall
was played all over again. No sooner had I read the Genesis
story from the Torah to my family—assembled as one unit
in the synagogue—than I saw them split again into different
factions. After the service, my mother and father made two
separate bar mitzvah parties for me. My mother's family
went off to one catering hall, my father's to another. I was
shuttled back and forth like some exhibit animal in the cir-
cus. I wish I could suggest that this was just a lapse in
judgment by otherwise well-meaning parents, but the same
dual celebration (if you can call it that) was held for both
my brothers. Six bar mitzvahs for three boys.

A few years later, when I could see the absurdity of this
—how family animosities could not be set aside for the
moment of our individual joy—I harbored a fantasy. I
dreamed that someday I would get married and invite all of
my relatives, on both my mother's and father's sides, to a
festive wedding banquet. I would have them all together in
one room, and it would be up to me to make the seating
arrangement. My mother and father would be at the same
table. My aunt who filled my ears with ugly gossip about
my grandmother would be seated next to her. The people
who disliked each other the most, that is, would be forced to
smile and be polite. The main course would be rib steak, and
the table would be set with steak knives so sharp that they
would catch the glimmer of the chandeliers. In the middle
of the meal, just as all the family, exercising the greatest

politeness, would be lifting their knives to cut into the steak, I would sneak outside and pull the main power switch so that the hall would be cast in total darkness.

Would anyone survive, I wondered, or would it be like the last scene in *Hamlet*, where hatred triumphs and no one lives?

So much for fantasy. The wedding Shira and I had on Labor Day 1983 was considerably different. For one thing, the food was vegetarian, so there was no need for razor-sharp knives. Family members on both sides had mellowed considerably. The wedding was held on the well-groomed grounds of the Connecticut home of my mother and her second husband. Despite his refusal to walk down the aisle since the wedding was at my mother's house, my father graciously attended with his new wife. The old fights, if not the old animosities, had subsided.

But the old scars remained.

# CHAPTER 5

# Veritas

Said Rabbi Bunam: "The Lord selected Truth as his seal, because any other virtue may be a clever imitation of the true form, whereas any imitation of the Truth is falsehood."

The emblem is ubiquitous at Harvard. It is on sweatshirts in the bookstores, on sculls on the Charles River and on flatware in the dining halls. Surrounded by a wreath and shaped like a shield, the Harvard coat of arms has a rendering of three open books, and written across them is VERITAS, the Latin word for "Truth."

A brief item in the *Harvard Divinity Bulletin* caught my eye one morning. It pointed out that "Veritas" was not the original motto of Harvard. When Harvard was founded in 1636, it was dedicated *In Christi Gloriam*, "To the Glory of Christ." "Veritas" didn't come along until seven years later, when Henry Dunster, the Hebraist and first president of Harvard, proposed it to the Board of Overseers.

The article in the *Divinity Bulletin*, published during Harvard's celebration of its 350th anniversary, was quite confident that Dunster's "Veritas" was just another, shorthand way of recognizing Jesus Christ, who was seen as the ultimate Truth. The three books, no doubt, represented the

Trinity—the Father, Son and Spirit who are One—and the book, no doubt, represented the Bible, the bulletin reasoned.

It was a minority opinion. For most at Harvard, the "Veritas" of their symbol represented a greater, that is, broader, generic Truth. And the three books were there to stress the importance of the training of ministers, magistrates and merchants in the three languages of antiquity—Hebrew, Greek and Latin.

Harvard, like Yale and Princeton and many other schools founded for religious purposes, cast off its original sectarian mandate to become the Great American University. Now, 350 years after the school's founding as a training ground for Puritan ministers, the place of religion at Harvard was uncertain. Where did religion fit in an America that had practically made a religion out of the separation of church and state? And what was the place of religion in a great university, where ideas were supposed to flourish without the fetters of faith?

For decades, the answer at Harvard was the Divinity School, which became the university's ghetto for the study of religion. Matters of faith had their place, but it was a limited, underfunded place that was distinguished but largely ignored by the rest of the university. Ask an undergraduate in Harvard Yard directions to the Divinity School, and you'll get the answer—as I did when I first arrived— "Divinity School? There's none here, I can tell you that."

It was not until 1974 that students at Harvard College could major or "concentrate" in religion. And even today there is no religion department, but a committee made up of professors from different disciplines (among them, Philosophy, Fine Arts, English, the Classics, Anthropology, as well as the Divinity School) that oversees this small major.

In her first lecture on "World Religions," Professor Eck dealt briefly with the place of religion at Harvard. Clearly, Harvard's uncertainty about where to put religion reflected a larger American discomfort with the subject. And if this discomfort with religion exists with Christianity, it only increases when the traditions encountered are those of others. "There is a sense that religion is what *we* do," Eck was saying. "What others do is superstition."

This is seen dramatically in the Christian dogma of exclusivism: "Outside the church there is no salvation." This didn't necessarily damn everyone else to hell; Catholics, for example, had long had the notion of "invincible ignorance," which reasoned that those who didn't know any better could also find salvation by the grace of Christ.

The idea of exclusivism was further modified by the Second Vatican Council of the mid-1960s, which promoted a modified form of inclusivism. "Non-Christians," the council said, "can be saved, but only in Christ." The Catholic theologian Karl Rahner called them the Anonymous Christians, the people who unknowingly receive the grace of Christ even though they are outside the church. Rahner recognized the God-like element in other faiths as somehow representing or reflecting Christ's metaphysical presence.

While all of these ideas strained to give some validity to non-Christians, they smacked of a kind of Christian imperialism that seemed to say that, whether knowing or unknowing, all grace came through the church. Missing here, of course, is a genuine pluralism that recognizes separate paths to salvation, be they through Judaism, Islam, Hinduism, Buddhism, Shintoism or others. Eck nicely framed the question of how we regard the religions of others with a quotation from Chaim Potok's *The Book of Lights*. A Jew in Japan was watching a Shinto priest in the most blissful meditation. "Is God listening?" he asked a friend. "If not, why not? And if so, what are we all about?"

The purpose of the course in world religions was to take a look at each faith from within, through the eyes of the believer. In so doing, Eck was saying, it is important to remember that in many cases the believer does not make the distinctions that the outsider does. "A Hindu does not see Hinduism. He sees life."

This attempt to see religion from within may seem obvious, but it was not always so. Well into the 1950s, it was acceptable for scholars of religion to study faiths that they never observed firsthand. Books, articles and occasional interviews were considered sufficient for this enterprise. A scholar of African religion no more had to live among a tribe than a biologist had to live in a petri dish or an astronomer had to fly to the stars. Physical detachment did not hinder exploration.

All this changed, however, as the world got smaller. Thanks to airplanes and other travel conveniences, it no longer took a death-defying journey to visit Africa or India. And, maybe more significant, it was no longer unusual to have a neighbor who was a Buddhist or, in some parts of the country for the first time, a Jew. This is especially true today in Europe where, with the wave of immigration from the East, Islam is the fastest-growing religion. Leicester, England, has become the largest Hindu city in the world outside of India. New York has long been the largest Jewish city, inside or outside of Israel. By the same token, Christianity was spreading through Asia, Africa and Latin America. Owing to the conversions and the sizable birthrate in Latin America, a monumental shift took place in the 1980s: there are now more Christians living in the Southern Hemisphere than in the North.

Another noteworthy development in the academic study of religion has been the ability of scholars of religion to admit that they too—on occasion—are men and women of faith. The distinction between believers and scholars was fast coming apart in a reaction to the objective study of religion that had been prevalent at the university for decades. Suddenly, faith was seen as an edge in the study of religion. As a result, ministers and priests, long valued at seminaries, were finding greater acceptance at Harvard— and not just at the Divinity School.

All of this, I knew, had implications for another profession in which objectivity was held sacred: journalism. If academics suddenly had license to experience the faiths they were teaching, could journalists also? Or did the journalist have to remain the outside observer?

My romance with newspapers began when I was eleven years old. It was 1960, and I was living with my mother and brothers in Queens. Through the fifth grade, I had been attending a modern Orthodox yeshiva, Dov Revel, where boys and girls took classes together, were inculcated with Zionism and learned conversational Hebrew. But suddenly, and without warning, my parents decided that it was time for a change. I write the words "parents decided" glibly, but in fact I remember the major telephone fights between my mother in New York and my father in Hartford that preceded this—and any other—important decision regarding "the boys." The peace promised by their separation and divorce never came; the fighting only continued long distance.

The decision was to transfer me, and later my brothers, to an all-boys yeshiva, the Rabbi Jacob Joseph School on the Lower East Side of Manhattan, an hour-long subway ride away from my mother's apartment. There were no girls in sight, Zionism was regarded with suspicion and Yiddish was preferred over Hebrew.

Whatever the reasons, I now found myself on the subways a full two hours a day. And what do people do on the subways? Read newspapers. This was the early sixties, when there were seven daily newspapers in New York. And you didn't even have to buy one. On the seat here someone left a *World-Telegram*, there was a *Mirror* and there a *Journal-American*. The best find of the day was the *Herald Tribune*, which fast became my favorite. I was quickly turning out to be the subway version of my grandfather.

The subway was taking me to my right-wing Orthodox yeshiva, where I learned about my Jewish heritage, but the newspaper was giving me a world tour. In its pages, I learned about politics, following the Nixon-Kennedy campaign with keen interest. When Kennedy was elected, I sat on the subway memorizing, for my own enjoyment, the names of the members of his cabinet. The papers were filled with news of the "space race" spurred by the Soviets' launching of *Sputnik* in 1957. I, the descendant of Russian Jews, was convinced that Yuri Gagarin, the first man in space, and I had the same first name but that mine was the Hebraicized version. I shivered at the implications of the Cuban missile crisis and read all about how children around the country were ducking under their desks in preparation for nuclear war. (Somehow, this civil-defense technique was never practiced in the yeshivas that I went to. But I wasn't surprised —we seemed to live in the time of Moses or Maimonides, not in the age of Khrushchev and Kennedy.) The papers also taught me about sex. Sex crimes—rapes, sodomy and homosexual acts, which were then considered criminal—fascinated and horrified me. I read of the Profumo scandal as if it were a sex manual.

My wonderful two hours a day in subway-newspaper fantasyland were endangered, however, when my parents, after another telephone fight, decided to switch me to yet another yeshiva. It was called Crown Heights Mesifta, and it was taking me further to the Orthodox religious right. Not only were there no girls, but there was less and less time for secular studies. In the yeshivas I had attended before Crown Heights, the school day was evenly divided between Jewish studies, usually in the morning, and secular pursuits such as English, math and science in the afternoon. The Jewish component was divided into segments on the Bible, Hebrew, Jewish history and ritual and, as I got older, the Talmud.

At Crown Heights, where I entered ninth grade, Jewish studies consisted solely of Talmud study. The school followed the model of the East European study halls, where Talmud was everything. The argument made for this approach is that Talmud embodies everything since it is not just a book but a virtual library of Jewish history, philosophy, ritual and Scripture.

In my new school, we approached the Talmud as the rabbis did in prewar Europe. We sat in twos at long tables in the *bais medrash,* the synagogue–study hall of the yeshiva. In our own thirteen- and fourteen-year-old ways, we were supposed to decipher the Aramaic text, check the biblical references and study the commentaries. As we studied in singsong voices and conversation, a bearded rabbi, known as the rebbe, would pace up and down between the tables. A wave from a student would bring him, bending over a shoulder to help out with a difficult word or concept. The rebbe was also there to make sure the conversations did not stray too far from the agenda set by the Talmud. The study hall exchanges were held for three hours each morning, from nine to noon.

After an hour-long lunch, during which we burned off our teenage energy romping in the neighborhood and school yard, we gathered in a classroom where the rebbe would give his lesson on the Talmud, known as the *shiur.* In a format not unlike that of a law school seminar, the rebbe would question us sharply to see how well we prepared. The *bais medrash* of the next morning would be to review the rebbe's shiur and to prepare material for the new text we would study that afternoon.

At about three in the afternoon, when most teenagers were getting out of public high schools around the city, we began our secular studies. From the yeshiva's point of view, this worked out very well, since their science, math and English teachers were drawn from the public schools. At three o'clock, they were free to teach us.

At this hour, however, neither the teachers nor the yeshiva students were in the best of shape for the learning process. Many nights I finished school at 7:00 P.M. and then faced an hour-long subway ride home to Queens.

While the schedule was grueling, there was something comforting about all of it for a teenager from a broken home. The better rebbes, like Rabbi Siegel, were strong and warm father figures. Their aim in teaching the Talmud was to produce not only scholars but good, disciplined Jews who would go on to lead a moral life. I also drew sustenance from the spiritual dimension of the school, expressed in the fervor of the thrice-daily prayer and in the singsong recitation of the Talmud. Before a holiday, we would dance in a circle holding hands and singing God's praises.

The long school day interrupted my newspaper reading, since the only time to do homework was on the subways. (Luckily there was no homework for Jewish studies, since we had the study hall each morning.) I began doing homework on the subway ride home and reading the newspaper on my way to school. Each morning I would walk into the study hall with a *Trib*, found abandoned on a subway seat, tucked under my arm.

After a few months, my rebbe, Rabbi Siegel, confronted me about my newspaper reading in an aside during his Talmud shiur. We were learning the Talmudic tractate of B'rachot, which deals with what blessings are said over different foods and experiences. In one of the wonderful diversions that the Talmud takes, it began to tell the story of a man who tied a rooster to his bedpost to wake him up in the morning in time for prayers.

Rabbi Siegel, warm even in rebuke, used this as an occasion to remind us that the first thing we should do in the morning is praise the Lord. "You should not fill your heads with the filth of the marketplace," he said. "It is not right that you should read newspapers the first thing in the morning," he continued, looking directly at me. He reached into his briefcase and took out a small blue volume of penitential readings, known as the *Mesillat Yesharim* ("The Path of the Upright"), an eighteenth-century book popular in the European yeshivas of the nineteenth century. "Read this," he said, gently handing the book to me. "This is how a Jew should start his day, with a mind purified by Torah."

I thanked him and put the book in my schoolbag.

That night on the subway I opened the *Mesillat Yesharim* and read:

> If a man is allured by the things of this world and is estranged from his Creator, it is not he alone who is corrupted, but the whole world is corrupted with him. But if he exer-

cises self-control, cleaves to his Creator and makes use of this world only insofar as it helps him to serve his Creator, he himself rises to a higher order of being and he carries the world along with him.

This was no normal high school. To keep us aloof from the corruptions of "this world," we were instructed that we should not watch television or read popular magazines. In 1964, I watched the Beatles' first appearance on *The Ed Sullivan Show* with fascination but was unable the next day to talk about it openly in school. Out of earshot of Rabbi Siegel, I whispered about the program to another TV-watching classmate. We talked about the group's jaunty manner and the mops of hair on their heads. It was something called sex appeal, but we couldn't name it. And, even among friends, we didn't mention the most intriguing part of the whole spectacle—the teenage girls screaming their delight in Ed Sullivan's studio audience.

We were teenagers who were told to ignore our emerging sexuality. Social dances were out of the question; there were no girls anywhere near our school. There was no sex education, leaving me, at least, to profound confusion about the whole issue. For some of us, this meant masturbation in the bathroom during recess or in the silence of our bedrooms while siblings slept.

For others, it meant sitting very close to your study partner in the study hall and maybe caressing his knee or, for the adventurous, his groin. Although it was never spoken about, homosexuality is the dark, dirty secret of the right-wing Orthodox yeshiva. I saw it in the study hall and in the right-wing summer camps, where teenage boys would huddle together in bed, ostensibly to tell each other secrets or keep warm. The rabbis knew it was going on but looked the other way. Of course, it was forbidden by the Torah they so revered and followed letter by letter. "Thou shalt not lie with a man, as with a woman; it is abomination," Moses tells the Jewish people in Leviticus 18:22. I don't know, maybe our rebbes reasoned that the boys would grow out of

it, as most apparently do. In any case, they probably felt
that it was easier than having girls around.

Girls were creatures from another planet. On the subway,
I would stare at their bosoms and legs, wondering what it
felt like to be them, wondering what it would be like to touch
them. In school, we were taught that the mere act of touching girls before marriage was a sin. This was an especially
difficult message to assimilate for those of us who were
clandestinely listening to the Beatles croon "I Want To Hold
Your Hand."

The injunction against touching girls stems from their
"unclean" state following their menstrual flow. The way to
undo this uncleanliness is for a woman to bathe in a *mikveh*,
or ritual bath. Orthodox women who are married visit the
mikveh after their period in order to resume sexual relations
with their husbands. (According to Orthodox law, intercourse is prohibited during the menstrual flow and for the
seven days following its cessation.) The mikveh option,
however, is not offered to single girls or women. Hence,
they remain in a perpetual "unclean" state until the waters
of the mikveh purify them before their wedding night.

My yeshiva environment, with its demanding schedule
and numerous rules, was repressive, to be sure, but I was
not going to let it all stand in the way of my journalistic
growth. I carried that small blue penitential volume with me
every day, just in case Rabbi Siegel should suddenly appear
on the D train, saying "purify your mind with Torah." But
I read the *Trib* faithfully. I just threw the paper away before
I got to school.

# CHAPTER 6

# Hinduism

Said the Koretzer: "God and Prayer are One.
God and Torah are One. God, Israel and Torah
are One."

PUPIL: How many Gods are there?

TEACHER: 3,306.

PUPIL: How many?

TEACHER: 33.

PUPIL: How many?

TEACHER: 1½.

PUPIL: How many?

TEACHER: 1.

This dialogue, from a traditional Hindu legend, is a far cry from anything that would have taken place in the yeshivas of my youth. Yet the ultimate answer is the same. The belief in one God is, of course, the cornerstone of Judaism, and it is also a tenet of Christianity, with its three-in-one Trinity. Islam also proclaims,

"There is no God but Allah and Muhammad is His Prophet."

In my world religions class, Professor Eck related the dialogue between Hindu teacher and pupil to illustrate a very different concept: the idea of the "manyness" of God. It is an idea alien not only to the Western religious imagination but to our entire cultural construct. All of modern Western thought could be said to be grounded in monotheism. We all believe in One Truth. In our minds, there is only one Cadillac, one president, one cola ("the Real Thing"), one Harvard.

Hinduism does not have one creed, one founder, one prophet or one central moment of revelation. It is the product of five thousand years of religious and cultural development in Asia. Over that time, it assimilated many ideas and ideologies. As in the pupil-teacher dialogue quoted, the right answer depends on your *darsana*—your point of view. A strictly numerical answer to the pupil's question about the number of gods is unimportant. The important lesson conveyed is that the question of God, like so many other questions, can be seen from different valid angles. "Truth is one and the wise call it by many names," goes an ancient Hindu saying.

All of this reflects a humility about human understanding that is almost unknown in the West, where we want to explore everything from the tiniest cell to the farthest corners of the universe. The Rig Veda, an ancient holy book of Hindu lore, says that mankind knows only one-quarter of all the speech that exists. When the universe was created by the gods, they used only this limited amount of speech. Reality, then, far exceeds what we can ever imagine or express.

So Hinduism introduced me to a new concept: henotheism. Rather than the worship of one single God, henotheism is the worship of one God at a time. Each God fills the whole horizon when it is worshiped. No other God, no matter how great on the celestial hierarchy, can compete. At the moment that man calls, the God invoked is the only God.

Which God created heaven and earth? It depends on your point of view. Here is one story: The Gods Vishnu and Brahma meet and argue over which of them is the ultimate Creator. A fight ensues. Brahma enters Vishnu's body to consider the validity of his opponent's view. Vishnu enters Brahma's body to do the same. So impressed are they by the new perspective, that they give up the fight and decide to honor each other as Creator. As they are congratulating each other on their greatness, a great fire—the God Shiva—consumes them.

Not all these tales make a great deal of sense to me, but their imagery is astounding. Here is one of my favorites: In the toenails of one God is reflected all of the Universe.

Given this diversity of gods, each Hindu person is free to choose his or her own god or goddess. (Interestingly, however, men more than women tend to choose goddesses.) In Hinduism, man chooses God from among all the gods. There are 800 million people in India and 300 million gods.

For me, this is a whole new way to view God. Man choosing God is in stark contrast to the Jewish idea that God chooses man, and more specifically that once, long ago, God chose the Jewish people. If Jews are the Chosen People, Hindus are the People who Choose God.

My guide through this multiplicity of gods was Gandhi. In class, we studied his life and his writings, one of which became emblematic of my year at Harvard. It was called *All Religions Are True*. Mohandas Karamchand Gandhi grew up in a close-knit Hindu family compound in Gujarat in western India. His mother would recite to him from the Koran and the holy books of the Sikhs as well as the Hindu Upanishads and Bhagavad Gita. What emerged in the philosophy of his adulthood was the doctrine of *ahimsa*, or nonviolence, which he believed was the way to achieve the realization of God. For Gandhi, this was the finest harmony of religion and politics.

In the struggle to free India from British domination, Gandhi employed ahimsa not as a passive philosophy but as a way of political action. Although it might sound like a contradiction in terms, passivity as action is not all that alien to the West, Professor Eck pointed out. Consider Jesus on the cross. In his passive suffering, Christians believe mankind was redeemed from sin and death.

It was for this reason that the cross was a favorite symbol of the Hindu leader, who used it in worship and as a rallying point in his nonviolent demonstrations. The wide range of his Hinduism, in fact, made incorporation of such a symbol only natural. "Since my youth upwards," Gandhi writes in *All Religions Are True*,

> it has been a humble but persistent effort on my part to understand the truth of all the religions of the world, and adopt and assimilate in my own thought, word, and deed all that I have found to be best in those religions. The faith that I profess not only permits me to do so, but renders it obligatory for me to take the best from whatsoever source it may come.

This acceptance of diversity, however, has a down side. Apparently for all religions to be true, they all have to be imperfect. After all, if any one religion were perfect, it would be better than all the others. "The Vedas, the Koran and the Bible are the imperfect word of God," Gandhi writes, if only because they are conveyed through imperfect human beings. "Whilst I believe that the principal books are inspired, they suffer from a process of double distillation. Firstly, they come through a human prophet; and then through the commentaries of interpreters. Nothing in them comes from God directly."

Today's fundamentalists disagree with Gandhi, but his outlook gave him a wonderful opportunity for openness sorely lacking in most religious philosophies. At the same time, Gandhi's openness did not dilute his own religious conviction. He rails against conversion, especially the efforts of Western Christian missionaries in India who came to "win souls for God."

"It is idle to talk of winning souls for God," he writes. "Is God so helpless that He cannot win souls for Himself?"

Conversion, he adds, is a pointless exercise. "All religions are branches of the same mighty tree, but I must not change over from one branch to another for the sake of expediency. By doing so, I cut the branch on which I am sitting."

Gandhi's ideas are beautiful. Still, there is one section of *All Religions Are True* that disturbs me. With all his tolerance, all his diversity, he writes that he is repulsed by parts of the Old Testament. Apparently, it is too violent, vindictive and vengeful for this apostle of nonviolence. "Between the Old and the New Testaments, there is a fundamental difference," he writes. "Whilst the Old contains some very deep truths, I am unable to pay it the same honours I pay the New Testament. I regard the latter as an extension of the teaching of the Old and, in some matters, a rejection of the Old."

Still, Gandhi redeems himself, in my eyes, with these concluding paragraphs:

> Nor do I regard the New as the last word of God. Religious ideas, like everything else, are subject to the same law of evolution that governs everything else in this Universe. Only God is changeless; and as His message is received through the imperfect human medium, it is always liable to suffer distortion in proportion as the medium is pure or otherwise. I would, therefore, respectfully urge my Christian friends and well-wishers to take me as I am.
>
> I am convinced, I know, that God will ask, asks us now, not what we label ourselves, but what we are, i.e. what we do. With Him *deed* is everything; *belief* without deed is nothing. With Him doing is believing.

My friend Gary, one of the handful of Jewish students at the Div School, was spending his time there exploring the historic and theological links between Judaism and Hin-

duism. He divided his time between classes in Hebrew
and classes in Sanskrit. I expressed surprise at his course
of study, saying that I thought the two faiths—one
monotheistic, the other polytheistic—have little in common.

That appears to be true, he said, only because Judaism as
we know it was so influenced by Christianity. "What I'm
trying to do is to look at Judaism as it was in the post-Biblical
and pre-Christian times," he said. "There are many more
similarities, for example, in the myths of the Gita and the
Mahabharata and the Torah."

We don't normally think of Jews and Hindus living together, he said, but there have long been Jewish communities in India and Persia. "Did you know that the Lord
Krishna is mentioned in the Book of Esther?"

I looked it up. It was a tale that I had read each year on
the holiday of Purim since I was a boy, but never took note.
But there it was in the text. When Ahasuerus, the Persian
king who is almost duped by Haman but is set straight by
Queen Esther, is deciding what to do with his first wife, he
consults "the seven princes of Persia," among them a deity
named Krishna.

Gary was twenty-four. He was of slight build, had blond
hair and wore a small gold earring in his right ear. He had
grown up in a comfortable home just south of Los Angeles,
a home with strong Jewish identification but little Jewish
observance.

In high school, however, Gary got interested in his Jewish
heritage and began to study with a Hasidic rabbi. Later,
when he went on to college at Berkeley, he became active in
the Hillel, the Jewish campus organization. On occasion he
would join in the charismatic prayers at the local Chabad
House, which is run by the Lubavitch Hasidic group.

"At Berkeley, I was a premed student majoring in religion," he said. "But I soon realized that I didn't want to go
to medical school. I dropped out of college, lived on a farm

for two years and then went to a small college in Connecticut. I decided to study something that really interested me. I began to study world religions.

"When I got out of college, I applied for a Fulbright to study in Vienna. When I didn't get it, I decided to go anyway. I took an apartment, sat in on courses at the university, talked to professors, sat in the coffeehouses, made a lot of friends."

Since leaving California, Gary was coming to terms with more than his distaste for medicine as a profession. He was trying to come to terms with his homosexuality or, as he put it, "I've been coming out of the closet ever since I dropped out of Berkeley. I wasn't fully out until I got to Divinity School."

The Div School has a reputation for being particularly accepting of homosexuals. "There aren't a lot of other seminaries in the country where it is okay to be gay," Gary said. "Here it's not an issue." At most seminaries, being homosexual is a cardinal sin; at the Div School, the cardinal sin is being homophobic—that is, discriminating in any way against homosexuals.

Gary felt welcome both at the Div School and in the larger Harvard community, including the Harvard Hillel. With his earring in place and a talith on his shoulders, he frequently led Friday-night prayers at the Conservative service at Hillel, one of the four Sabbath services held there. (The others were Orthodox, Reform and Traditional Egalitarian, which was liturgically Orthodox but in which men and women participated as equals.)

Was he interested in becoming a rabbi?

"I've considered rabbinical school," Gary said, "but I wouldn't go back into the closet to go to seminary." The Jewish Theological Seminary, which trains Conservative rabbis, does not accept openly gay men and women into its rabbinical program. The openly gay are accepted by the Reform seminary, Hebrew Union College–Jewish Institute of Religion, but, Gary said, "I wouldn't want to go to a Reform

seminary." He believed that the Reform, with its innova-
tions in Jewish tradition, has strayed too far from classical
Judaism. "Right now, being a rabbi interests me, but not
rabbinical college."

Another student exploring Hinduism at the Div School
was Diane, who, like Gary, was twenty-four years old and a
homosexual. In her last year of college, Diane also applied
for a fellowship to study abroad, but, unlike Gary, she got
it. She came to the Div School after spending six months in
India, where she had been studying the role of women in
traditional Hindu families.

Diane, a member of the United Church of Christ, a Protestant denomination once known as Congregationalist, had
a seriousness about her that seemed incongruous with her
looks. She was just a little over five feet tall and wore her
blond hair stylishly short. Her red cheeks were so pudgy
that it seemed she had to make an effort not to smile.

"There are a lot of us here," she said of the school's gay
and lesbian students. "If you asked, maybe ten percent of
us would raise our hands, which means there are a lot more
than ten percent." Students estimated that one-quarter to
one-third of the student body of the Div School was gay.

"At the conservative college I went to," Diane continued,
"the Gay and Lesbian Caucus had maybe eight people. It's
much more comfortable here. We're not walking around
wearing signs; for us, being gay is a perfectly normal
thing."

Still, she added, being a gay seminarian had its anxieties.
"For a lot of people, their careers depend on keeping their
gayness a secret." As a result, gay students who could be
very open on campus, walking arm in arm with a lover, had
to be more discreet about their sexual orientation back in
their denominational churches.

Nearly all the Protestant denominations in the United
States explicitly exclude homosexuals from the ministry.
The liberal ones do this even while vigorously advocating

equal rights for gays in housing and employment. The denominations draw the line at accepting gays into the ministry for a variety of reasons, including the belief that
homosexuals would not provide the right kind of "family
role models" for congregations and because of the clear Biblical injunction against homosexual practice.

Motions to ordain homosexuals are offered regularly at
the annual conventions of many denominations, including
the Presbyterians, the Methodists and the Episcopalians.
Advocates of equality for homosexuals in the ministry routinely lose these votes but say that their cause is gaining
momentum. The margins of defeat are shrinking. Homosexuals are nonetheless ordained into these churches; they
just keep quiet about their sexual orientation.

Diane's denomination, the United Church of Christ, is
one of the few that has adopted a national policy in favor of
ordaining gay ministers. However, the national denomination holds little power over the individual congregations. Of
the more than one thousand Congregationalist churches,
fewer than twenty have shown a willingness to appoint a
homosexual to the pulpit.

Diane grew up in a churchgoing home in suburban Detroit
but never gave much thought to entering the ministry, even
when she saw a woman ordained in her church. By the time
she went off to college, Diane had stopped going to church
altogether. "When I would visit home, I remember going
and finding it all so meaningless," she said.

Back in college, however, she found another spiritual out-
let, witchcraft. She joined a coven, a small group of women
who commune with spirits, and participated in their
monthly "full-moon ritual." The group would gather once
a month in what they called a "magic circle" in a quiet
clearing just after the moon rose. They would light candles
and then wait for the wind to blow them out. One by one,
the women would call out in each of the four directions,
evoking the elements attributed to each: East to air and the

mind; South to fire and energy; West to water, emotion and sexuality; North to earth and the body. Together they might chant:

> All-dewy, sky-sailing pregnant moon,
> Who shines for all.
> Who flows through all . . .
> Aridia, Diane, Cybele, Mah.

As it turned out, some of Diane's friends from the magic circle were also churchgoers. "I would go to the ritual on Saturday night and join them in church on Sunday morning," she said. "I found that some of the same sense of empowerment that I got from the coven, I would get from the church." Diane began to explore these feelings in religion courses. "I found it intellectually challenging and personally challenging," she said of her study.

When she entered the Div School, however, she was unsure of her goals. "I was torn between the ministry and the academic world," she said, explaining that she did not know whether she wanted to be ordained in her church or pursue a Ph.D. in theology. Midway through her first year, she was leaning toward the ministry, albeit with some reservations. "In the parish you live in a fishbowl, and that can be difficult with the whole lesbian issue," she said. "Yet it is in the parish where all the dimensions of ministry come together—teaching, counseling, preaching." Diane told me that she was glad she had another two and a half years at the Div School before she had to make the decision about her future, adding: "This is a good place to sort it all out."

# Buddhism

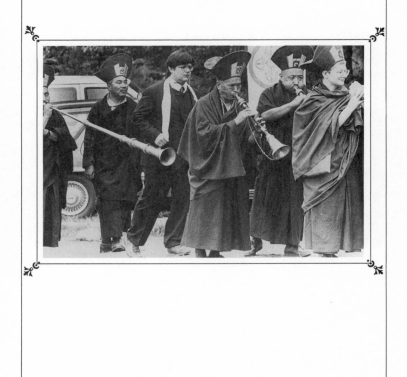

The Bratzlaver said: "Meditation and prayer
before God is particularly meritorious in grassy
fields and amid the trees, since a man's soul is
thereby strengthened, as if every blade of grass
and every plant is united with him in prayer."

I n a matter of lectures we went from Hinduism, with its millions of gods, to Buddhism,
with none. "None" is an even harder concept for Western-
ers to swallow. Professor Eck recalled one former student's
reaction to Buddhism: "You mean they don't even believe
in God? That really grosses me out. And they don't want to
live forever? You call *that* a religion?"

Yes, we do. And in so doing I am introduced to the idea
that a belief in God may not even be a prerequisite for a
religion. After all, we are talking about Buddhism as a religion (from "binding back") rather than in the God-talk of
theology. And Buddhism binds the believer back to a period
some five hundred years before Jesus.

The Buddha, Siddhartha Gautama, was a human being, a
seeker, who became free. He was born to a privileged family
in the north of India and was raised a prince. His father, the
raja of Kapilavastu, had a vision in which he saw that his
son would be either a beggar or a king. He sought to protect

the youth from the harsh realities of life. The prince lived comfortably in the palace, took a wife of his father's choosing, who bore him a son. His privileged life insulated him from the realities of the world, realities he only glimpsed when his coachman drove him through the streets.

On one journey the prince saw old age. Then he saw disease and then, in the figure of a corpse, death. On his final trip, he saw a mendicant, a man who had renounced worldly goods to go through life begging for alms in the streets. The prince returned home, kissed his wife and son as they slept and told his servant to prepare his white horse. The prince galloped to the outskirts of town, dismounted, set his horse free and became a seeker.

At first, he searched for knowledge in the traditional Hindu way, striving through rigorous yoga exercise to unite himself with the world. But this failed. He continued through harsh physical denial, living on one sesame seed a day, until he was near death. Ultimately, he rejected the ascetic life and turned to meditation. Sitting under a fig tree, he gained Enlightenment.

The cause of all unhappiness, the Buddha reasoned, is desire. The ills of life all flow from the lust for power, success, sex and material pleasures. Give up the desire and one can attain truth. In Leviticus, the God of the Hebrews declares that one must love one's neighbor as oneself. To Buddha, one need not love even oneself.

Even after the story, the question remains, what kind of religion is this? In class, we read Walpola Rahula's *What the Buddha Taught*. Rahula describes Buddhism as more of a therapy than a philosophy and Buddha as "a physician not a metaphysician."

In one three-word saying of the Buddha I find an entire lesson in comparative religion. "Come and see," the Buddha tells his followers. It is not the "Come, follow me" of Jesus and it is not the "Come and learn" of the rabbis of the Talmud. For Buddhists, it is come and see . . . for yourself.

My first reporting experience with Buddhism, which came soon after I left the Div School, seemed a long way from the ideals described in the Harvard classroom. I journeyed to a clearing in the Vermont woods for the cremation of a Tibetan teacher who had helped bring Buddhism to the West. His name was Chogyam Trungpa Rinpoche, and he died at the age of forty-seven of what his critics described as excess. Too much food, too much liquor, too much sex. His American followers saw his great appetite for life as a virtue and attributed his death to a heart attack. Although AIDS was never mentioned in connection with Trungpa's death, the man who succeeded him as leader of the sect, Osel Tendzin, died of the disease in 1990, also at the age of forty-seven.

On the spring morning of the cremation, there was a mood of restrained celebration. The followers preparing for the rite were an interesting assortment of 1980s yuppies, people who had been attracted to Trungpa in the tumultuous sixties and remained under his influence even as they settled down and prospered.

The ceremony, to which several thousand followers flocked, gave me an opportunity to write about Trungpa's life, how he fled from Tibet in 1959 and became a major exponent of Buddhism in the West, and about the dramatic cremation rite, complete with ringing handbells and Zen archers performing a choreographed ceremony around the burning pyre. In my piece, I was also able to give a sense that, although a funeral, this was a kind of Woodstock for grown-ups, noting the blankets, insect repellent, lunch coolers and backpacks for toddlers. But my favorite, if whimsical, quote fell prey to one of my straitlaced editors: "This is not a wake," I had quoted one follower, "it is awake."

"Awake" is the goal of every Buddhist, and that is what Trungpa's death meant. In death, Trungpa came into full enlightenment and shared that spirit with his followers. "Although the body of the teacher has died and will be consumed by flames, his mind still exists and pervades all space," David Rome, an aide to the holy man, explained at a press briefing the day before the cremation. The moment of the cremation, he added, would be a propitious moment during which the followers could "connect with the mind of the teacher and accomplish a greater realization of ourselves."

Aside from his Buddhist connections, the fortyish Rome was a descendant of Salman Schocken, a department store owner in Germany who in 1932 became a book publisher. When, under Hitler, Aryan companies could no longer publish books by Jewish writers, Schocken acquired the rights to Kafka's works, which the company still holds. Like most of the two thousand people who gathered for the Buddhist funeral rite, Rome was born Jewish.

In my article, I did not mention the large Jewish presence at the Buddhist leader's cremation. (*The Times*'s policy is not to note religion or race unless it is "relevant" to the article, a judgment call exercised by editors.) Nor could I relate what Emily Wolitzky, another devotee of Trungpa in her forties, told me: "I always wanted to be awakened by Judaism, but as a woman there was nothing there for me." Emily was not just another woman in the crowd; she had been my older brother's girlfriend some fifteen years earlier.

Emily's complaints about Judaism were something I had heard from other Jewish women. At a Buddhist study center in western New Jersey, a woman who grew up in an Orthodox Jewish home told me: "If I were twenty today, I'd probably want to become a rabbi, but I'm forty and a Buddhist." The first women were admitted to the Reform rabbinate in the early 1970s. The Conservatives began to ordain women in 1985; the Orthodox still do not and probably never will.

While some Jewish women were drawn to Buddhism because they felt excluded from Judaism, Buddhism holds other attractions for Jews. It is a faith that makes few demands on its adherents; you don't even have to be a Buddhist to participate. An outsider is welcome to draw what spiritual nourishment he or she wants from the faith and leave the rest. For Jews alienated from Judaism, Buddhism provides an alternative that isn't Christianity. As disillusioned as many of these Jews were with their own faith, they had been conditioned by their upbringing to seeing Christianity not merely as a substitute for but as a repudiation of Judaism.

For this reason, Buddhism is especially attractive to Jewish-Christian couples. Instead of setting up a struggle over who, the Jew or the Christian, should give in, it offers a third alternative—take on a new faith that is broadminded enough to encompass the practices of the old ones.

Not long after the Trungpa cremation, I covered the first dialogue between the Dalai Lama, the leader of Tibetan Buddhism, and a group of Jewish scholars. The meeting was held at the impetus of the Dalai Lama, who lives in exile from his native Tibet and makes frequent visits to the United States. The Dalai Lama said that he wanted to better understand "the secret" of Jewish survival through two thousand years of exile. He also wanted to learn more about Judaism, he said, since so many of his American followers were Jews. I spent some time with the Buddhist organizers of the event, all of whom were born Jewish. Then I met their wives, virtually all of whom were born Christian.

With my Orthodox background, however, I felt alienated from Buddhism. I could neither bow nor light candles to a statue. At the cremation in Vermont, though, I was clearly in the minority. No one, it seemed, was as hung up about these things as I. I was surrounded by people with names as Jewish as my own who were using Tibetan words to describe their spiritual life (dharma, samsara, nirvana) and meditating on their knees before the burning stupa of their teacher, who had been preserved in salt, covered in purified butter and wrapped in silk.

I thought back to the time when Shalom and Emily had dated. I cannot picture Shalom alone during those years, only with Emily at his side. He was tall and bearded, his red hair in a ponytail. She was petite and curly haired and favored loose-fitting peasant dresses. Once on a visit to the brownstone Emily and Shalom shared in Brooklyn's Park Slope section (to the horror of my parents), I saw Emily kneeling silently in a darkened room as she lit a candle at an altar in front of a corpulent wooden Buddha. As someone who then knew just one religion—Judaism—I wondered what was wrong with her. But now, in Vermont, with a basic understanding of Buddhism, I wondered what was wrong with me. After all, was lighting candles before the Buddha all that different from lighting candles to welcome the Sabbath on Friday night?

# Sabbath
# Candles

When an old woman who had served in her
youth in the household of Rabbi Elimelech was
importuned for stories about the master and his
ways, she said: "Nought has remained with me
in my remembrance, save only this. During the
week, there were often quarrels in the kitchen,
and upbraidings between the maidenfolk, as in
other households. But in this we differed from
others: on the eve of each Sabbath, we fell
around each other's neck, and we begged
forgiveness for any harsh words spoken during
the week."

F or me, Sabbath candles still held their
magic. There was a perfect moment of silence when Shira would light them in our apartment in
Somerville as the sun went down Friday evenings. She
would wave her hands three times over the blue-and-white
flames, cover her eyes and recite her private prayers. "What
do you say?" I would ask when she had finished, knowing
that, for her, the formulaic blessing ("Blessed art thou . . .
who sanctified us with the commandment of lighting Sabbath candles") would not suffice. Shira would always answer
my inquiry with a smile, which was all I really wanted
anyway.

With the arrival of Shabbat, as we called it, our house
would be transformed. The TV, the radio, the record player,

the food processor and the word processor were shut off. Cooking and cleaning ceased. Exams and terms papers were behind me. Deadlines and interviews were behind Shira. There were only the three of us.

Adam, just a few months past his first birthday, was at a most delicious stage—half boy, half baby. He would toddle, cuddle, giggle and tumble, never letting go of the bottle in his mouth. He was trying out his first words, one of which was "light," which took on new meaning for him when he pointed to the candles ablaze over the white Shabbat table-cloth.

At times we would open up our little circle and invite a few guests for the Friday-night dinner. When we lived in Manhattan, these were usually Jews who, if not observant, were at least familiar with our Sabbath songs and the blessings we made over the wine and challah. In Somerville, we decided to open things up even more. After all, at the Div School, I was interested not only in learning but in sharing.

The cross-cultural possibilities were exciting. One Friday night we had over Jan, a Roman Catholic student who lived in Poland and was given a special visa to study religion at Harvard; Fran, a graduate student in the Div School who worked part-time for her church, the First Church of Christ, Scientist; and Anna, a bright undergraduate religion major who was Jewish and in my world religions class. On another occasion, two other classmates—Gary, my gay friend from California, and Edward, who was straight and from England —joined us. My dream was to get my two favorite teachers there on one night, but it couldn't be arranged. Instead, Rabbi Louis Jacobs came with his wife, Shula, one night and Professor Eck came another.

The discussions at our Sabbath table ranged widely and deeply, going well beyond the formality of a classroom or the niceties of a dinner party. Shira and I found that the sharing of our Sabbath rituals broke down barriers rather than created them. As we made the blessing over the wine, ritually poured water from a cup on our hands and cut the

83611

challah, our guests questioned and compared and shared their own religious experiences. They talked about their lives, their families, their religious awakenings and disappointments and the meaning they derived from them.

On one Friday night, Lisa, a classmate who once managed a health food restaurant, joined us with her live-in boyfriend, Jim, a graphic artist who had trained at the School of Visual Arts in Manhattan. Lisa and I talked about the courses we were taking and general Div School gossip that nobody but a student there could care about, like whether the seminar on the morality of nuclear war should be open to undergraduates. Shira and Jim were talking about the virtues of living in Boston versus New York. Jim didn't show any interest in things religious until we gathered around the Sabbath table and I recited the Hebrew prayer over the wine. "What does that mean?" Jim asked.

"It's from Genesis," I told him, offering a rough translation, "And God finished creating the heavens and the earth and rested on the seventh day."

"Chapter two, verse one," Jim said, with a nod of his head. "Thus the heavens and the earth were finished, and all the host of them." He went on like this, quoting the King James Bible in perfect preaching cadence. He saw he had a surprised and appreciative audience, so he continued with such fervor that I was afraid he would wake Adam. "And the name of the third river is Hiddekel: that is it which goeth toward the east of Assyria. And the fourth river is Euphrates." He didn't stop until he had finished the chapter. "And they were both naked, the man and his wife, and were not ashamed."

"I am the son of a Southern Baptist preacher from Louisiana," Jim told us over dinner. "It was a bit like growing up as a monk, except that you still had to live with your family. Grace before eating. Study the Bible, the unerring word of God. And beware of Catholics. And girls? Oh, there were girls, but don't get caught with one. Remember, social dancing is the work of the Devil!" We laughed and talked about growing up until the differences between a Southern Baptist from Louisiana and an Orthodox Jew from New York seemed minuscule.

As they were ready to leave, Lisa and Jim asked us the question we got most often about our Sabbath ritual: "You do this every Friday night?" We had to answer in truth that we did. There was no party, no show, no dance, no assignment, no opening that could stop us. "Why?" No, it was not the Biblical mandate to observe the Sabbath or its rabbinic interpretation, although these figured into our observance. Our greatest motivation was also the most inexplicable: It was the magic that happened when Shira lit the candles.

One Friday night, after a house full of company, I fell asleep and dreamed I heard a knock on the door. In my dream, I arose, opened the door and saw Rabbi Siegel. "Rebbe!" I said with surprise. He walked right past me and into the kitchen. First he looked into all the cabinets, checking for the kosher symbols on each product—the *o* with the little *u* inside, indicating the approval of the Union of Orthodox Jewish Congregations; the *VHM*, the Vaad Harabanim (Rabbinical Council) of Massachusetts or the less preferable *K*, signifying kosher but not telling by whose authority.

Then he held his hand over the top of the range to make sure it was warm. Since Jewish law forbids turning the stove on and off on the Sabbath, it is customary to leave one burner on to heat up food.

Then Rabbi Siegel turned to the table, all covered with white, except for a half-empty bottle of Sabbath wine. He spoke for the first time: "Were there goyim here tonight?"

The word stung my ears. I knew why he was asking. If a Gentile pours from an opened bottle of wine, the wine is rendered unclean and cannot be used for kiddush.

"Yes, there were goyim," I told him, using the word against my will. "But, Rebbe, I did the pouring."

Religious diversity was not something that came naturally to me but a taste acquired in adulthood. At the right-wing Orthodox high school I attended, there was no acknowledgment that anyone but us, sitting there poring over the Talmud, had any religious validity. Christianity was unmentionable. (When we said "X-mas," it was not some cute shorthand or an abbreviation substituting the Greek letter *chi* for Christ, but a way to avoid uttering the word *Christ*.) We were also taught to shun those in the more liberal Reform and Conservative branches of Judaism. Just as one was not permitted to enter a church (even if only to escape the rain), one could not walk into a Reform or Conservative temple. Who knows who might snatch you at the door!

Likewise, so-called secular knowledge—math, science, literature—was given second-class status. "Real" knowledge was knowledge of the Torah; the rest was only a concession to a world into which we would have to go out someday and make a living. College was frowned upon, although the right-wing rabbis looked the other way if you studied Torah during the day and went to college at night. Night school, after all, was a place to earn credits, not a laboratory for new ideas. And besides, there weren't that many girls who took courses at night at Brooklyn College, the school popular with yeshiva boys. But even better than college, we were told not too subtly, was a rich father or, if you missed out on that, a rich father-in-law, someone who would free you from the worldly concerns so that you would have time for the important thing in life—Torah study.

Because I had a father of only modest means and was not dating anyone (rich or otherwise), college was definitely in the cards for me. My grades, however, did not exactly mark me as "college material." The rigorous dual program of my yeshiva high school, plus the long subway ride from Queens and later from Manhattan, where we eventually moved with my mother, had taken their toll. Secular studies were so deemphasized in my school and my home life was so tumultuous that I was barely passing some of my courses and routinely failing the New York standardized tests known as the Regents. My parents, who hoped and expected that I would go to college, woke up to this fact late in my high school career and worried that no college would want me. After I failed biology in my junior year, my father took me out of Jewish summer camp in the Poconos (where my mother had sent me), brought me to his house in Hartford and enrolled me in summer school. There, finally, I passed bio. Given my new academic success, I remained in Hartford and finished my last year of high school there. It wasn't as if my parents actually made the decision for me to stay in Hartford. It was more a factor of inertia. I was there already, so there I stayed.

So, at the age of sixteen, I enrolled at Weaver High School in Hartford and had my first educational experience outside of a strictly Orthodox environment. I was going to school with Catholics and Protestants and Jews of all different stripes (except the familiar Orthodox). There were blacks and Hispanics too. And girls.

My first crisis was whether to continue to wear a yarmulke, the cap that is supposed to remind us of a "higher power" atop our heads. In yeshiva we had been taught not to walk four cubits without a hat or cap covering our heads. (As any *real* yeshiva boy can tell you, a cubit is a Biblical measurement equal to the distance from the tip of the middle finger to the elbow.) At home, my brothers and I wore yarmulkes all the time; we went to sleep with the yarmulkes on our heads, although we usually found them somewhere under our beds in the morning. We wore them on the streets, on the subway, at the movies. Most important, we needed yarmulkes to make b'rachas, for how could we bless the food we were about to eat before God with heads uncovered? All these rules made perfect sense in the world of the yeshiva and the Orthodox home. But what about at Weaver High School on Blue Hills Avenue in Hartford, Connecticut?

The principal of my new school advised me against it.

Wearing a yarmulke would be looking for trouble in a school that was then 60 percent black, he counseled. It was, after all, 1966, just a few years after violent race riots had ripped through New York, Newark, Los Angeles and Chicago. Much of the hostility was directed at the white merchants, many of them Jewish, who owned stores in the ghetto.

I insisted, however, on wearing my yarmulke when I ate, so the principal gave me special permission to go home for lunch. Luckily, my home for the year, where my father and his parents lived, was just two blocks from Weaver High.

School was eye-opening. In history class, I learned about the Reformation and finally figured out why there were Protestants *and* Catholics. For the first time, I took a real gym class, complete with a running track and showers, where, for the first time also, I saw uncircumcised males. (In yeshiva high school, gym meant playing stickball in the parking lot.) And, because I loved to sing (mostly the songs of the synagogue), I somewhat naively enrolled in an honors course in music.

Sitting in the music class, along with the top members of the Weaver High School Orchestra, I was short on musical sophistication but long on innate musical appreciation. Thanks to the nurturing of the wonderful woman who taught the class, a Mrs. Martin, I felt instantly at home with Mozart, Mahler, Wagner and Bartók. And, most of all, she gave me Handel. At first George Frederick Handel and I did not get along. Christmas was approaching, and Mrs. Martin was examining with us Handel's most famous work, the *Messiah*. How could I—still the yeshiva boy at heart— study an oratorio about the Coming of Christ? How could I listen to a libretto that distorted the meaning of the Jewish Prophet Isaiah ("For unto us a Child is born" or "And behold, a Virgin shall conceive") for Christological ends? Even worse, how could I hear the promises of the New Testament ("Behold the lamb of God, that taketh away the sins of the world," or "Since by man came death, by man came also the resurrection of the dead")?

"I don't want your soul, just your heart," Mrs. Martin

told me when I protested. "You can remain a good Jew and still love this music. And I'll make a deal with you. Listen to this and I will add an oratorio on a Jewish theme that the whole class will learn—just because you are here with us."

I studied the *Messiah*, even learned of the tradition of standing during the "Hallelujah Chorus." What beautiful music. But even more astounding for me was what came next: Handel's *Israel in Egypt*. It was as if he had written it for me. I loved the plaintive "And the Children of Israel Sighed," the pastoral "He Sent a Thick Darkness" and the galloping "The Horse and His Rider, the Horse and His Rider, Hath He Thrown into the Sea." I cannot think of those words without hearing Handel's glorious music in my ears.

Surely Mrs. Martin did not want to see me convert. In fact, more than anyone Jewish I had known, she encouraged me to become a cantor. "What a wonderful career," she said, thinking it over out loud, "singing for God."

Despite my parents' worst fears (or maybe because of them), I made it into college. I entered the undergraduate school of Yeshiva University in the fall of 1967. It was, in a real sense, my family's school. My father had gone there, as had innumerable uncles and first, second and third cousins from both sides of my family. (The man my mother was to marry several years later, when I was a senior at Yeshiva, was also a graduate.) In 1976, when Dr. Samuel Belkin, the president of the university, died, two of my uncles (one on my mother's side and one on my father's) vied for the presidency. One of them, Dr. Norman Lamm, got it; the other, Rabbi Israel Miller, already a vice president of the school, was reappointed to his post.

The philosophy of the school was as different from that of Weaver High School, where I graduated, as it was from that of the right-wing Crown Heights Mesifta, where I'd spent the first three years of high school. If Weaver represented secular America, Crown Heights represented Eastern

European Orthodox Judaism. The goal of Yeshiva University was to "synthesize" the two into a unique brand of American Orthodoxy, something we called back then "Modern Orthodoxy." The school's motto has long been "*Torah U'Maddah*," which loosely translated means "religious studies and secular knowledge." In this approach, the humanities and the sciences are not necessary evils, as they had been to my right-wing rabbis, but valid intellectual pursuits which also are to be revered and explored as the handiwork of the Almighty. While secular studies were downplayed at my Orthodox high school, they were central to the Yeshiva College curriculum. And Yeshiva was proud of its graduate schools of medicine, law and social work, as well as its affiliated Orthodox rabbinical school, the Rabbi Isaac Elchanan Theological Seminary.

My cousins, also the children of Yeshiva University graduates, were sent to elementary schools and high schools that shared the liberal Torah U'Maddah philosophy, places like Ramaz on the East Side of Manhattan. But my brothers and I, owing in large measure to the confusion that followed our parents' divorce, were educated in the extremes. (Curiously, several of these moderately raised and educated cousins are now Gush Emunim—Block of the Faithful—settlers in Israel who carry guns on the West Bank in the name of Biblical Judea and Samaria.)

Despite the emphasis at Yeshiva on secular learning, I remained largely oblivious to my courses once there. The only thing that really interested me was the school newspaper, the *Commentator*. Instead of studying in the library, I would interview my classmates, write articles and then join the newspaper editors at a printer in Lower Manhattan late at night to "put the paper to bed." I loved every part of the process, especially the writing. In my sophomore year, I wrote a feature story about a Yeshiva senior named Harry Weiss, who served as the campus correspondent, or stringer, for *The New York Times*. I wrote a nice story about him that answered the question, Why would *The New York*

*Times* care about Yeshiva, anyway? I explained that Yeshiva was a place where *The Times* could take the pulse of the American Jewish community, get answers to questions about Jewish practice and see how students react to the 1960s student rebellion at a conservatively religious but politically liberal campus. When Weiss graduated, he recommended me to *The Times* as his successor. I was hired as a *Times* stringer. My toe was in the door.

While newspaper writing was my primary concern, I also absorbed a good deal of the Yeshiva philosophy. It said, in effect, that Orthodox Judaism is not made for the ghetto but for the world. One could be involved in the world and all its challenges of science and philosophy and still be a good Jew. The persons we most esteemed were those who were at the cutting edge of medical research—and still remained observant; those who argued cases before the Supreme Court— and still remained observant; those who made a killing on Wall Street—and still remained observant. And observance didn't only mean that they kept the letter of the law, abstaining from forbidden foods and from work on Saturday, but meant that they also kept the spirit of the law, being moral and ethical in their personal and professional lives.

I came to see Orthodox observance as a system that was supposed to enrich a life, not frustrate it. I greatly admired the people who succeeded in their professions while grappling with the constraints of *halacha*, or Jewish law—the shopkeeper whose business thrived even though he closed on Shabbat, as well as the shopkeeper who, using a halachic loophole, took a Gentile partner who kept the store open on Shabbat. I heard tales of lawyers who asked judges to stop court proceedings because a Jewish holiday was coming at sundown and who then walked to their hotels and made a solitary kiddush in their rooms. I learned also that the law has certain flexibilities. For example, a doctor who is dealing with matters of life and death is not only permitted but has an obligation to treat patients on Saturdays. He can talk on the telephone, drive his car, perform surgery—and be living in accordance with Orthodox Jewish law.

To my mind, the law is meant to be challenged in the real world. That is where it comes alive, not in "safe" professions, like teaching, or the Orthodox-dominated world of Forty-seventh Street, where deals on diamonds are sealed with a handshake and the Yiddish words "*Mazel and Bracha,*" luck and blessings. It is easy to keep the ostensible mitzvahs there. But just think of the challenges . . . I made up scenarios for Orthodox Jews who would live in accordance with the Torah in all different professions: firemen, cowboys, forest rangers, Third World diplomats. More than anyone else, I decided, I would admire the first observant Jewish astronaut, who figured out how to observe Shabbat while orbiting the earth at supersonic speeds. To me, that person, more than anyone on the earth, would sanctify God's name.

# CHAPTER 9

# Catholics

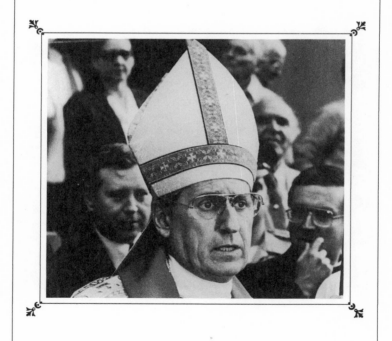

The Kobriner Rabbi turned to his Hasidim and said: "Do you know where God is?" He took a piece of bread, showed it to them all and continued: "God is in this piece of bread. Without the manifestation of His power in all nature, this piece of bread would have no existence."

At the Div School I discovered that Roman Catholics, like Orthodox Jews, have had their troubles in reconciling their faith with the real world. In fact, there was a whole course in the subject at the Div School. It was called "The American Catholic Bishops and Public Policy: A Feminist Perspective," and, as is evident from the title, it wasn't exactly a dispassionate look at the issue. The course, an examination of how American Catholics balanced church-state issues, ended up being an unrelenting attack on the antiabortion agenda of the Catholic church.

Given the strong feminist leanings of the school, this stance was not surprising. At the same time, however, it would be unfair to characterize the Div School as anti-Catholic. While most of the students were Protestants, the individual Christian denomination represented in greatest number was Roman Catholic. So it was more likely for me to be sitting next to a Catholic in class than next to an

Episcopalian or Methodist or even a Unitarian, the denomination that once ran the Div School. Why the Roman Catholics were there wasn't entirely clear to me. Just as no rabbinical school would ordain you on the basis of a Div School education, no Catholic seminary would. As best I could tell, these were not Catholics who wanted to be priests under the present rules, which allowed only celibate men. These were men and women who were married or planning to be married. Some were gay.

The Catholics at the Div School were there because they had an unfulfilled longing to be involved with their church in a manner that was consistent with their consciences and life-styles. Some said that they planned to be Catholic educators; others just wanted to be knowledgeable and active Catholic laity. For them, this course of action was the best way to change a church that they saw as out of step with modern realities. By and large, the Catholic students were not radicals; they were seekers.

"When I was young I thought I would become a member of a religious order," my friend Justin told me one day after class. "That vocation is still present within me."

In church parlance, the word *vocation* means more than a job. It means "a calling," especially to priesthood. At age twenty-three, Justin said he still had the calling but wasn't sure that he was going to answer it in the traditional Catholic way.

Justin, with the dark complexion of his Lebanese mother and the chiseled features of his German father, sang in the choir at St. Paul's, the Catholic church just off campus where George MacRae's funeral had been held. Aside from the Sunday mass, he attended the Wednesday night mass that Catholic students held at the Div School.

Even so, the priesthood did not seem in the cards for Justin. He had a girlfriend, Chris, whom he'd met at a Lutheran college in Minneapolis. Chris, a nurse, moved to Boston to be with Justin while he studied at the Div School.

Justin grew up in a small, depressed Ohio town not far from the silenced steel mills of Youngstown. He was the youngest of ten children, all of whom were given names that start with the letter *J*. There was Jack, Joan, Jeanette, Judy, Joli, Jeff, Jerry, Janice, Jane and, finally, Justin. The parents were John and Josephine. Justin once asked his mother, who gave birth to all ten children within eleven years, why she had so many. "I've wondered about that too," she told him with a smile. "But which one of you could I do without?"

The family lived in a three-bedroom apartment over the woman's clothing store that Josephine ran while John worked in a steel plant. "It was a very organized household," Justin said. "We had triple-deck bunk beds." There was one bathroom, not counting the one in the store for those willing to navigate the nineteen steps down from the apartment. "At night, that took courage," he recalled.

The family was not particularly devout, Justin said, although all the children started out in parochial schools. "I did well," he said. "I got two awards from Bishop Malone for Greek and Latin. I went on to study the classics and religion at St. Olaf's."

Of the ten children in his family, Justin said, seven have repudiated the Catholic faith and two became "ultraconservative traditionalists" who would be happy to see the revival of the Latin Mass of the pre–Vatican II era. Justin sees himself holding the middle ground, a good Catholic, but not extreme.

When Justin finished college, he applied to several graduate programs in religion in the hope of becoming a religious studies teacher in a Catholic high school. He sent applications to Notre Dame and Catholic University in Washington and then, almost as an afterthought, he applied to Harvard Divinity School. He thought Harvard was a long shot, but, in fact, he was just the kind of applicant the Div School was looking for: a good student with clear goals in religious education.

Justin got into all three schools and began to compare the

programs. Harvard offered him a generous financial aid package, and, although it wasn't Catholic like his other two choices, it had three other things that attracted him: George MacRae, Henri Nouwen and the Weston School of Theology. He decided on Harvard, only to find out later that George MacRae, the Jesuit scholar and the acting dean, had died and that Henri Nouwen, an inspiring teacher and expert in Catholic spirituality, had left the school. Weston, the Jesuit seminary just a few blocks from the Div School, was still there and open to cross-registrants from Harvard. "I figured, one out of three wasn't bad," Justin said with a wry smile.

Justin took about half of his courses at Weston, where he enjoyed the spiritual life of the "tight-knit group" of students, faculty and priests from the religious order. "I find the ideals they set there to be very appealing," he said.

When I asked Justin about "spirituality" at the Div School, he gave a hearty laugh. "There's a glorious side to Harvard and a not-so-glorious side," he said. "The glory is in walking down my hall and having a Jew, a Catholic, a Muslim all living and studying together. Everyone believes in God, but differently. The sad part is that there is no spiritual cohesion here that can bring us all together."

Catholics at the school got together each Wednesday for a mass. The students did their best to modify the ritual in an effort to encourage people to participate, but the service remained, at its heart, an orthodox ceremony. Sometimes women would read or a few topical hymns and readings would be added. "We bent the ritual a bit, but there was nothing off the wall," Justin said. For example, while some feminists wanted a woman to consecrate the wine and the wafer, as has been done in radical Catholic women's worship, the Catholic celebration at the Div School stuck to the traditional model of the male priest saying the Mass.

While they generally stayed in line when it came to the church liturgy, Catholics at the Div School took great liberties when it came to theology. Mary Segers, the instructor of the course on the Catholic bishops—and a former Catholic nun—is an outspoken feminist, writer and teacher. In class she asked students to critique Vatican documents, including the 1974 "Vatican Declaration on Abortion." "This is pitiful," a student began. "The document's strongest argument is from tradition. But it does even that badly." The Pope and all his men, from Joseph Cardinal Ratzinger to John Cardinal O'Connor, were the unmistakable villains of this course.

Few Catholic thinkers, in fact, escaped the wrath of the instructor and her students. One of the few treated with anything resembling reverence was John Courtney Murray, the Jesuit thinker who in the 1950s delineated the fine line between church and state, a distinction that helped set the stage for John F. Kennedy's campaign for president in 1960. Murray, born in New York City in 1904, labored through his writings to broaden the narrow scope through which American Catholics saw themselves as participants in American democracy.

First, during the Second World War, Murray wrote essays urging Catholics to get involved in interfaith dialogue with Protestants and Jews. These essays came, of course, before the Second Vatican Council of the mid-1960s gave any serious religious credibility to the beliefs of others. In keeping with the church's notion at the time that salvation came only through Catholic beliefs, Murray did not advocate theological dialogue but argued that non-Catholics had to be engaged if matters of social justice or human life were at stake.

In writing on church-state issues, Murray said that the church should not try to impose its will on society through legislation that would outlaw for all citizens those practices forbidden to Catholics, such as divorce. (Today, Murray followers might add such practices as birth control and homosexuality, maybe even abortion, all issues unthought of in the context of church teaching in Murray's day.) Rather than try to impose the Catholic will on others, Murray said, the church should present its positions on the basis of moral values and reason and thereby try to influence both its own members and society at large. Such a position, Murray admitted, did "not promise to transform society into the City of God" but only to prescribe "that minimum of morality which must be observed by the members of society if a social environment is to be human and inhabitable."

Murray was widely attacked in his day by conservative Catholic theologians, who argued that his vision of religious pluralism risked a watered-down Catholicism. These critics also said that the church had an obligation to pursue a legislative agenda in line with church doctrine. Criticism of Murray damaged his standing in the church; his works were excluded from academic conferences, and in 1958, under pressure from the Vatican, Jesuit authorities denied Murray permission to publish papers on church and state issues.

The theologian, however, lived to see his ideas vindicated. For one thing, his notion of the separation between church and state was expanded on by John Kennedy, who publicly confronted the issue in a major campaign address before a group of Protestant ministers in Houston in 1960. Kennedy assured the ministers and the nation that his first responsibility was to uphold the Constitution, not the dictates of Rome. "I do not speak for my church on public matters," the senator from Massachusetts said, "and the church does not speak for me." If a conflict arose that would put his constitutional duty in conflict with his Catholicism, Kennedy promised he would resign the presidency.

Pope John XXIII, who called the Second Vatican Council soon afterward, also helped to resurrect Murray. (Ironically, Murray's major backer was the conservative Francis Cardinal Spellman, archbishop of New York, a predecessor of Cardinal O'Connor.) One of the Vatican Council's major documents, "The Declaration on Religious Freedom," was written in part by Murray. In it the church went even further than recognizing the separation between church and state. It affirmed that each person has "the duty, and therefore the right, to seek the truth in religious matters."

A year and a half before I arrived at the Div School, I had had an encounter with a Catholicism of a different kind when I met John Joseph O'Connor, who was then bishop of the diocese of Scranton, Pennsylvania. In a surprise appointment on January 31, 1984, Pope John Paul II named O'Connor archbishop of New York. It had been a surprise because O'Connor was a relative unknown among the nation's three hundred bishops and New York, with 1.8 million Catholics, was one of the mightiest archdioceses.

O'Connor, known to his friends as J.J., was a Philadelphia priest who had spent twenty-seven years as a chaplain in the navy, where he gained a reputation as a pro-military conservative. In 1968 he wrote a book defending United States involvement in the Vietnam War, a work he would repudiate in the 1980s. When he retired from the navy in 1983, with the rank of admiral, O'Connor was made a bishop and served as an auxiliary to Terence Cardinal Cooke, the former archbishop of New York, who also held the title military vicar. O'Connor was put in charge of Cooke's military role, which meant ministering to Catholics in the United States armed services around the world. When the nation's bishops were preparing a pastoral letter on the morality of the use of nuclear weapons, O'Connor was put on the drafting committee. Auxiliary Bishop O'Connor was seen as a conservative, pro-military voice and a balance to such liberal, antiwar prelates as Thomas J. Gumbleton, an auxiliary from Detroit. The day the bishops released their final draft—which took a strong stand against the use of nuclear weapons—O'Connor got the word that he had been given a diocese of his own, the diocese of Scranton.

After only eight months in Scranton, during which Cardinal Cooke died, the Vatican announced that O'Connor would be going back to New York as the new archbishop. Suddenly, O'Connor became big news in New York. When he was about to preach his last mass in Scranton, my editors sent me to see what kind of reception he would get. Shira was five months pregnant with Adam at the time and, it being a Sunday, joined me for the three-hour ride to Pennsylvania. As most expectant fathers have learned, car trips with pregnant women require frequent stops. So when we finally got to St. Peter's Cathedral in downtown Scranton, Shira ran ahead to find the ladies' room. On the way out, she bumped into a tall, bespectacled man wearing a bright purple robe and gold crucifix, who greeted her, "Hi, I'm Bishop O'Connor."

By the time I'd parked the car, Shira and the bishop were chatting away. (He seemed to have a special affinity for pregnant women; maybe it had something to do with his strong stand against abortion. He always said he was a "friend of the unborn.") In his sermon at the morning mass, he welcomed "two Jewish visitors, Mr. and Mrs. Goldman from *The New York Times*." We both cringed; I felt horns sprouting under my hair. After the service, O'Connor embraced us warmly and invited us to join him for lunch in the rectory. We sat at a huge table in the dining room, frescoes and icons all around us. The bishop had seated Shira immediately to his right, while I was put at the opposite end of the table, among monsignors and men I was supposed to call "Father."

The first course arrived. It was chicken soup. While chicken soup is one of the most famous "Jewish dishes," it isn't kosher unless it is made from a ritually slaughtered chicken; the chicken from O'Connor's kitchen wouldn't do. Shira and I just stirred our servings until they were removed. Then came the main course: roast beef. Again, meat that can be prepared according to kosher specifications, but not so in this instance. We declined. Finally, the salad arrived. I began heaping it on my plate with glee. Then I looked up at Shira and saw her shaking her head. I looked closer; inside the salad were tiny, yet ubiquitous, shrimp. By this time O'Connor was beginning to notice that we were not eating.

"Oh my," he said slapping his head with the palm of his hand. "I'm so embarrassed. Here I invite you to lunch and I give you nothing you can eat. I should have known you are kosher."

By then we were both shaking our heads, saying that we had had a late breakfast and that we really "only came for dessert." But O'Connor was already ringing a buzzer under the ledge of the dining table. Two nuns flew out of the kitchen door. "Get these people some salad. Just plain lettuce and tomato." And then, turning to us, "That's okay. Just salad. Yes? I'm just so embarrassed."

Shira and I happily ate our salads and gobbled down dessert, a scrumptious strawberry shortcake baked for the bishop by an admirer in the diocese. We then left O'Connor as he prepared for the afternoon mass, which was held at the gymnasium of the University of Scranton. It was a gala affair, with a procession of uniformed Knights of Columbus festooned with feathered hats and sabers, an ecumenical delegation and speeches by local politicians. Everybody loved "J.J." and, God knows, he loved them back. "I have lived virtually throughout the world. And I have never met a people who surpassed you in goodness. You do not know how good you are." (It was a theme he was to use repeatedly in his first few months in New York, claiming then, of course, that New Yorkers were the greatest people he'd ever met.)

If he was to be remembered for anything, the bishop told his Scranton audience, he wanted it to be his unswerving opposition to abortion. Abortion, he said, is tantamount to murder, and he lamented its victims—"four thousand babies each day in the United States."

I employed Shira as my legwoman, a task she performed enthusiastically, getting colorful quotes for me from the participants. I called *The Times* to check in with Steve Rago, who was then weekend editor, and told him that I had a one-thousand-word story coming and that the lead would be O'Connor saying that he would press his antiabortion fight in New York. Rago, himself a Catholic, said that the idea of a bishop pressing the abortion issue did not seem like a strong story. After all, what would you expect O'Connor to do?

Instead, Rago said that I shouldn't stretch so hard for a news angle but should write a feature story emphasizing the outpouring of affection shown for O'Connor, who had been bishop of Scranton for only eight months. Within the body of the story, Rago suggested, I should get into abortion and other issues with which O'Connor had become identified. If I did a good job, he said, the story could land on Page 1.

I unpacked my laptop word processor and began, aided by the challenge of Rago and the quotes Shira was feeding me. At five o'clock, as the shouts of farewell still rang out from the stadium, I dialed *The Times*, pressed the right computer buttons and filed the story in time for deadline.

On Page 1 the next day, under a Scranton dateline and my byline, the first paragraph read as follows: "Thousands of people made their way through steadily falling snow here today to bid an emotional farewell to Bishop John J. O'Connor, who will be installed next week as the Roman Catholic Archbishop of New York."

The story was just a prelude to the enthusiastic reception that met O'Connor in New York, where he was installed at St. Patrick's Cathedral amid rites of splendor and majesty. The honeymoon did not last long, however. O'Connor soon found himself tangling with Mayor Koch, Governor Cuomo, New York's sizable Jewish community and New York's sizable gay community. In the next few months, I was involved in covering all these controversies, a fact that did not always endear me to the archbishop. But before the honeymoon was over, I got an invitation to lunch at the chancery, the headquarters of the archdiocese of New York on First Avenue.

Shira had been invited as well, but morning sickness kept her home. When I entered the dining room, I could not believe my eyes. There, set out on the archbishop's table, were plastic plates, knives and forks. On each plate was a leaf of lettuce topped with a freshly opened can of tuna fish. Matzoh crackers and parve margarine rounded out the meal. And the kosher food was not prepared just for me; the archbishop and his aides—three middle-aged priests—also ate kosher.

From the way Archbishop O'Connor spoke, it seemed that he had never heard of John Courtney Murray. There was nothing subtle in O'Connor's attempt to influence public policy. He went right for the jugular. The most merciless example of this involved the 1984 Democratic nominee for vice president, Geraldine A. Ferraro. Soon after she was picked by a euphoric Democratic convention proud of its historic choice of a woman, O'Connor accused her of "misrepresenting Catholic teaching on abortion." Two years earlier, it seemed, Ferraro had been among a group of Catholic legislators who argued that there was a "diversity of opinion" among Catholics about abortion. While she was personally opposed to the procedure, she explained, she supported a woman's right to choose abortion.

O'Connor responded that there was only one Catholic position on abortion: you can't do it. He delivered that message on the steps of churches around New York while he stood arrayed in the symbols of his office—the bishop's miter on his head and the shepherd's crook in his hand.

Ferraro and her running mate, Walter Mondale, would no doubt have lost the 1984 election without the drubbing they took from O'Connor, but the archbishop's actions troubled many because they muddied the already turbulent waters of religion and politics. O'Connor continued the assault by fighting New York City's gay rights bill and sparring with Mayor Koch over the hiring of homosexuals in programs paid for by the city and operated by the archdiocese. (The two bachelors later patched up their differences and became good friends, even co-authors of a 1989 book called *His Eminence and Hizzoner*. Likewise, O'Connor's relationship with the Jewish community improved markedly. He won high marks from Jewish leaders for being accessible and largely sympathetic. His fierce loyalty to the Vatican line, however, sometimes reopened the tension with the Jewish community; for example he went on *Nightline* in 1987 to defend the Pope's decision to meet with Kurt Waldheim.)

One area where O'Connor seemed especially pleased with my coverage was in giving him an opportunity to rebut a *New York Times* editorial that criticized his comparison of abortion with the Nazi Holocaust. He had drawn the analogy even before he arrived in New York, saying in response to a question posed by the television journalist Gabe Pressman: "I always compare the killing of four thousand babies a day in the United States, unborn babies, to the Holocaust." The *Times* editorial called the analogy "highly offensive" and suggested that when O'Connor came to New York "a change of tone would be welcome."

I called O'Connor on the day the editorial appeared, and he let loose, saying he was "outraged" at the inferences it drew. He stood by his analogy. "The abortion mentality that has swept the country, that has simply declared the unborn to be nonhuman—that is what I compare to the Holocaust. I very sincerely believe that an abortion mentality, structured and legalized in this country, does not differ in essence from that mentality that legalized putting Jews to death in Nazi Germany."

My position on abortion is closer to Ferraro's than to O'Connor's, but I thought it important that he have his say. The story appeared under the headline "Bishop Rebuts Criticism of a Holocaust Analogy." He called me the next day to thank me.

Over the next few months I followed O'Connor everywhere. I was with him on a visit to a maximum-security prison upstate and tagged along as he took the ferry to Staten Island to greet Catholic schoolchildren. I covered the first mass he celebrated in Spanish before ten thousand Hispanics, thus fulfilling a promise he made at his installation that he would learn the language of one-third of the 1.8 million Catholics in his new archdiocese.

He was always colorful and quotable. He made good copy that got him—and me—into the paper. O'Connor and I were getting along so well that when my son, Adam, was born, in August 1984, I told O'Connor that I would invite him to the bris. O'Connor said that he had never been to a circumcision ceremony and welcomed the opportunity.

Jewish males are normally circumcised on the eighth day, but Adam had been born seven weeks prematurely, at four pounds five ounces, so his bris was postponed. O'Connor sent us a beautiful bouquet of flowers and left an enthusiastic message on our answering machine at home: "Welcome to the world, Adam J. Goldman," he said.

It was around this time that the Ferraro story began to heat up. I continued to cover O'Connor fairly, but the attacks on him began to get more severe, especially when Governor Mario Cuomo, who already was engaged in a debate with O'Connor over abortion, came to Ferraro's defense. I reported on both O'Connor and his critics.

Five weeks later, when Adam's weight was over five pounds and he was released from the neonatal care unit of Lenox Hill Hospital, we took our son home and began planning the bris. By this time, I had been assigned by *The New York Times Magazine* to write a profile of O'Connor. Given that assignment and the stepped-up attacks on the archbishop that I was covering, I thought it would be inappropriate for me to invite him to the ceremony. We scratched his name off the guest list.

The night of Adam's bris, as a matter of fact, I spent in the office finishing the 5,600-word magazine story. In it, I was tougher on O'Connor than I had ever dared to be in the staid news pages of the daily paper. I recalled some of O'Connor's bons mots (like the time he told President Reagan that he would trade his Madison Avenue residence behind St. Patrick's for the president's on Pennsylvania Avenue "if Nancy stayed" in the White House) and quoted his admirers ("I hope he learns a little couth") and his detractors ("O'Connor acts like he's at a Kiwanis Club meeting"). I also pointed out his penchant for ecclesiastical garb, noting that he had recently "posed for a newspaper photographer wearing his black cape and gold pectoral cross to show how he makes coffee for himself in his kitchen."

On the Sunday the magazine article appeared, I heard through others, including Mayor Koch, whom I ran into at a West Side street festival, that O'Connor was not pleased. "I told him I thought it was great," Koch said. O'Connor let me know his feelings indirectly by cutting off the easy access that I had been given to him in his first few months in New York. In fact, after the magazine piece was published, it was six months before he granted me a one-on-one interview.

It wasn't easy to arrange. I had been rebuffed so many times by his ever-evasive spokesman, Father Peter Finn, that I decided to take matters into my own hands. Early one Sunday in March, Shira and I bundled Adam up in our Snugli baby carrier and went to the 10:15 mass at St. Patrick's. I figured O'Connor could turn me down, but how could he turn down a new mother and her cute little kid? Adam slept through most of the service. Afterwards we approached O'Connor, and he was charming, giving Shira a hug and pinching Adam's cheeks in an avuncular way. "Can I have an interview?" I asked. He told me that he had heard of my requests for time with him made through Father Finn, but that he had been extremely busy. In fact, he was flying down to Washington the very next day for a bishops' meeting. "Can I come and interview you there?" I asked. O'Connor said that he was "booked solid" in Washington. I proposed that I interview him on the plane on the way down. Finally, he agreed.

I got up early the next morning and caught the New York Air flight to Washington with O'Connor. We shared the airline's "Flying Nosh"—a bagel with cream cheese and coffee—and got down to business. The peg for the interview was O'Connor's first anniversary in the New York job. I found him a lot more low-key and pensive than when I first got to know him. He had just returned from two missions abroad—one to El Salvador and Nicaragua and the other to

Ethiopia—and said that he was feeling tired. His quick sense of humor also seemed to have vanished on this early Monday morning. We reviewed the lively events of his first year; O'Connor expressed no regrets. In a quiet moment of reflection as we were about to land in Washington, O'Connor admitted that he had tried to cooperate with the "liberal media" in New York, meaning *The New York Times*, but had given up hope. "We just have a different agenda," he said, somewhat sadly.

I said good-bye to O'Connor at the Washington airport and caught the next shuttle flight back to New York, where I wrote a news story about our conversation. After that, my access to O'Connor improved slightly, but it never returned to the rapport that we had struck up in Scranton and during his first weeks in New York. There were no more kosher lunches at the chancery.

Not long after our flight together to Washington, I was trying to reach O'Connor, but even his secretary could not track him down. It was a Thursday, so I left my home number, asking for a call over the weekend. O'Connor returned the call early Friday. "What are you doing home?" he asked.

"This is my day off," I explained. "I work Sunday through Thursday, and I'm off on Friday and Saturday."

"Now that's a great workweek," he exclaimed. "How do I get days off like that?"

Before I had a chance to respond, the Roman Catholic archbishop of New York answered his own question: "I know, I'll become an Orthodox Jew!"

# Orthodoxy

Several university students, unmistakably Jews, passed the Belzer Rabbi on the thoroughfare. The Rabbi sighed and said: "I am not opposed to non-Jewish education. Even our father Jacob adopted Esau's garments in order to obtain a blessing. I sigh, however, because, unlike our father Jacob, they do not return to the culture of Israel after they have received the blessing of secular learning. For the most part, they decline to remove the garments of Esau."

"*Boring!*"
It was a word that I rarely invoked in my year at Harvard Divinity School, but that is what I scrawled across the top of a page in my notebook in my course on Jewish law. Rabbi Louis Jacobs, the man who had so thrilled and intrigued me in the opening days of school, was now boring me. "Jacobs is approaching the Talmud with a sluggishness that is driving me crazy," I wrote. "This is the second week of his introduction. He is proceeding as if he were afraid to begin. As an example of how Jewish law develops, he is using the Fifth Commandment, Honor Thy Father and Mother. . . . Boring. I don't like his manner either, making jokes like, 'These days, it is the parents who have to fear the children.' Rabbi jokes—I hate them."

In retrospect, there was more that was bugging me about

Louis Jacobs than I was willing to admit at the time. His course was giving me a new perspective on Judaism, a perspective that challenged many of my Orthodox assumptions. Like myself, Jacobs was firmly rooted in the Orthodox world. As a yeshiva student in the English industrial town of Manchester, he had dreamed at a young age of going to Lithuania to study at the great Talmudic academy at Telshe. He got a visa and was ready to leave when the Second World War broke out on the Continent. Prevented from traveling, he completed his studies at the rabbinical academy in Manchester, where he followed in the line of brilliant scholars. He was ordained by Rabbi Moshe Yitzhak Segal, who was himself ordained by Rabbi Yehiel Michel Epstein, author of the Arukh Ha-Shulchan, an authoritative code of Jewish law written at the turn of the century.

After distinguishing himself at the Orthodox seminary, Jacobs was named the rabbi of a prominent Orthodox congregation in the Kensington section of London called the New West End Synagogue. Widely recognized as a fine scholar and erudite speaker, Jacobs probably could have remained comfortably there for many years and, some say, could have risen to the post of chief rabbi of Great Britain. In 1959, however, he published a book that would later sabotage his career in the Orthodox rabbinate. In the book, *We Have Reason to Believe*, Jacobs raised doubts about the divine authorship of the Hebrew Bible, engaging in that anathema of the Orthodox, Biblical criticism, in which the Torah is seen against the backdrop of historical scholarship.

The book drew little attention until several years later, when London's Jews College, the primary training ground for Jewish ministers in England, expressed interest in appointing Jacobs to its top academic job, that of principal. Jacobs left his synagogue to accept an interim position at Jews College as moral tutor, a post that his supporters expected would lead to the top job upon the principal's retirement. At the last minute, however, his promotion to principal was blocked by England's chief rabbi, Sir Israel Brodie. Opponents of Jacobs had brought his unorthodox writings to the chief rabbi's attention. But Brodie did not stop there. He sought to prohibit Jacobs from returning to his old synagogue.

The congregation was a member of United Synagogue, an organization chartered by the Chief Rabbinate. In order to serve there, a rabbi needed what was in effect a license from the chief rabbi. Jacobs and his supporters argued that he already had the license since he had served there previously. But Chief Rabbi Brodie said that he was considering Jacobs as a new applicant for the position and, after reviewing his credentials, had decided that he should not be allowed to serve as the head of an Orthodox congregation. The wardens of the congregation took a vote and decided to stand by Jacobs. The Chief Rabbinate dismissed the wardens and sent Jacobs a letter barring him from preaching at the New West End Synagogue.

At that point, the end of 1964, Jacobs's supporters picked themselves up, left the congregation and founded a new one on the northwest side of the city. Known as the New London Synagogue, the congregation is to this day headed by Jacobs and remains unaffiliated with the Chief Rabbinate's United Synagogue.

More than twenty years later at Harvard, I asked Jacobs how he had made the leap from the Orthodox world of the yeshiva to the thorny world of Biblical criticism. He said that it boiled down to a realization that it was the Oral Law (the Talmud) that was governing and shaping the Written Law (the Torah) and not the other way around, as most Orthodox rabbis would have you believe. For example, in explicating the Fifth Commandment, the Talmud asks, Why does the Torah say "Honor thy Father and thy Mother," when it could have simply said, "Honor thy Father and Mother"? The Torah does not waste words, so why the extra *thy*? As is often the case, the Talmud uses the repetition as the basis for adding a new law. " 'Thy' teaches to include your older brother," the Talmud explains, saying that older brothers must also be respected.

Ninety-nine out of one hundred Orthodox Talmud teach-

ers would say, "Look at the economy of the divine Torah
[the Written Law] and see how it shows the way for the
Talmud [the Oral Law]." But Jacobs refused to believe that
the Talmud really figured out a coded message from the
Torah. What was happening, he said, was that the Talmud
was calling the shots—it was in effect deciding what the
Torah should say. Jacobs explained: "The rabbis didn't de-
rive the law about the older brother from the word *thy;*
they had an ethical idea and looked for a source. They found
an extra word and had backing for their idea." In a sense,
the Talmud was already engaged in a form of Biblical criticism. To Jacobs's mind, he was working within the tradition
of questioning and exploring the Torah.

What I found most intriguing about Jacobs was that his
inquiry did not diminish his Jewish observance. In his au-
tobiography, *Helping with Inquiries,* he explains his approach to halacha, or Jewish law:

> I see no reason why following the ideal of critical investiga-
> tion into the Jewish classical sources need prevent acceptance
> of Halacha, albeit with a sense that Jewish law has had a
> history and did not drop down ready-made from heaven.

While this approach is similar in many ways to that of
Conservative Judaism, a uniquely American branch that has
no real following in England, Jacobs writes that he has a
"problem" with the Conservative notion of a "genetic fal-
lacy" that assumes that since the Torah is not divine (only
divinely inspired) it does not have the full authority to direct
the lives of modern-day men and women. The Conservatives believe that the Torah has authority but that it must,
in effect, share that authority with contemporary scholars,
who have license to reinterpret the tradition in light of our
times.

Jewish law is not debased by critical inquiry, Jacobs ar-
gues, but finds new authority, if not from Sinai, then from
"the historical experiences of the Jewish people," which in

itself, he writes, is a type of revelation. "There has to be a different concept of revelation from that which obtained before the rise of critical scholarship," he writes.

As for religious observance, he adds, "I [have] lived an observant Jewish life, and still do, since my whole contention was that to keep the mitzvot did not depend on a fundamentalist understanding of the doctrine 'The Torah is from Heaven.'"

I thought his position admirable. After all, he was a man who had given up so much for the sake of intellectual integrity. I'm certain there are a lot of Orthodox rabbis with doubts who keep their mouths shut (and their pens still) for the sake of expedience. Louis Jacobs spoke out and paid the price.

The Catholics, Methodists and Unitarians in my class at the Div School loved him, as did the handful of Jewish students there. Not too many of them worried over the meaning of Jewish revelation. I loved him too, but as the term progressed, I wondered if I should not be more skeptical. After all, I was the only person at the Div School with an Orthodox yeshiva education. Was I doing my background justice? Maybe I should be the one to challenge Louis Jacobs; or, at least, maybe I should be the one person to be critical about his unorthodox (and un-Orthodox) approach.

One day when I got to Jacobs's class a few minutes late there were no seats available, so I went to a darkened neighboring classroom to find myself a chair. As I picked it up to bring it next door, I felt Rabbi Siegel tugging at the other end. "The voice is the voice of Jacob, but the hands are the hands of Esau," my rebbe whispered. It was a quotation I knew well from the Genesis account of Jacob tricking his father into giving him the blessing intended for Esau. "Don't be fooled," Rabbi Siegel said. "In every generation there come those who deceive and make us stray from the holy Torah. Some do it through tyranny, but the ones who are more dangerous do it through sweetness." His hold on the chair became more firm. "How long do you think this

man's Torah will last? Don't be fooled because he puts a
talith over his head in shul. If he doesn't believe in Torah
from Sinai, his Torah will be forgotten." We stood there a
long time, Rabbi Siegel and I, pulling the chair back and
forth between us.

When I was in college at Yeshiva University, Orthodoxy
never presented a conflict, in an intellectual or practical way.
The food was kosher, there were no classes or exams on
Friday nights, Saturdays or Jewish holidays and the horizons for an Orthodox person seemed limitless. Upperclass-
men were going on to careers in teaching, medicine, law,
even politics.

Orthodoxy also did not keep my classmates and me from
being part of the student revolution of the late 1960s. We
campaigned for Bobby Kennedy and Eugene McCarthy and
organized an active chapter of the Vietnam Moratorium
Committee. We sang Bob Dylan and Phil Ochs songs and
wore our hair long and wild, although we kept our knitted
yarmulkes pinned to the mops atop our heads. We washed,
bleached and tore our blue jeans before putting them on,
smoked marijuana and collected peace buttons; we even had
our own button made up with a picture of a dove and the
word *Shalom*.

When students around the country closed down campuses
for a day in 1970 to protest Nixon's bombing of Cambodia,
we shut down Yeshiva too. The killings of four protesting
students at Kent State University by National Guardsmen
later that year brought further turmoil to college campuses.
Under intense student demands, schools around the nation
were canceling final examinations and giving everyone a
passing grade for the semester.

The crisis forced Yeshiva to confront what it really was: a
school of Jewish studies? or an American university? Under
mounting student pressure, the administrators resolved the
dilemma in an appropriately Solomonesque way. They
closed down the college but kept the Jewish Studies Division
open to the very end of the school calendar.

Educational reforms also came to Yeshiva in that era. Required courses were trimmed from the curriculum, pass/fail grading options were instituted and the taking of attendance was dropped, to be replaced by a system that was music to my ears: "unlimited cuts." In theory, you did not have to go to class once all semester; all you needed to do was fulfill the required papers and lab work and take the final. We also campaigned for a Student Senate and a student voice on the university's Board of Directors. Indeed, the college I graduated from in 1971 was radically different from the one I had entered in 1967. The Yeshiva part of Yeshiva College, however, remained pretty much the same.

The unchanging nature of the Jewish studies component was in many ways comforting. And it served to support my belief that one could be part of the rough-and-tumble of society and still maintain an Orthodox life. Yeshiva undergraduates were given the option of enrolling in one of three Jewish studies programs as they pursued their liberal arts degrees in the college. For those who had limited background in Judaism, there was the Jewish Studies Program. Many of the students who enrolled in JSP, as it was called, were from nominally Orthodox homes from around the country; most had not attended yeshiva high school but had had a few years of after-school synagogue programs, known as talmud torahs, at least until their bar mitzvahs. The second program was the Teacher's Institute, ostensibly for those interested in careers in Jewish education but more practically for yeshiva high school graduates who wanted a broad-based Jewish education that included philosophy, history and Hebrew language. This school, known as TI, was popular with premed students and others who wanted to put their main energies into their college programs. And finally, there was the Rabbi Isaac Elchanan Theological Seminary, Yeshiva's rabbinical school, known as RIETS. A student with a good background in Talmud could start RIETS in his freshman year and be ordained as a rabbi seven years later, that is, three years after finishing college. Most of the RIETS undergraduates—like myself—left after the first four years without a Jewish studies degree but with an ability to pick up a Talmud and study.

If there was a European vestige at Yeshiva, it was to be found in RIETS. A few of the older rabbis, with their long black gaberdine coats and white beards, were refugees from the great centers of Jewish learning in Europe. But most of the others were American-trained and -bred rabbis, clean shaven and modernly dressed, who excelled as teachers and Talmudists. The course of Talmud study at RIETS was less intense than the program at Crown Heights Mesifta, although it followed the same basic format. The day would begin with study in small groups in the study hall, which were followed by a shiur, or class led by a rebbe.

I enjoyed studying the Talmud even when my afternoons were spent drawing up banners for an antiwar protest and my evenings were spent at the printer's putting out the next issue of the college paper. The Talmud, compiled five hundred years after Jesus, is a world unto itself, a collection of Jewish law, folklore, history and mysticism.

It wasn't until years later that I developed a theory about the relationship between the Talmud and journalism, but I think I knew it on some level even in my student days. The Talmud never seems to settle for only one opinion. The famous Hillel makes a statement, and his colleague Shammai takes issue. Rabba disagrees with Abaye, and Rav and Shmuel are always at each other's throats. In short, there are always at least two ways of looking at a situation—and, remarkably, they can both be right. One of my favorite stories from the Talmud concerns a heavenly voice that is heard in the study hall as two rabbis are engaged in a vigorous academic argument. *"Aylu va'aylu divrey elohim chaim,"* the voice declares. What this one says *and* what that one says—both are the words of the living God.

So too in good journalism. There is always more than one opinion. The prosecutor says this, the defense says that. The cops disagree with the robbers, the Democrats with the Republicans. And, again remarkably, they can both be right.

As in the Talmud, there is no opinion that is invalid, all are worth listening to and recording.

The links between journalism and the Talmud even extend to structure. The Talmud begins with a Mishna, a summary statement of law compiled around the year 200, and then expounds on the Mishna in the Gemara. A good Mishna contains the who, what, where, when and how, and the Gemara fills out the details. For me it has served as a model for news writing in the perfect pyramid style: Begin with a good strong summary in the lead, then follow up with the details and lively arguments in the body of the story. With logic and perseverance, the Talmud strives for equality and justice. No part of life is excluded, from business to prayer to sex. To me, it is the ultimate newspaper of Judaism.

The affection I had for music, fostered by my father in the synagogue and by my public high school teacher, Mrs. Martin, also flourished at Yeshiva. I took courses at Yeshiva's Cantorial Institute but found that my voice—which had carried me beautifully through my bar mitzvah—had lost its timbre and extraordinary range. I enjoyed singing, but others stopped enjoying listening. Still, I played my acoustic guitar and led my fellow antiwar protesters in "If I Had a Hammer," "Blowin' in the Wind" and "I Ain't Marchin' Anymore."

The Yeshiva dormitories in upper Manhattan were just a subway ride away from Carnegie Hall and Lincoln Center, where I would buy a third-tier seat for classical music concerts when I wanted to escape. I began with orchestral music but soon found that my ears and eyes would always follow the cello section. There was something that intrigued me about the instrument. Maybe it was its sensual lines, not unlike those of a full-bodied woman, and the way the cello is played, embraced by the musician's arms and legs. Or maybe it was the range of the cello, which, more than that of any other instrument, mirrors that of the human voice. The cello, in fact, retained the vocal range that I had lost in becoming a man. It retained the innocence of my bar mitzvah, when my voice still soared high through the octaves, and linked it to the deeper timbres of adulthood. I became a cello fan and rounded out my record collection of folk music with Casals, Rostropovich, Starker and Feuermann. I dreamed of someday learning to play the cello.

I would also think back to the choral music Mrs. Martin had introduced me to in my year at Weaver High School. At family Passover seders, I introduced the songs of Handel's *Israel in Egypt,* leading my cousins in choruses of "Their Land Brought Forth Frogs" and "The Horse and His Rider Hath He Thrown into the Sea."

One year at Christmastime, I picked up two tickets for the *Messiah* and—after failing to find a real date—asked my best friend and classmate, my cousin Michael, to join me. I had already introduced Michael to *Israel in Egypt* and wanted him to experience Handel's other great work. He was horrified.

"Are you going to take off your yarmulke?" he asked.

"Of course not," I told him. "Michael, this is New York, you can go hear the *Messiah* with a yarmulke. Will you come with me?"

"How could I go to anything called the *Messiah?*" Michael asked.

"It's just music," I assured him. "Come on. Why don't you ask your rebbe if you can go?"

His rebbe, a popular American-born Talmudic scholar, said he saw no problem with going. "Just don't stand for the 'Hallelujah Chorus,' " he warned. "Now there is a worldly man," I told Michael. But Michael was not persuaded. Even though he had the green light, he decided not to join me. I went down to Carnegie Hall myself, sold my extra ticket before reaching the door and took my seat. I may have been the only person sitting during all the "Hallelujahs!" but I didn't give a damn. I was an Orthodox Jew, yarmulke firmly on my head, enjoying the best of modern culture. I sang the whole blessed oratorio in my head.

My religious, academic, musical, professional and activist worlds were in a wonderful harmony in my college years, but as I neared graduation, a problem loomed. I knew that I was going to have a career in journalism—with my love of writing and newspapers I saw no alternative—but how could I be both an Orthodox Jew and a newspaper reporter? The potential for conflict seemed formidable. An Orthodox Jew is forbidden to work, travel or even pick up the telephone on the Sabbath, but newspapers come out seven days a week. I knew that reporters do not have a nine-to-five, Monday-through-Friday workweek, and, even if they did, they have to respond to emergencies on the weekend. How could I cover a war, a mobster trial or labor negotiations and know that I would be free from it all when the sun set on Friday night? There were also the dietary laws to contend with. It isn't just pork that is forbidden to Orthodox Jews. Meat and fowl have to be slaughtered according to Jewish law under the supervision of a rabbi to be labeled kosher. Shellfish are verboten. Foods and utensils have to be separated for meat and milk. In an Orthodox household there are separate dishes, silverware and cups for meat and milk. How could a reporter, with his trench coat and beat-up typewriter, traveling around the world and dining with potentates and peasants, possibly keep all of those intricate laws of *kashrut*?

I lay awake nights trying to figure out how I was going to do it all. It's funny, but I never entertained the thought of abandoning either my life of observance or my ambition to be a reporter. Somehow I believed that they both could be accommodated, although I wasn't sure how. I knew I had two passions—Judaism and journalism—and I was going to hold on to them both.

My Orthodox friends, even the worldly ones, thought I was nuts to believe I could have both. Even Danny Greer said that it couldn't be done. Danny was one of those people the modern Orthodox pointed to proudly to demonstrate how worldly an Orthodox person could be. Danny was an undergraduate at Princeton, where he roomed with Jerry Brown, a former Jesuit seminarian who went on to become governor of California. Danny used to boast that at Princeton, Jerry Brown was his "Shabbos goy," a Gentile who performs tasks, such as turning on electric lights, for a Jew forbidden from such activities on the Sabbath. Danny went on to Yale Law School and held a commissioner-level post in the "young and fresh" administration of Mayor John V. Lindsay of New York.

I got close with Danny in 1972, when he was running for a State Assembly seat on the West Side of Manhattan. It was the year after I graduated college, a year that I had a lot of free time. I had hoped to go to the Graduate School of Journalism at Columbia that year but didn't get in. I did, however, make the waiting list, which I took as a sign that it was worth another try. I decided to reapply for the fall of 1972, hoping that my luck would change. While waiting, I became the campaign manager for Danny Greer's legislative campaign.

I discussed my dilemma with my friend. It seemed he had it all—an Orthodox life and exciting careers in law and politics. How can I do the same with journalism, I asked him one day.

"You can't," Danny said flatly. We were in the apartment he lived in with his wife, Sara. He pointed to the window overlooking Riverside Drive. "Your chances of being an Orthodox journalist are about as good as sitting outside that window and expecting not to fall."

Had I been sold a bill of goods? I had gone through Yeshiva believing that a Jew could be observant and modern. Religion is supposed to enrich your life, I was taught, not frustrate it. I was torn apart by the Judaism-journalism conflict. I could not accept that I would have to make a decision between them.

I let it ride for a while, living with the tension through journalism school at Columbia and through my early days as a copyboy and news clerk at *The New York Times*. Then, shortly before I was promoted to reporter trainee at the paper, I went to see a rabbi, himself a Yeshiva University graduate, whom I had always admired for his scholarship and moderation in religious matters. I will call him Rabbi Z.

I told Rabbi Z about my problem and about the unbearable set of choices that I felt I was being asked to make. How could I forsake my faith, yet how could I ignore my journalistic calling? I told him that I felt that I, an Orthodox Jew, was on the threshold of a career as a reporter at *The New York Times.* "Rabbi, tell me, what should I do?"

Rabbi Z was warm and sympathetic. He listened intently and helped me examine my feelings. Finally, with pain in his voice, he said that I would have to forgo the job offer when it came. "Just think of the *kiddush hashem,*" he said, using the term meaning "the sanctification of God's name." (It is a term fraught with historical significance since it was often used to describe the Jews killed in the Nazi Holocaust.) "You have worked hard to fulfill your dream. You will have the satisfaction of knowing you could have made it if you wanted to. But you are going to give it all up because you want to maintain your life-style as an Orthodox Jew. Ari, I know it will be hard, but it will be a real *kiddush hashem.*"

I left Rabbi Z's office with tears streaming down my face.

The one who saved me was my mother.

My mother, an Orthodox woman who to this day asks me if I recited my prayers and put on my tefillin "this morning," encouraged me not to abandon either my journalistic longings or my Orthodox heritage. But what would happen when conflicts arose? What about Shabbat and kashrut? "Don't anticipate problems," she would say. "You'll deal with each conflict as it arises. I have confidence in you. You will know what to do. Things will work out because you will make them work out."

I was not the first in my family to balance the religious and secular. Both of my paternal great-grandfathers were

Eastern European refugees who settled on the Lower East Side, then pulled up their roots again to find better economic opportunities in New England. They were peddlers who, with packs on their backs and their young families in tow, headed north. The story about one of them, Ephraim Zalman Finkelstein, was that he was bound for Boston on the railroad but accidentally got off the train early. Once in Hartford, he found he had some *landsleit*—people from the same Russian town—so he decided to stay. By that time, another of my great-grandfathers, my namesake, Louis Goldmann, had already set up a dry-goods store there on Temple Street, just a block from the federal courthouse. It was a convenient location since Louis worked as the Polish translator at the court, helping other immigrants adjust to the New World system of justice. When he was needed at the courthouse, he would close down his shop. It was a good business decision since he knew he would make twenty-five cents an hour working as a translator, whereas business at the shop was at best uneven.

Louis's business succeeded, but his health was failing. He died at the turn of the century at the age of fifty-four. A short while later his wife, Rachel, died, leaving five children, among them my grandfather Samuel, orphaned at age thirteen. While Lou and Rachel Goldmann had kept some of the religious traditions from the Old Country, these traditions were forgotten by their children after their death.

After coming of age in an orphanage, Samuel Goldman (he dropped the second *n* in the family name after his father's death) went to work as a salesman for Ephraim Zalman Finkelstein, who had prospered. Ephraim Zalman had established his own dry-goods store, called Cheap Johns. Ephraim Zalman, "John" to his Christian friends, was a pillar of Hartford's Jewish community, a builder of the local synagogue and the ritual bath. His participation in the building of the bath was one of the most significant things about him, I was told as a youngster, although I didn't understand why cleanliness had been so important to him. It wasn't until years later that I learned that it was ritual rather than physical cleanliness that Ephraim Zalman had focused on. Under Orthodox law, the bath prepares women to resume intercourse with their husbands after their periods.

While the ritual bath was a priority for my grandfather, so was the Sabbath. An hour before sundown and the arrival of the Sabbath each Friday, he closed down Cheap Johns, and he kept it closed on the busiest selling day of the week, Saturday. During the winter months, when the early-setting sun meant that the Sabbath would be over sooner, he would open up the store for a few hours of business on Saturday nights.

The traditions of Ephraim Zalman and the assiduous manner in which they were kept made Sam Goldman think of his own parents. Sam—resolute, disciplined and good-looking, with curly blond hair—eventually fell in love with the boss's daughter, Nettie, a lively and petite dark-haired girl with big brown eyes who was eleven years his junior. Ephraim Zalman at first did not approve of Sam's courtship of Nettie because the young man was not Orthodox. He finally agreed to let him have Nettie's hand in marriage when Sam promised that he would be faithful to the old traditions.

Sam eased nicely into the Orthodox world of Hartford. Although he had no formal Jewish education, he quickly adapted to the traditions and became a respected member of the synagogue and trustee of the ritual bath. He was devoted to his newfound Orthodoxy as well as to his business and related political interests. Over the years Cheap Johns—later renamed Finkelstein's—expanded from men's clothing to accessories, such as boots and watches, guns and fishing tackle. It also sold uniforms to police and fire officials. Sam thought it would be good business to get involved in politics. In 1911, three years after marrying Nettie, he was elected a Hartford city councilman. In 1922, the year my father was born, he was appointed the city's police commissioner. In the 1930s he was street commissioner, and in the 1940s he was elected a city alderman.

When I was young, I often heard stories about how the

family business was always run in accordance with Jewish traditions despite the pressure of politics and the marketplace. There was one story about a city official who came to the house one Sabbath afternoon insisting that Grandpa Sam sign the payroll for the Police Department. Sam made him sit and wait until after sundown. Then there was the time there was a flood at the store. A messenger brought word, but no one in the family went downtown until after sundown. The Sabbath took precedence over all worldly matters.

When Ephraim Zalman died, Sam and his brothers-in-law took over Finkelstein's and kept it going into the late 1950s, when the federal government built a highway through downtown Hartford. Rather than relocate the store, the Finkelstein heirs decided to take the money from the government and prepare for early retirement. When the store closed in 1958, it had been in business for sixty years and had never opened on the Sabbath.

Initially, my father showed little interest in business. In fact, after graduating college my father had been accepted into dental school, but he had just met my mother and wanted very much to get married and begin a family. He decided against dental school, got married and settled in Hartford, where he went into real estate.

My mother's family was remarkably similar, Orthodox yet worldly, although not quite as prosperous as my father's family. My maternal grandfather, Sholem Mehler, was a salesman for a New York bra and girdle manufacturer. He spent his days with lingerie and gorgeous models, the family lore went, but still he went to synagogue for services each morning. He had a beautiful singing voice and often served as the informal cantor, leading the services with joy in his Orthodox congregation. And his musical interests extended beyond the synagogue liturgy. Sometimes he would take the family to the free Brooklyn Philharmonic concerts in the park on Saturday afternoons. Today, the Orthodox say it is wrong to hear live music on Saturdays, but Sholem told his family that music is entirely consistent with the spirit of the Sabbath. Since business transactions are prohibited, however, only free concerts are allowed. If the music is there for the listening, he would argue, why deny yourself?

Sholem had the same feeling about professional boxing. He would never turn his radio on to listen to a fight on the Sabbath, but if it was a pleasant afternoon and his eldest daughter wanted to take a walk, why not saunter down to the corner bar? Of course they would not enter the bar, but there was no harm in standing casually on the sidewalk and listening, he reasoned.

His wife, Tillie, bore him five children, including one set of twins, the elder of whom was my mother, Judith. Tillie and Sholem raised their family in the Crown Heights section of Brooklyn. When I was growing up in the 1950s in front of a television set, I always heard stories about my mother's house in Crown Heights, where everyone read books—all the time. I loved hearing these stories so much I would even turn off the television to listen to them when my mother spoke.

In the home of Judy's childhood, everyone always had his or her nose in the pages of a book—romances, thrillers, histories, anything, it seemed, with the printed page between two hard covers. My grandfather was proud of all this reading but lamented the lack of normal communication between the members of the household. He recalled his own impoverished youth, when books were a luxury and families actually spoke to one another. One day, to underscore his point, he set the dining room table for his wife and five children with books. Surrounding the books were flatware and napkins and glasses, but no plates. For that meal, at least, my mother recalled, the family laid aside their books and enjoyed a good dinner conversation.

With their good manners and matching dresses, the twins, Judy and Jean, became the toast of Thomas Jefferson High School and later Brooklyn College. The highlight of their social lives was the five o'clock tea dances that were sponsored by the Orthodox Mizrachi organization. (Social dancing, today disdained by Orthodox organizations as being immodest public behavior—even between husband and wife—was then de rigueur among the Orthodox.)

At one such dance in the early 1940s, when the twins were eighteen, Judy met a handsome young naval ensign. Not only was he tall and a good dancer, but he was well read and aspired to be a writer. He was also very interested in Judaism, but a brand of Judaism different from that of my family. The naval ensign was a committed Reform Jew, a branch of Judaism that says that the old traditions of Sabbath observance, kashrut and the laws of purity are outmoded. Reform Judaism says that in the modern era Judaism has more important things to contribute to society —moral values, monotheism and an ethical system for living.

The ensign was articulate and intriguing. Judy went home after the dance and excitedly told her mother about the stranger. The mother, however, did not share her daughter's enthusiasm. She forbade Judy to see the ensign. When he called, her mother would not pass on the messages. Judy and the ensign managed to get together secretly, but the opposition of her mother was too great for Judy to bear. As all this was going on, Judy met a young, good-looking Orthodox college student from Hartford. His name was Marvin Goldman.

Three children later, when Judy and Marvin's marriage was unraveling, my mother cried to her mother, whom we all called Bubba. You should have let me marry the ensign, my mother complained. "Look," my grandmother told her, "I had four other children. I could not let my eldest daughter marry a Reform Jew." It is ironic, but when my mother remarried some fifteen years after she divorced my father, she married a knowledgeable but nonobservant Jew. Bubba, nearing eighty at the time and still outspoken, saw how much they loved each other and held her tongue.

My mother remarried when I was a senior at Yeshiva College. Despite the fact that her new husband, a corporate executive, was not observant, she vowed that she would remain faithful to Orthodoxy. To the surprise of many inside the family and out, through the two decades of her second marriage she has kept her word.

She and her husband travel widely, but my mother will not get into a car or an airplane on the Sabbath, even if it means traveling a day later than her husband. They eat at fine restaurants and in the homes of corporate presidents, but my mother always makes sure that she has a kosher dish prepared for her. She has a home in Connecticut and an apartment in Manhattan, both of which are strictly kosher. (Her Connecticut home has two dishwashers—one for milk and one for meat dishes.) And if her husband is foolish enough to light up one of his cigars before the stars come out Saturday night, my mother good-naturedly sends him out of the house until the cigar is finished or the Sabbath is over.

So when my mother advised me to pursue my dual passions—journalism and Judaism—she was in part passing on the lessons of my shared family history. Both Sam Goldman, the police commissioner, and Sholem Mehler, the bra and girdle salesman, knew how to keep a balance between their secular and religious lives. She knew I too would find a balance. At the same time, my mother was passing on to me the lessons of the journey of her heart. She knew the mistake of trying to compromise. She had compromised on love in her youth because of religion but proved in adulthood that she could be both religious and in love. She did not want to frustrate my life by forcing me to compromise.

Although I wasn't sure just how, I decided that I would be Orthodox and a reporter. "I have confidence in you. You will know what to do," my mother assured me. "Things will work out because you will make them work out."

CHAPTER 11

# *The Times*
# and Judaism

Rabbi Ishmael ben Elisha told Meir the Scribe:
"Be careful in your work, which is a divine art,
for by omitting or adding a letter, you may
cause the world's ruin."

— Sota 20a

While I was agonizing over whether it was right for me—an Orthodox Jew —to become a reporter at *The New York Times, The Times* was also wondering about me. Years later Arthur Gelb, the managing editor who had been in charge of metropolitan coverage when I was hired, told me, "We never heard of such a thing: a reporter who couldn't work seven days a week." But times were changing.

*The New York Times* had been a Jewish-owned newspaper since it was purchased in 1896 by Adolph Ochs, the son of German Jews who came to America in the years before the Civil War. Still, as best I could tell, I was the first person hired as a *Times* reporter who was a Sabbath-observant Jew. Judaism to *The Times* publishers had long meant Reform Judaism. In 1883, thirteen years before he purchased *The Times*, Adolph Ochs married Iphigenia Wise, the seventh child of Rabbi Isaac Mayer Wise, the father of Reform Judaism in the United States. Ochs believed that Rabbi Wise's liberal brand of Judaism would sweep the land.

Rabbi Wise had little use for tradition. In Albany, New York, his first pulpit, he proposed that the men take off their hats and that the women come down from the balcony. The reaction was so violent, according to one account, that he had to escape through the back door. He began his Reform ministry in earnest in Cincinnati, Ohio, where he proclaimed the kosher laws irrelevant. "My soul is not in my stomach," he declared, "so it doesn't make a difference what I put there, so long as it is digestible."

In a 1981 memoir, Rabbi Wise's granddaughter, Iphigene Sulzberger (the daughter of Adolph and Iphigenia Ochs), said of her famous rabbinic ancestor: "He had many followers, and his new approach to Judaism might well have overcome the old in this country had it not been for the great influx of Jews from Eastern Europe. Those immigrants were practically medieval in their religious practices." The immigrants she was referring to were, of course, my great-grandparents, the unwashed, unlettered and superstitious peddlers who were an embarrassment to the German Jews who had come a generation before.

Iphigene Sulzberger's perceptions of Judaism were not insignificant in shaping The Times's attitudes. She was not only the daughter of the first publisher (Adolph Ochs) but also the wife of the second publisher (Arthur Hays Sulzberger), the mother-in-law of the third publisher (Orvil Dryfoos) and the mother of the fourth publisher (Arthur Ochs Sulzberger). She died in early 1990, at the age of ninety-seven, as her grandson, Arthur Ochs Sulzberger, Jr., was being groomed to be the fifth publisher of The New York Times.

I, like many others, always assumed that Arthur, Jr., who is about my age, is Jewish. But I heard him offhandedly deny it one day when he was doing a stint in The Times's third-floor newsroom as an assistant metropolitan editor— an assignment he carried off with considerable talent and poise, putting everyone at ease with his humor and casual manner, which included walking about the newsroom in his

stocking feet. "No, no, not me," he said when another reporter talked about Arthur as Jewish. "I'm an Episcopalian."
While he bore a famous Jewish name, he explained, his
mother was not Jewish.

Several years later, as I was finishing this book, I asked
Arthur about his response that day in the newsroom. In the
intervening years, he had done the grand tour of *The Times*,
working in management positions in various news, business
and production departments of the paper. He now holds the
title of deputy publisher and he no longer walks around in
his socks. Still, approaching forty, Arthur Ochs Sulzberger,
Jr., retains much of his youthful charm.

"I'm really betwixt and between," he told me. "I'm not
Jewish and I'm not Episcopalian." Arthur's parents were
divorced when he was a small child, and he was brought up
in his mother's faith. Though he was baptized and confirmed, Arthur left his Christianity behind in his late teens.
Many years later, however, while on an Outward Bound
trip in the South, he began to explore his Jewish roots
through books and conversations with friends. But his
search yielded little. "I'm not a religious person," he concluded, "and I'm not raising my children in any particular
faith." He added, however, that he has taken his young son
and daughter to Passover seders and other Jewish observances so they would be familiar with the tradition. "I don't
want them to be alienated from Judaism," he said, "the way
I was."

Though not raised as a Jew, Arthur has a Jewish identity.
"Ninety-nine out of one hundred people consider me Jewish," he said. "How could a Sulzberger not be Jewish?" And
then he noted somberly, "I'm well aware that if I lived in
Germany under Hitler I'd be on my way to the ovens."

Arthur added that his alienation from Judaism was not
characteristic of his generation of the "*Times* family," the
descendants of Adolph Ochs, several of whom occupy management positions at *The Times*. He noted that a few of his
cousins have recaptured some of their lost Jewish heritage.

When one cousin recently made a bar mitzvah for her son, Arthur said, "it was probably the first bar mitzvah in the family in ninety years."

In his 1969 book about *The New York Times, The Kingdom and the Power*, Gay Talese observed that the paper has long labored against the perception that it is a "Jewish newspaper." "Indeed," he added, "it is not, and it will bend over backwards to prove this point." I know precisely what Talese was referring to, for I have seen the extra measure of care taken on certain sensitive stories. I've seen it not only on articles about Israel and Jewish issues, but also on stories about Catholicism, race relations and homosexuality. *The Times* does a lot of bending over backwards to be fair. The Jewish bending is but one aspect of that concern, and I see it diminishing as the paper becomes less and less self-conscious of its Jewishness.

Perhaps Talese's most memorable examples of how in the 1930s and 1940s *The Times* tried to avoid the Jewish label are his stories of how the paper used to credit articles by reporters with Jewish-sounding names. In those years, bylines were given out parsimoniously, and Abraham Raskin, promoted to *The Times* staff in 1934, had to wait five years to get one. The story of how this finally came about, as told by Talese, is worth repeating.

One day in 1939 Raymond H. McCaw, a senior editor, particularly enjoyed reading the carbons on one story that was about to go into the next day's paper. He walked over to the City Desk and asked who had written it.

"Abe Raskin," came the reply.

"Put a byline on it," McCaw said, and then, as an afterthought, he asked, "What's Abe's middle initial?"

"H."

"Well," McCaw said, "sign it 'A. H. Raskin.' "

Another young reporter of that era, Abraham Rosenthal, the son of a Russian Jewish housepainter, also struggled for years to get a byline and eventually was rewarded with "by A. M. Rosenthal." Beginning in 1946, he was assigned to the nascent United Nations, at the time still a place of influence and of hope for world peace. His coverage of the debates and personalities of the United Nations brought him the admiration of his colleagues and compliments from his editors but not the assignment to a foreign capital that he so much desired. It was eight years before Rosenthal was given a foreign post, and when he finally got one—India, in 1954, followed by Poland and Japan—he changed the face of foreign reporting. Foreign correspondents had long covered wars and conflicts, filing dispatches with the news that the readers back home desired. Rosenthal, of course, did the news reporting ably, but he went one giant step further. Finally liberated from the tedium of New York, Rosenthal was intoxicated by the sounds, the smells, the colors of the cities and towns he visited. He wrote about people and places in a way that newspapers had rarely looked at them before. His approach reached an art form in a short piece he did for *The New York Times Magazine* on August 31, 1958, called "There Is No News from Auschwitz." In one arresting paragraph in that piece, he explained the obsession that drove him to write:

> And so there is no news to report about Auschwitz. There is merely the compulsion to write something about it, a compulsion that grows out of a restless feeling that to have visited Auschwitz and then turned away without having said or written anything would somehow be a most grievous act of discourtesy to those who died here.

After distinguishing himself as a foreign correspondent, Rosenthal returned to New York and—as city editor, managing editor and executive editor—changed the face of *The New York Times*. More than any other person, Abe Rosenthal was responsible for taking what was known as the Old Gray Lady, the stodgy yet thorough "newspaper of record," and giving her blush, mascara and a fashionable wardrobe. Rosenthal revamped the way *The Times* wrote about theater, health, movies, books, fashion, food and life-styles.

The results—among them "Science Times," "Home," "Living" and "Weekend"—have become part of the regular newspaper diet of more than a million people each day. And, most remarkably, Rosenthal revolutionized the paper without compromising the thorough news coverage that made *The Times The Times.*

I first met Rosenthal in the summer of 1972, soon after my friend Danny Greer lost his bid for the New York State Assembly and I, his campaign manager, found myself out of a job. By that time, I had been admitted to Columbia Journalism for the 1972–73 school year and was looking for a summer job. I went to see Peter Millones, who was then an assistant managing editor, about getting hired as a copyboy. Millones knew my work as the college correspondent from Yeshiva, and we had spoken before about getting an entry-level position at *The Times.* He also knew I was a Sabbath-observant Jew.

"Can you work weekends?" Millones asked casually when I inquired about a summer job.

"Sure," I said, shifting uncomfortably in my seat.

"Let me check the schedule."

He got up and left me sitting at his desk. I took one of the paper clips out of a small glass cup on his desk, unraveled it and twisted it until it broke into two worthless pieces of wire. What would I do if Millones came back and asked me to work on Shabbat? I knew that this could be more than a summer job. It could just be the Big Break into journalism that I had been dreaming of. How could I turn it down? But how could I accept it?

I looked out the window and thought I saw Rabbi Siegel. In my imagination, he was standing, Moses-like, on a cloud high above Times Square holding above his head the two tablets of the Law. His voice echoed past the massage parlors and dirty book stores and X-rated movies, and stung my ears:

> Remember the sabbath day, to keep it holy. Six days you
> shall labor, and do all your work; but the seventh day is a

sabbath to the Lord your God; in it you shall not do any work, you, or your son, or your daughter, your manservant, or your maidservant, or your cattle, or the sojourner who is within your gates.

I closed my eyes tight and shook the rabbi's image from my head. I resolved to banish him forever. When Millones came back, I was going to tell him that I was available to *The New York Times* twenty-four hours a day, seven days a week. I had banished the hobgoblin of religion, and I was ready to proceed with my brilliant career.

"We have an opening for August," I suddenly heard Millones say. I opened my eyes and saw him standing there with a smile on his face. "You can have the job, but you will have to work on Sundays. Your days off are Friday and Saturday."

I was so stunned I didn't know what to say. Here I had prepared myself to work on Shabbat, and the luck of the draw (or the sympathy of Millones—I wasn't sure which) had given me the perfect days off. My dreaded conflict didn't materialize after all.

"Is that okay?" Millones was saying.

"Perfect," I stuttered.

I quickly invited the hobgoblin of religion back into my head. Rabbi Siegel was still there, holding the Ten Commandments, and he too was smiling. Maybe, just maybe, somebody is watching over me. And maybe I shouldn't give it all up so easily, I thought.

A copyboy's lot is not always a happy one, but August was magical. This was the summer of 1972, just a few years before computers were installed at *The Times*. It was a time when copyboys did everything that computers now do and then some. A reporter would yell "copy," and a copyboy— or on rare occasions a copygirl—would race down the row of desks and bring a page or "take" of his—inevitably *his*— story to the front of the newsroom, where another copy person would rip out the carbons and distribute the ten copies to the various editors who had to see the story. The top page became "the hard copy," which would be read and corrected by an editor who would then shout "copy" when his task was done. A copyboy would grab the copy and put it in a pneumatic tube, which would suck it up to the fourth floor, where a pressman would set the story in the old movable system known as hot type.

Copyboys would also fill the editors' paste pots, answer the telephones or run across the street to get a container of coffee or get a reporter out of Gough's, the Forty-third Street bar popular with pressmen and reporters. At about 2:00 A.M., when the last deadlines were being met, the copyboys on the "lobster shift" would take the day's discarded memos, wire stories and proofs off the editors' spikes and roll them in newsprint into huge balls on each desk. The rolls, a kind of precomputer "memory" function, would be marked with the name of the desk—City, Foreign, National —and the date and placed on shelves in a special storage room. Somebody (certainly not a copyboy) had the idea that all these discarded papers would prove valuable in a libel lawsuit or, more practically, would settle an office argument over who was responsible for an error that had slipped into the paper.

I was one of twenty copyboys on the night shift, which ran from 3:00 in the afternoon to 11:00 P.M.; sometimes I would work the lobster (a name derived from its similarity to the hours worked by lobster fishermen), from 7:00 P.M. to 3:00 A.M. While copyboy was the lowest job in the newsroom, I was soon to find that even among copyboys there was a hierarchy. The supervisor of the copyboys, a jockey-sized man with a sadistic streak named Sammy, had his favorites. Sammy, who was so short and so skinny that he used to buy his clothes in the boys' department at Alexander's, knew how to build loyalty by dishing out the good assignments to his favorites. The senior copyboys would get to fill in for vacationing clerks at some cushy desk job while the rest kept running. But maybe the best job of all—reserved for Sammy's special favorites—was the "*Daily News* run." This was an amazing night on the town that involved going uptown to Reuters to pick up some wire service photos and then heading across town to the Daily News building to pick up their "Night Owl Edition." Night after night I would watch Sammy choose one of his favorites for the task, put two subway tokens in his hand and send him out the door. Two or three hours later, the copyboy would saunter in with a stack of *Daily News*es under his arm and tantalizing stories about women met in Times Square and Broadway shows snuck into after intermission. And somehow the copyboy always managed to stretch the money given for carfare into dinner or at least drinks. (This was all the more remarkable since the subway fare was thirty-five cents.)

One night in late August, Sammy surveyed the cavernous newsroom and signaled me to come over. He put two tokens in my hand and barked "*Daily News* run." I couldn't believe my good fortune. Finally I had made it. I was part of the inner circle. I wondered what adventures awaited me. My joy ended when I got to the first-floor lobby and looked out the revolving doors. Rain. And not just a drizzle—a summer storm, complete with lightning and thunderclaps. It is a wonder I hadn't heard it in the newsroom. Everyone else apparently had.

I stepped out into the rain for the bus. Missed it. I began to run uptown in the downpour. An hour later I did my best to hold my head high as I walked back into the newsroom, my sneakers squishing water and a stack of soggy *Daily News*es under my arm. I was greeted with smiles, applause and slaps on my wet back.

Oddly enough, after that incident the newsroom felt like a friendlier place. Sammy even sent me on the *Daily News* run when it was nice out. I got to know reporters and spoke to editors about writing some pieces for the back of the Sunday paper, a place that welcomed copyboy contributions.

On one of my rounds one day, I saw Abe Rosenthal standing outside his office near the Forty-third Street end of the newsroom. Wearing a dark, ill-fitting suit, Rosenthal, standing alone, looked out on the newsroom and puffed on a cigarette. He was a journalistic legend, "the most powerful man in American journalism" the newsmagazines called him. I swallowed hard and strode up to him with all the confidence I could muster. "Hello," I said extending my hand. "I'm Ari Goldman, a new copyboy. I just wanted to introduce myself."

Rosenthal reacted warmly. He shook my hand and asked where I was from and what journalism background I had. I told him that I had already been around the paper for a few years as the Yeshiva University stringer.

"Oh, you're the one," he said. "You won't work on Saturdays. Well, let me tell you, that could be a problem in this business. But don't worry. I know the Pope, I'll arrange for a dispensation."

Just then somebody yelled "copy," so I excused myself and was off on my rounds. Rosenthal's comment was so bizarre that I didn't know what to make of it. I almost would have taken it as an insult had he not been so friendly. I decided it wasn't all bad. After all, maybe his friend the Pope would give *him* a dispensation to hire me as a staff reporter.

I was having such a good time at *The Times* that I did not want to leave when September came and J School was starting. In my classically unrealistic style, I decided that I was not going to give up either. I would go to Columbia during the day and work nights at *The Times*.

J School was a full-day program run on the model of a newspaper, with professors serving as editors and students running out to cover events on deadline. After a full nine-to-five day of school, I grabbed dinner and headed downtown to work the night shift at *The Times*. I started each night at 7:30 and ended at 3:00 the next morning with "rolling" the desks.

The dual schedule was brutal but valuable in that it gave me a chance to weigh the relative merits of each experience.

I soon realized that nothing would be as exciting for me as working at *The Times*, even as a copyboy, but, in doing that, I wasn't really learning a lot about writing. More than excitement, I needed to become a better reporter. And Columbia was the place to do it. After two weeks, I quit *The Times* and became a full-time journalism student.

There was much for me to learn. At Yeshiva, most of the journalism I had done was about Jews and Israel. I needed to be broadened, and if there was one man at the J School who opened me up to different reporting experiences it was Mel Mencher. I had Mencher for the basic first-semester course appropriately called "Reporting and Writing I." Mencher, a demanding and irascible man (and a gifted teacher) who walked around the school in his stocking feet, had an agenda for his students. We could not complete his course until we reported a news story at each of the following locations: a police precinct, a hospital, a welfare office, a courthouse and a racetrack. We learned more than just where these places were—we learned how to find information at each, and that meant knowing how to find the desk sergeant, the hospital administrator, the government bureaucrat, the judge's clerk and the stable grooms.

J School also helped me discover my strengths and weaknesses within journalism. I took a wonderful course in editing with Irv Horowitz, an adjunct at the J School who was an assistant national editor at *The Times*. Word processors were still a few years away from arriving at *The Times's* newsroom, so Horowitz taught us the old editor's symbols, the little arrows, circles and squiggly lines that were used to mark copy. At the beginning of each class, Horowitz would hand out a mimeographed sheet of "hard copy" for us to edit. As we worked, he would sing loudly, carry on conversations with imaginary friends or simply pace back and forth. All this, he said, was to simulate the environment of a real newsroom. "Get used to it," he would reply if we asked him to keep it down.

One of my favorite Horowitz exercises was an obit just

three paragraphs long reporting on the death of one Oscar Paddleford. The first paragraph said that Paddleford died "last night" at the age of thirty; the second graph said that he had worked as a lifeguard and the third graph said that he died under "unusual circumstances" while bathing.

I knew right away what to do. I moved all the elements together into the lead and then wrote the following headline: "Lifeguard Oscar Paddelford, 30, Dies in Tub." My news judgment and my writing were impeccable, but I committed the gravest journalistic sin: I spelled the guy's name wrong. It was *Paddleford*, not *Paddelford*. I learned many things from the editing class, but, maybe most important, I learned not to become an editor.

Toward the end of my year at the J School, while most of my classmates were making plans to find jobs on small-town papers, I decided to give *The Times* one last shot. I returned to Peter Millones with my journalism degree in hand, and he said that maybe—just maybe—I could have my old copyboy job back. I was shocked. For this I went to journalism school?

I hadn't expected to waltz into *The Times* and be hired as a reporter, but I was hoping for a step up from copyboy. Millones said nothing was available. I couldn't see working as a copyboy again but refused to abandon all hope of working at *The Times*.

Again, I sought my mother's advice. "Is there an empty desk in the newsroom?" she asked.

"Sure," I told her. "There are always empty desks, especially during the summer."

"Well, find an empty desk and sit there."

I took my mother's advice and set up shop at a desk in full view of the Metropolitan Desk editors. I told them I was working on some free-lance assignments for the short-lived Brooklyn–Queens–Long Island supplement (assignments that were not yet assigned) and that I might be available, if they really needed me, to help out. It was a hot summer, and there was a thin reporting staff of prima donnas who did not want to be bothered with the routine fires and murders. I liked nothing more. I ran all over the city, covering these minor disasters and racing for phones to give the reporter in the office facts, color and quotes. Eventually, the editors would even let me write the story myself—with no byline, of course. I wasn't even on staff, just helping out.

By the end of the summer, a job as a news clerk on the National Desk opened up. I was the natural choice for it. Work started at 3:00 in the afternoon, just like it did in my old copyboy job, but now I got a desk to sit at and had much more of a chance to learn. I sorted wire service stories for an assistant night national editor, a kindly longtime newspaperman named Bill Lamble, who spent all night blowing smoke from his pipe in my face. With a flick of his wrist, Lamble would impale one piece of copy after another on his silver spike until something caught his well-trained eye, some story that had the right combination of information and irony that would make it worthy of a few lines in *The New York Times*.

I spent my nights working for the National Desk and my days writing features and doing legwork for the Metropolitan Desk, compiling a clip file with over one hundred unbylined stories. Even though I was off from the National Desk on Fridays, I came in to write. Saturdays I stayed home.

After eighteen months of National Desk duty, I got the finest clerk job in the newsroom. I was made Abe Rosenthal's office boy. I helped answer his mail, keep his liquor cabinet stocked and usher visitors in and out of his office. I was but a footman at the center of power, but it afforded me great status in the newsroom. Everyone assumed that I knew everything that was going on and that I was a confidant of Rosenthal's.

The two previous clerks who had held the job had been promoted to reporter, and I knew I too was on my way. Still, when it happened, when Rosenthal called me into his office with a mock-stern "Ari, come in here," and spun around and gave me a handshake that was soon an embrace,

I was on top of the world. "You made it," he said, reaching for a bottle of champagne that he had chilled for the occasion.

I made it with no strings attached and no commitments. I could be who I was, observe my Sabbath and still be a *Times* reporter.

I can only guess why my Sabbath observance—which had loomed so large for me as an issue for so many years—was not a problem for the paper. A dozen years after I was hired, when Abe Rosenthal had retired as executive editor to be a columnist and I was writing this book, I sat with him in his new wood-paneled office and asked if my observance had been a factor when I was promoted to reporter. "No," he said. "You were a good reporter. And that is why we hired you."

You weren't worried about my inability to work on the Sabbath?

Rosenthal said, yes, now that I mentioned it, there were some questions raised about the issue, but they were quickly put to rest when he asked a rabbi friend about it. "He told me that if you had to make a living, you were allowed to work on the Sabbath," Rosenthal said.

I looked at him with disbelief. Who was the rabbi? Rosenthal said he could not remember. He certainly wasn't my Rabbi Z, or any other Orthodox rabbi I ever heard of. To them, one could violate the Sabbath only if life itself hung in the balance. I was brought up with stories of families who went hungry because the man of the house refused to open his store on the Sabbath. (Of course, the stories would end with their being rewarded by some fantastic stroke of luck for their sacrifice.) For a moment while sitting in Rosenthal's office, I wondered if there was some Reform rabbi out there somewhere whose name I did not even know who was responsible for my being hired at *The Times.*

Could religion have been so peripheral a concern for the editors that they could not even comprehend the power of it in my life? Did they just dismiss my Sabbath observance as something that would slip away when it was deemed troublesome? I think not.

My theory is that my promotion at *The Times* was an almost unconscious coming to terms with the paper's long-suppressed Jewish heritage. The seventies, after all, were a time when society was rediscovering its roots. Black was beautiful; the Italians and the Irish and the Polish were proud. Jewish studies was booming on the nation's campuses. And, at the same time, feminism was no longer seen as a hysterical, radical movement but a trend that would change society forever. All of this, of course, was being recorded almost daily in the pages of *The Times*. It might have escaped the paper's soul, however, were it not for hiring requirements imposed during that decade as a result of suits by groups of blacks and women at the paper. Suddenly, a paper that had had few of any of them was vigorously recruiting women, blacks and later Hispanics for reporting and editing positions.

Was I, with my kosher diet, Sabbath observance and Hebrew name a recognition of Jewish heritage? I asked.

"Absolutely not," Rosenthal said. "You were a good reporter. And that is why we hired you."

Still, I wonder.

# CHAPTER 12

# Other
# Christian
# Voices

Said the Baal Shem Tov: "The Lord does not object even if one misunderstands what a man learns, provided he only strives to understand out of his love of learning. It is like a father whose beloved child petitions him in stumbling words, yet the father takes delight in hearing him."

One of the great delights of my year at the Div School was Professor William R. Hutchison. With a wit so dry that many students refused to believe it existed, Hutchison taught a class called "American Religious History: Colonial Era to the Present." Either you liked Bill Hutchison or you didn't get it. But I was a fan. Hutchison, a tall, gangly and graying Quaker, held the Div School's Charles Warren Professorship of the History of Religion in America. I took his course because I wanted to find out why there are so many Protestant denominations in the United States.

I had sat through many a church service as a reporter but still had trouble sorting out the Baptists from the Methodists and the Shakers from the Quakers and the Lutherans from the Episcopalians. The American religious history course had the reputation of being a heavyweight, with oodles of readings and papers, so I decided just to audit and show up when I had the time. As it turned out, I never

missed a Hutchison lecture. My class notes are filled with
odd notations, songs, bar graphs, quotations and drawings,
only some of them relevant and others irreverent.

To be sure, there was a weightier side to Hutchison, with
lectures called "The Triple Melting Pot" and "Pluralist and
Unitive Ideals." I sat through them, not always fully com-
prehending, and waited around for the gravy. There was
plenty. Hutchison gave us religion statistics from the 1790
census, played music from the Colonies on his tape recorder,
showed slide after slide on his projector and spouted obscure
quotes, such as Harry Truman on economists. ("They're
always telling me, 'On the one hand this; on the other hand
that.' What I need is a one-handed economist.") When we
studied Jews in America, he couldn't resist playing Tom
Lehrer's "National Brotherhood Week," which includes
these rhythmic lines:

> Oh, the Catholics hate the Protestants,
> And the Protestants hate the Catholics
> And the Hindus hate the Muslims
> And everybody hates the Jews.

Hutchison even gave out song sheets.

To demonstrate how America was perceived as "the New
Zion" by the Puritans, he pointed to a takeoff of the Jewish
lament "By the Waters of Babylon" that went something
like this: "By the waters of Watertown, where we sat down
and there we wept for old England."

In the middle of one of Hutchison's famous slide shows,
depicting the persecution of Mormons in the nineteenth
century, complete with mob violence in which Mormons
were beaten and their homes burned, he'd throw in a political cartoon. My favorite one appeared in a newspaper after
the death of Brigham Young and showed his widows in
mourning: twenty women, all in modest nightgowns and
sleeping bonnets, sat dabbing their eyes in a vast communal

bed. In the center was the embroidered pillow of their late husband.

In the course of all this entertainment, I did learn about the different roots and philosophies of the various Protestant denominations, how they had been shaped by their European origins and American experiences.

Hutchison brooked little tolerance when it came to one of the homegrown American religious movements, the Fundamentalists. During one slide show, he presented a recent cover of Jerry Falwell's *Fundamentalist Journal* that depicted a little red schoolhouse on a hill with neatly dressed, blond-haired children playing outside. In the foreground, one tow-headed boy was giving his prim, bonneted teacher a shiny red apple. The caption read: "Let's Get America Back to Our Roots."

"Fundamentalist propaganda," Hutchison roared. It was an important lesson. The White-Anglo-Saxon-Protestant America the Fundamentalists say they are trying to "get back to" never really existed. From the beginning, this country had American Indians, Jews and Catholics, as well as Protestants. They had red skin and black skin and white skin. To be sure, not all these groups were treated equally. It was most often the whites who subjugated the others; maybe that is the America to which the Fundamentalists want to return. But, for most Americans, the thought of returning to slavery, anti-Catholicism and anti-Semitism or anti–American Indianism represents America gone awry and not "America Back to Our Roots."

One of my Hutchison classmates, Fran, could have stepped right out of one of Hutchison's slides on indigenous American religious movements. Fran was a Christian Scientist, a member of a faith founded in 1879 in Boston by Mary Baker Eddy, who said that she had been miraculously cured of an illness after reading an account in the New Testament of Jesus healing the sick. Mrs. Eddy's faith is most famous today for its opposition to medical intervention for the sick. When illness strikes, Christian Scientists believe that healing comes from within a person and from spiritual understanding. Special healing practitioners, who use a combination of Scriptural readings and prayer, are summoned.

Fran was one of my best friends at the Div School. We had signed up for many of the same classes and often ended up sharing notes, studying and having lunch together. She became a regular guest at our Friday-night table.

Fran, with short, black hair and modest in dress, was twenty-two but looked more mature than her years. She was a deeply rooted Christian Scientist and, curiously, had entered the Div School with some of the same hesitations that I had about studying Christian theology. "Scholastic theology doesn't go over big with Christian Scientists," she said. Mrs. Eddy warns in her book *Science and Health* against the overintellectualization of religion as one of the things that "fetters faith." The others are the study of civil law and medicine.

Before enrolling in the Div School, Fran consulted members of her church. No one could remember a Christian Scientist ever enrolling at Harvard Divinity School. But that didn't bother Fran; she was accustomed to being a pioneer. Fran had been one of the few Christian Scientists at Brandeis, a largely Jewish school, where she did her undergraduate work in history. For her senior research paper at Brandeis, Fran had examined the "God is Dead" philosophy that had swept the country in the 1960s. She needed a book —*Religion in the Secular City*, Harvey Cox's sequel to his best-selling *The Secular City*—and she couldn't find it in her local bookstore. She journeyed from Brandeis, which is in the Boston suburb of Waltham, to the Div School in Cambridge, where she was sure she would find it in the bookstore since Cox had been a longtime Div School faculty member. "I was amazed at how friendly everybody was," she said of her initial visit to the Div School. "It was the first time I had been to Harvard, where everyone was nice to me, unlike Widener Library and other places, where they don't talk to you unless you are a Harvard student."

Fran also recalled being taken with the whimsical murals of Biblical scenes painted on the walls of the basement hallway of the Div School. "I saw that mural of Shadrach, Meshach and Abednego smiling in the furnace. And the other one of Sarah laughing outside her tent. They were childlike drawings and really inspiring in their simplicity. It was that day that I decided to apply to the Divinity School."

Once at Harvard, Fran was interested in examining church history, in particular the role of women in the nineteenth century. With her vision clear about what she wanted to study, Fran saw no conflict with her church's reluctance to engage in "scholastic theology." "I looked at myself not as a theology student but as a historian," she said. "I was not going to the Divinity School to try to define God for myself or come up with a better definition than the Bible or *Science and Health* provide, because, for me, that's complete."

How did the people in her church feel about her going?

"They were very proud and supportive," Fran said. "They felt I was a kind of missionary, bringing Christian Science to the Divinity School."

"I think I've failed miserably in that mission," she said with a laugh. "But that wasn't *my* mission anyway."

Although she won no converts, she did, often unwittingly, help explain Christian Science to her classmates, just as I, also unwittingly, found myself explaining Judaism. In Hutchison's class, Fran was called upon to talk about an indigenous American religion and I about a faith transported from Eastern Europe.

Fran was initially delighted with the Div School. It lived up to her expectations as a friendly, tolerant place, until one day in "Contemporary Theology" she found that there was little tolerance for one way of thinking. The discussion turned to the debate over whether there is such a thing as life after death.

Fran, who had read the Bible from the time she was a small child, raised her hand confidently and said, "There is proof from John, Chapter 11, where Jesus raises Lazarus from the dead." There were audible snickers in the room. In certain academic circles, especially at Harvard Divinity School, the Bible can be picked apart, examined, debated and condemned but never, never accepted at face value as historic fact.

When the snickers died down, the discussion continued as if Fran's suggestion that the Bible is history had simply not been made. It was apparently too outrageous even to contemplate. "I was shocked, hurt and offended," Fran said of the response.

After that, Fran stayed away from theology courses at the Div School. She continued to fulfill her requirements, taking a course in Scripture and another in world religions, but she took her electives in Harvard's History and Literature departments. "I'm an English major at the Divinity School," she would joke, with only a touch of bitterness.

Her specialty was, as she had intended, the role of women, a course of study that, she said, "helped me find my footing as a feminist." Fran was quick, however, to distinguish her feminism from that which dominated the Div School, where women's studies were often coupled with "a declaration of war on men," as she put it. "I think that is what I disliked most—the belief, which is rampant at the Div School, that anger is a positive force for change."

The diversity of Christian experience demonstrated by Professor Hutchison and my fellow students served as an important reminder that the Div School brand of ultraliberal Christianity did not represent the faith, belief or politics of most Christians in the United States. Polls show that most take the Bible a whole lot more seriously, adhere to conservative politics and are still coming to terms with women in the workplace, let alone the pulpit.

Diana Eck, for all her strengths in presenting world religions, came up short in her course when it came to teaching about how Christians, like herself, feel about their faith. In each of the other world faiths we studied (Hinduism, Buddhism, Judaism and Islam), she helped us understand the faith from within. Through lectures, assigned readings, slides and movies, she gave us a flavor of what it is like to worship a Hindu goddess, follow the Buddha, revere the Torah and embrace the Koran.

Perhaps she felt it was not necessary to present the insider's view when it came to Christianity because most of her students were, after all, Christian. But I was disappointed. In class, she spent more time examining what Christians feel about non-Christians than looking at what they believe themselves. She could not, it seemed, get beyond the Harvard tendency to embrace religious relativism rather than religious truth.

For example, Eck favored the names *Hebrew Bible* and *Greek Bible* to the standard terms *Old Testament* and *New Testament*, saying that *Old* and *New* sounded like value judgments. While I appreciated her sensitivity, I thought it unnecessary. For a believing Christian, *Old* and *New* seemed to me like perfectly appropriate terms. No apologies needed.

The assigned reading for the Christianity section of her course was John A. T. Robinson's *Honest to God*. Robinson, a bishop of the Church of England, was a British forerunner to the 1960s debate in the United States about whether God is alive. (The most famous manifestation of the American debate was the cover of *Time* magazine on April 8, 1966, which asked in red and black: "Is God Dead?")

However, Robinson's book, a best-seller after it was published in 1963, was a sorely inadequate tool with which to view Christianity in the 1980s. Robinson struggled with literalism—the virgin birth, the divinity of Jesus, among other issues—and concluded that new theological language was necessary "today." But Robinson's "today" was over twenty years old. Whatever demythologizing had been done in the 1960s was getting remythologized in the eighties. You didn't have to be a reporter to know this; you just had to follow politics and read the daily papers. Ronald Reagan had been elected to the White House by an alliance of Fundamentalists and conservative populists. Bible-thumping evangelists were filling our television screens with messages that the Bible is to be taken literally. Membership in the liberal Protestant denominations was down, and Fundamentalist churches were thriving. Why were we reading John Robinson and not Jerry Falwell, I wondered.

In fact, in her four lectures on Christianity, Eck never mentioned the most vital and dynamic force in Christianity in the mid-1980s—Evangelical Protestantism. Instead, she wrapped up our tour of Christianity with a slide show of the 1983 meeting of the World Council of Churches in Vancouver, British Columbia. One of the high points was a slide showing Christians and Native American Indians raising a totem pole together, interfaith cooperation at its best. I have nothing against the ecumenical movement or totem poles. But I was hoping that the Div School would teach me about how Christians feel about themselves. This educational encounter with Christianity was a disappointing one.

# CHAPTER 13

# Student Life

Thus taught the Baal Shem Tov: "Study for the sake of scholarship is desecration; it is a transgression of the commandment against bowing before alien gods, the idol being mere learning. The study of the Torah is a matter of the heart's devotion."

Throughout my year at Harvard, I never got over the sheer joy of being there. I arranged my schedule so that I would be on campus five days a week, beginning each day with a ten o'clock class. This gave me time to drop Adam off at his day-care center and then take the mile-long walk down Massachusetts Avenue to school. Three days a week I would head right for the Div School; the other mornings my classes met in Harvard Yard. The walks through the Yard were my favorite. I passed through Johnston Gate, given by a member of the Class of 1855, past red-brick residence halls where members of that class and hundreds of others had lived during their undergraduate years. Members of future graduating classes —teenage boys and girls in sweatpants and blue jeans— were coming out of those very same dorms as I arrived each morning. We crossed the Yard together on the narrow concrete walks that cut across the verdant lawns.

In the middle of the Yard is University Hall, with the

statue of John Harvard sitting in bronze in front of it, looking quite pleased with the school that he had helped found
350 years earlier. On the other side of University Hall is the
humongous Widener Library, with 3.5 million books, the
largest of Harvard's one hundred libraries. It was named
after Harry Elkins Widener, a 1907 graduate who went
down with the *Titanic*. At the other end of the Yard is
Memorial Church, built for the Harvard men who fell in
World Wars I and II, and behind it, Memorial Hall, built in
memory of those from Harvard who fought and died for the
Union in the Civil War.

The church has a steeple with a bell tower that sets the
pace for the Yard. It rings mightily on the hour, signaling
the coming of classes, which start promptly ten minutes
after the bell stops ringing. My Harvard Yard classes were
in Sever, an inspiring Romanesque structure, and Emerson,
in the Baroque style with terra-cotta ornamentation. In the
lobby was a statue of Emerson, who studied theology at the
Div School in the 1820s, and over the entrance of the building was this quote from the Psalmist: "What Is Man That
Thou Art Mindful of Him?"

I delighted in every detail, from getting my identification
card—which proved (to me at least) that I was a Harvard
student—to buying a shoulder bag for my books. I got the
bag at the Coop, the Harvard Cooperative Society in Harvard Square, after deciding that at thirty-five I was just too
old to wear one of the rustic knapsacks favored by undergraduates. I wasn't too old to emulate their dress, however.
I put my workaday suits and ties away for the year and wore
jeans or cords, running shoes and sweatshirts (yes, even a
crimson one with HARVARD on it in big white letters).

Two days a week I had classes in the afternoons, but the
other days I was finished at noon. (It was hard to believe.
At *The Times*, my day would be just getting started at
noon.) I would grab a sandwich at the Div School's Refectory, a Harvard Square coffee shop or the Harvard Hillel and
then head for my favorite library. I had tried Widener but

found it just too large for human scale and a bit awesome, particularly the personal collection of Harry Elkins, which is still displayed behind glass seven decades after the *Titanic* went down. The whole thing seemed larger than life—or death. I also tried the Div School library, but it was a difficult place to concentrate because of the heavy and congenial Div School traffic. (The Div School library is rich with history. I once checked out a book—Louis Ginzberg's *Scholars, Students and Saints,* and commented to the librarian, "Look, no one has taken this book out since 1967. That's eighteen years!" She smiled, giving me a look that said, "Gee, you *are* new around here." Then she said with some pride: "The other day I stamped out a book that was last checked out in 1897." That was eighty-eight years!)

I also tried the science library and the education library among others until I found my favorite—Lamont. Opened in 1949 (the year I was born), Lamont is a six-story undergraduate library with a solid humanities collection. As in the other libraries, there are carrels for individual study, long tables for spreading out and easychairs for reading. But Lamont had one other thing—Farnsworth. Tucked away on the fifth floor of Lamont, Farnsworth is a library within a library. It was donated by Henry Weston Farnsworth, a 1912 graduate, and includes his collection of books on hunting, fishing, sports and law, all of which held only passing interest for me. What Farnsworth had that attracted me was a manly air, the spirit of a private men's club, complete with overstuffed leather chairs and ottomans. The walls were wood-paneled, and the light came from floor lamps with dim-watted bulbs rather than bright overhead fluorescents. Farnsworth also had self-standing ashtrays, a feature I liked even though I didn't smoke. There was always a nice musty smell in the air. This was a Harvard of a different era. And I liked it.

Farnsworth was my hideaway. Few people ever used it, and even if others were there, it would have been difficult to see them because the lighting was so poor. I had to push a floor lamp right up next to my chair to get enough light to read. But from there I read and read and read: histories and novels that I had always wanted to read but couldn't because of the press of normal adult life, and books for class on early Christianity and modern Islam.

To break up my afternoons of reading, I would walk over to the old Indoor Athletic Building to use the exercise machines, take an aerobics class or swim a few laps in the pool. Even the pool was historic. There was a metal plaque at the shallow end honoring John F. Kennedy, a member of the varsity swim team in 1937 and 1938.

My year at Harvard was a little like fulfilling a legion of New York intellectual fantasies. It was like reading *The New York Review of Books* and knowing that you would have time to read each new book reviewed. It was like seeing the list of oddball lectures in *The Village Voice* and knowing that you could make each one of them. It was like enrolling in every stimulating course offered at the New School, the Ninety-second Street Y and the New York Health and Racquet Club.

At least once a week, Shira and I used to give each other "nights off" so that one could be free to relish Cambridge while the other stayed home with Adam. Checking my diary entries, I find that on one not untypical spring evening I attended a Talmud class at the Harvard Hillel, heard a lecture called "Ben Franklin's Bible Hoaxes," took in some folk music in Harvard Square and then joined a late-night seminar called "Yoga: Relaxation or Meditation."

Despite my general euphoria, there was one disappointing episode during my first semester. I labored long and hard over a term paper and only got a B. This may not sound like a bad grade for someone who was returning to school after twelve years; indeed, in my college days I would have been pleased with a B on a paper. But I had so much hoped that my academic experience at Harvard would be different. I was older, matured by the experiences of life and, as Shira had reassured me on my first day of class, "from a happy home" rather than from the broken home of my childhood.

Although I was terribly upset at the time, in retrospect I see that the paper probably deserved a B. My problem was that I was accustomed to writing news articles, not term papers. Apparently it takes different skills to be a journalist and an academic. The paper was called "Judaism and Islam: Realities and Stereotypes," and was graded by a teaching fellow in my world religions class named Kuk Won Bae.

In my paper, I reviewed the historic links between the two faiths and how these parallels developed into strikingly similar religious traditions and rituals. Aside from the obvious common practice of circumcision and the prohibition against eating pork, both Judaism and Islam have similar systems of law, complete with written and oral traditions. There are links between the penitential periods of Ramadan and Yom Kippur; similarities between the Muslim hajj to Mecca and the Jewish pilgrimage to Jerusalem and parallels between the role of the rabbi in a synagogue and that of the imam in a mosque.

I worked hard on the assignment, reading a dozen books on Judaism and Islam and writing what I thought was a nicely crafted paper. I was prepared for some criticism of my scholarship but not of my writing style, especially from Kuk Won Bae, a doctoral student from South Korea.

"Each paragraph sometimes seems to be quite isolated from each other," he wrote in the margin. But this, I wanted to scream, is good journalism! Each paragraph has an idea so that if the story is cut virtually anywhere by the editors it will still make sense. My other academic sin was telling at the beginning of my paper what my conclusion was. That too is good journalism, but not necessarily good scholarship. The journalist reaches his conclusion at the beginning of the paper, while the academic comes to his at the end. Nonetheless, there was some satisfaction. In my journalism, I, like most reporters, work hardest on the first paragraph—that, after all, is my one and only chance to lure readers into the story. If I lose them in the first graph, they will turn the page and find something more interesting to read. Even in my academic paper I wrote a good lead. Diana Eck, who also read and commented on my paper, wrote "Great beginning" in the margin, although she agreed that the rest of the paper deserved a B. The paper began like this:

> *La ilaha ila'llah Muhammadun rasulu'llah.*
> *Shema Yisrael Hashem Elokeynu Hashem Echod.*
>
> The creeds of the Moslem and Jewish faiths, and the central role they play, are strikingly and—in the context of world events—almost frighteningly similar. "There is no God but Allah, and Muhammad is His prophet," is whispered into the ear of the newborn Moslem baby so that the words are the first the infant hears on this earth. "Hear, O Israel, the Lord is our God, the Lord is one," are the final words that should be on the lips of a righteous Jew before death.

My flexible schedule also gave me the opportunity to slip in and out of other courses when I heard something interesting was going on. One day while we were having lunch in the refectory, my friend Katherine invited me to come to her class in "practical ministry" the next day. The class was developing "new liturgies" for contemporary situations, and she and two classmates, Andrea and Terry, had put together a mock funeral service for an imaginary victim of AIDS. This was 1985, mind you, when AIDS was believed to be almost exclusively a homosexual disease. I went but wondered if this was not just another sign of the radicalization of the Div School by different interest groups.

In class, the two women, dressed in black tights, did a slow, mournful liturgical dance around the room. Terry, slim and handsome in tight black jeans, delivered the eulogy for the fictional victim, Jeffrey H. Webster (1956–1985) while sitting on the steps leading to the pulpit. I found his frankness astounding, even if it was about a fictional character. He told us—the class masquerading as a church con-gregation—that he was the dead man's lover and described how he and Jeffrey first met at a gay bar, their eyes locking in passion, and about a trip they took together to the Florida Keys. One line I remember because it was so unabashedly sexual: "We climbed to the roof of the Windsurf Motel and lay there naked, listening to the ocean pounding, pounding against the shore."

I was moved but skeptical. Only at the Div School, I thought. A few weeks later, Katherine invited me to another "new liturgy," this one a marriage rite for lesbian women. I politely took down the information but decided to skip it. Enough of sexual politics, I thought. After all, I came here to study theology, not to become radicalized.

It wasn't long after I left the Div School that I realized that what had seemed so extreme there might have, in fact, been prescient. In late 1987 I wrote a story about the Epis-copal bishop of Newark, the Reverend John Shelby Spong, a tall lanky southerner who favors the "blessing" of homosex-ual unions in Christian churches. He stopped short of saying that they should be officially married, noting that homosex-ual unions are not recognized by the state or the church. But he argued that over the centuries Christian clergy have offered their blessings on everything from the hounds be-fore the hunt to battleships going off to war. Why not gay couples? Such a rite, he said, would have the practical result of "reducing rather than encouraging promiscuity." Spong —married and the father of three grown daughters—said that his advocacy for homosexuals stemmed in part from his work in the civil rights movement. "We've got to deal with the fact that the church has been violently prejudiced against gay people," he said. "We've murdered them; we've burned them at the stake; we've run them out of town for some-thing over which they have no control. And that's im-moral."

In the 1960s, Spong took heat for being a southern

preacher favoring equal rights for blacks, and he was prepared to take the heat in the 1980s for favoring equal rights
for homosexuals. And heat he was getting. The Prayer Book
Society, a vocal right-wing Episcopal group, had tried to get
the House of Bishops to put Spong on trial for heresy. But
Spong continued with his crusade, publishing a book called
*Living in Sin?* in which he explores some of the "myths"
about human sexuality in the 1980s.

As I interviewed Spong in his office in Newark, I felt bad
that I hadn't accepted Katherine's invitation to attend the
Div School's "lesbian wedding." Who knows, I thought,
maybe the Harvard Gay and Lesbian Caucus would have
regarded Bishop Spong as a reactionary for giving them only
a bone—a "blessing"—when they wanted the real thing—
a marriage ceremony.

Another article that I wrote after leaving the Div School
also made me think back on the sexual politics of the place.
This wasn't some academic exercise but two real people who
were deeply wounded by the actions of New York's most
famous church, St. Patrick's Cathedral, the seat of the
Roman Catholic Archdiocese of New York. Their names
were David and Maria Hefner, and I heard about their story
through a friend who had used David as her hairdresser
when he worked at a Manhattan salon called Kenneth's.
David, a tall, fair-haired Texan, began cutting hair soon after
he came to New York in the early eighties with hopes of
becoming an actor. He had a six-month homosexual relationship with another hairdresser and then met and fell in
love with a customer, Maria Ribeiro, a Mexican woman with
jet black hair and a quick smile.

"We went down to City Hall and got married in 1984,"
Maria recalled. Two and a half years later, David was diag-
nosed as having AIDS. He deteriorated rapidly, leaving work
and becoming increasingly helpless as the disease sapped the
life out of his body. Maria left her job as a file clerk to care
for him full-time. She made him homemade soups and
breads, read escapist novels to him and told him stories

about what they would do when he got better. During his frequent hospitalizations, Maria went with him and slept on a cot in his hospital room.

"I had a lot of time to think," David told me when I interviewed them in their apartment on Second Avenue in January 1987. He sat in bed, propped up by a half-dozen embroidered pillows, two of them shaped like hearts. "There is not much I can do for Mara," he continued, using the nickname he had given his wife. "She does everything for me now." He noted that he was a Protestant and that his wife, a Catholic, always had wanted a religious wedding ceremony in her "dream church," St. Patrick's. She used to say it reminded her of the church in the little town where she grew up in Mexico. David decided to call St. Patrick's and was given an appointment to see an associate pastor, the Reverend John Clermont.

David and Maria went together. They told Father Clermont that they wanted a small wedding—only four guests would be there—and asked if someone could sing "Ave Maria." They also told Father Clermont that David had AIDS and might need a small stool or chair handy if he got tired during the ceremony.

"The priest said yes, he would celebrate our wedding," Maria recalled. "He said, 'I will make everything very comfortable for you.' " A time and date were set—9:00 A.M., February 14. Valentine's Day. Before they left, David and Maria talked about miracles with the priest and the possibility that David would someday recover. "Someday maybe we will have a child," Maria told him. "Maybe you will baptize the child for us." The priest smiled and said he would be privileged to.

The couple left the church full of excitement, talking about the clothes they would wear, the friends they would invite and where they would go for a celebratory brunch. They also reflected on the commitment they would make before God, a commitment they already had, to "love, cherish and honor" each other "in sickness and in health."

Two days later the priest called. "David was asleep," Maria recalled. She heard the priest say, "I cannot celebrate your wedding," hung up the telephone and wept. When David awakened, Maria encouraged him to call Father Clermont back. They were afraid no one would believe their story, so they recorded the conversation on their stereo tape deck. When I interviewed them, they stopped talking and played the tape. Maria and I sat on the floor in front of the stereo, and David sat up in bed.

"I'm sorry, David," the priest said, "you have a transmittable disease and we would be putting the church at risk to have you here."

"But, sir, it is transmittable only through sexual relations. In fact, the only person at risk by my going to the church is myself. I am extremely susceptible to infection."

The priest seemed not to hear. He continued: "David, I have to tell you, I got scared when your wife spoke of having a baby. You know the baby could be born with AIDS."

"Please, please. Mara was only joking, dreaming. We both know how sick I am. We have no intention of having a child. Because of my health, we have not had sexual relations for a year. And Mara has been tested three times for the AIDS virus, always with negative results."

The priest continued to express his regret but said there would be no wedding at St. Patrick's. He suggested that the couple try their local parish church. But David's sense of outrage was so strong—stronger than any illness—that he ended the conversation with words so eloquent that I looked across the room at him in admiration.

"It is very hard to have this illness and now to get slapped in the face like this. I just feel it is wrong. I cannot understand how the church of God would do something like this. If I were a killer, a hired murderer or a thief . . . ," he said, his voice trailing off. "But I am just a person who happens to have a sickness. My heart is very sick and I don't know what to say or do, but it's not fair, sir, it's not fair, and nothing good will come from this."

I left their apartment full of respect for the noble spirit of this couple and knowing that I had a great story, a story that could make a difference. It was one of those rare times that I've walked away from doing an interview knowing full well that once the story was told an injustice would be rectified. Sure enough, just a few days after my story appeared on the front page of the Metropolitan News section, Cardinal O'Connor reversed the decision of Father Clermont, who it turned out had been following the orders of his superior, Monsignor James Rigney, rector of St. Patrick's. David and Maria renewed their wedding vows at St. Patrick's on February 14, 1987. Valentine's Day. Cardinal O'Connor was there. Less than three months later, David succumbed to his illness. His funeral, like his wedding, was held at St. Patrick's.

In its own way, the Div School's radical approach, mock funerals and all, was preparing me for real life outside the walls of academia, whether I would continue in journalism or prepare for my ever-growing fantasy of being a rabbi.

The Div School atmosphere was clearly rubbing off on me. Here I was surrounded by people studying for the ministry who were different from the caricature of the self-centered, upwardly mobile, competitive student of the eighties. I loved being in a school where there were men and women interested in serving God and society in an age when many wanted to serve only themselves.

My neighbor Bill Doe, in his confusion about what I was doing at the Div School, had already decided I was a rabbi. Increasingly I began to think about it myself. After a day of struggling with John Courtney Murray, Maimonides and Karl Barth, I often found it difficult to read *The New York Times*. Newspapers had been a central part of my life since the subway-riding days of my childhood and, once I had set my sights on being a reporter, *The Times* became a kind of portable school of journalism. Once I was a reporter, the paper became indispensable. First, it told me what was going on in the world, and, second, of equal importance, it told me what was going on at the paper: who was getting the good stories, who was writing from abroad, who was stuck with the obits, who had a good lead and who was getting ignored. From the vantage point of the Div School, all of this seemed trivial. I wondered how it had all been so important to me. I tried to imagine a different life, the life of a scholar and a pastor. I would spend my days in book-lined rooms, surrounded by the wisdom of the ages, seeking answers to questions about man's relation to God. I would devote myself to sharing what I had learned with others eager for knowledge and spiritual guidance. I would teach classes every day of the week and preach on Saturday.

I liked it when Bill Doe called me "Rabbi," and I imagined giving up my byline for the title on a synagogue marquee: Rabbi Ari Goldman. As a rabbi, I could finally retire my reporter's notebook and experience life firsthand. Instead of writing wedding announcements, I could perform weddings and share in a couple's joy. Instead of writing obituaries, I could officiate at funerals and soothe the pain of the mourners. Instead of quoting someone else on the immorality of nuclear weapons or on the joy of the coming festival, I could say it myself. I could touch people's lives in the most direct way possible and in the process change my own life.

Just as the spring semester was beginning, Bill Doe disappeared from Chester Street. Soon afterward, I ran into Bill's friend the Judge and asked him what had happened to our garrulous neighbor. "He's at Mass General," the Judge informed me somberly. "Cancer."

When I got home, I called the hospital, and they put me right through to Bill. He sounded tired but was anxious to hear news about my family—"the rabbi's family," as he put it—and about the rest of the "celebrities" on Chester Street. When I asked him how he was doing, he sounded concerned but upbeat, in his finest military manner. "One operation down," he said, "and one to go." The first operation, he explained, had not been successful in removing all the cancer.

"Bill, tell me, is there anything I can do for you?" I asked with concern.

He didn't have to think. "Just pray for me, Rabbi."

"Of course, of course," I repeated nervously. And then I forced myself to say something rabbinic. "God bless you, Bill."

I hung up the phone wondering if I could really live out my rabbinic fantasy. Could I effectively hold the hands of the lonely, the dying, the bereaved? Could I in some way intercede in their behalf with my prayers? Wasn't I really better off being a step removed, protected by my reporter's notebook and my objectivity? I reached down deep into the well of theological studies into which I was steeped that year, but I found no answers to the suffering of my friend. And I knew that even if the ministry were to be my primary calling, the answers to some questions would remain beyond my grasp. Yet there was one thing that I had learned about all religious systems. There is a point when book learning stops and faith begins. The only thing I could do was what Bill had asked. I prayed for his soul.

# Reporting 101

Rabbi Bunam was wont to say: "When on the Sabbath day my room is full of people, I find it hard to interpret the Law. For each man needs his own law, and needs to be perfected therein; and what I interpret for all, I withdraw from each."

Although Bill saw me as a rabbi, at the Divinity School I was just another student. I didn't keep it a secret, but few of my classmates and teachers knew that I was a *New York Times* reporter, sent by my paper for an immersion in world religions.

I had not set out to be a religion writer. In fact, when I first became a *Times* reporter in September 1975, the last thing I wanted to do was write about religion. For one thing, it had a bad name at the paper. In the 1930s and forties, it was known as "Church News" and consisted of summaries of Sunday-morning sermons. It was a useful if largely meaningless way to help fill the Monday papers and give some experience to aspiring reporters. After Abe Rosenthal became a college correspondent for the paper in 1943, one of his first assignments was to cover church sermons. He'd rush from church to church collecting material and then write a few pithy paragraphs for each, earning three dollars a sermon.

My friend and early mentor Sam Hartstein was also among that honored cadre of sermon gatherers. Sam likes to tell how Ted Bernstein, *The Times*'s arbiter of style in that era, insisted on calling all ministers—Catholic, Protestant and Jewish—by the same honorific, "The Rev. Dr." Sam, who later went on to be the public relations director at Yeshiva University, bombarded Bernstein with notes until he relented and let rabbis be called rabbis.

These church roundups were under the direction of the religion editor, one of the first of whom was Rachel K. McDowell, a puritanical woman known around the office as the "Lady Bishop." If she is remembered for one thing, it is that she led a futile one-woman crusade to stop cursing in the newsroom. Legend has it that upon her death, she left her modest estate to the reporters' union with instructions that the money be used to set up a program to stop the use of profane language in *The Times* newsroom.

Years later, when he became executive editor, Abe Rosenthal would say that the heyday of religion writing at *The Times* came in the early 1960s, when John Cogley was brought onto the paper. Cogley, a liberal Catholic who had been editor of the Catholic magazine *Commonweal*, brought analysis to the religion beat at a time it was needed most—during the Second Vatican Council. The Roman Catholic church was undergoing a revolution, and Cogley was no less than a war correspondent, reporting the struggles and changes within the church. Cogley, who was at *The Times* only eighteen months before leaving on the advice of doctors after a heart attack at age fifty, also became the nemesis of every religion editor to follow him. "Remember what John Cogley did with the beat," Abe Rosenthal would tell the new recruit. Sometimes I thought that maybe what Rosenthal really wanted was another Vatican II rather than another Cogley.

By the time I became a *Times* reporter, the religion beat had less to do with big institutions like the Vatican and more to do with religion as a countercultural movement. From reading the newspapers of the late 1970s, it would seem that the greatest threats to young middle-class Americans were Eastern religious cults. The papers extolled the virtues of the "deprogrammers" who were working hard to rescue the boy next door who had shaved off all his hair, donned a saffron robe and spent the day dancing in a circle in Central Park. The Eastern religion craze of the seventies seemed only to increase the cynicism about religion that already afflicted most journalists I knew. I've found that reporters, who deal with the grimy underside of life, rapes, murders, wars— that, after all, is what makes news—are uncomfortable with religion. In fact, it wasn't until I became a religion writer almost a decade later that many of my colleagues confessed that they had any spiritual lives at all. Religion is not something talked about in polite journalistic company.

Right from the start at *The Times*, I was more open about my Judaism than anyone else. I did not work on Fridays and Saturdays, and my byline, with a Hebrew first name, stood out. Still, I was determined to keep my faith and my journalism separate. Besides, almost all the reporting I had done as a college correspondent from Yeshiva University and much of the writing I had done as a copyboy had revolved about Jewish issues. I was ready to branch out, broaden my horizons and begin building a solid record of reporting that would someday lead to the most coveted of *Times* assignments—foreign correspondent.

Of course, you begin small at *The Times*. My first assignment was to cover Long Island as part of a new effort the paper was launching in the suburbs. I was the first reporter for the "Long Island Weekly," a Sunday feature section that covered local news and personalities as well as the arts and new restaurants. It was quite an enjoyable job since I worked with one editor at a time (rather than the gaggle I had grown accustomed to on the Metropolitan Desk) and had one deadline a week. There were also perks, like a new Ford Pinto to get around the 120-mile-long island, and there were drawbacks, like the requirement that I live there too. I was single and had just broken up from an on-again-off-again romance, so I gave up my share in a Manhattan apartment (the other occupant was my brother Dov) and headed east. I found a spectacular place to live, the carriage house of an estate on forty acres overlooking Long Island Sound. I set up my office in my small apartment over the garage and went to work. I tooled around the island in my Pinto and returned to "my estate" to write. It turned out to be a glamorous but lonely existence.

I was twenty-six years old and, after years of striving in the world of journalism, had fulfilled my dream of becoming a reporter on *The New York Times*. But on Long Island, I found myself with plenty of free time on my hands. I decided to pursue an ambition that had been only a vague dream in college: I was going to learn to play the cello.

I had been looking for a cello teacher when, quite by accident, I found the perfect person: Heinrich Joachim. I met him one day in 1976 when I was late for an interview in a small office building in the town of Roslyn and accidentally knocked on the wrong door. A man of medium height with a shock of gorgeous white hair came to the door rubbing his eyes. The room behind him was dark, but, by the light from the hallway streaming into the room, I saw a dazzling wooden cello case with geometric inlay.

Forgetting why I had knocked on his door in the first place, I asked him, "Do you play the cello?"

"Yes," he replied in a German accent. "Do you want to become one of my students?"

"Yes," I said without hesitation.

A week later I returned to his studio, a simple room with the wooden cello case, two cellos, a piano, a full-length mirror, a mattress on the floor and a small round table with two chairs. Between lessons, Mr. Joachim, then in his sixties, would take short naps on the mattress. When a student came, they would begin by having a cup of tea at the table. A discussion would inevitably precede the lesson. Slowly, methodically, week after week, he taught me how to bring music out of my instrument.

The hours I spent with Mr. J, as I came to call him, were much like the warm musical walks to synagogue I had taken with my father when I was a young boy. Instead of singing the songs of the synagogue, I was playing simple pieces by Saint-Saëns, Purcell, Tartini and even Bach. We spent months on Max Bruch's "Kol Nidrei," a haunting cello solo that has much of the power and passion of the Yom Kippur prayer on which it was based.

My introduction to the cello came at the right time because, while living on Long Island, I had stopped going to the synagogue. Although I kept a kosher home, my Jewish connection was fading. There was no synagogue within walking distance of my isolated apartment, so I stopped going to services. The idea of driving to a synagogue on the Sabbath, acceptable in Conservative and Reform Judaism, was so alien to me that I thought it better just to stay home.

My official days off were now Saturday and Sunday, but this did not present the problem it had when I began working in Manhattan because on Long Island I had only one deadline to meet a week—on Wednesday afternoons—and could knock off on Fridays whenever I wanted. That was how I landed in Easthampton one Friday night in 1976. I was doing a story about the summer pleasures of Long Island during the day, expecting to return home by sundown to mark the coming of the Sabbath. But it was a beautiful day at the beach, and I lingered longer than I had planned. As I began to drive back, the sky was a magnificent shade of red, girls were skipping home in their bikinis and music was blaring from a hundred stereos on a hundred sun decks. And I—I was crying so uncontrollably I could hardly see the road. Amid all these worldly delights, my body ached for a cup of sweet wine so I could make kiddush and bless the coming of the Day of Rest. I wanted to abandon my car, the vehicle of my Sabbath desecration, and sit in the soft glow of candlesticks at a table with a pure white linen cloth, gleaming flatware and fine china. With all my being, I craved the Sabbath, needed it to wrap around me like the woolen prayer shawl I had left back home.

It was not the first time that I knew I was going to violate the Sabbath. I had done it before, but each time I came to regret my actions. It is not that I am afraid of sin or divine retribution or that my car will crash after the sun sets. Rather, I believe that there is an intrinsic value in my observing the Sabbath as an Orthodox Jew. For me, observing the Sabbath in an Orthodox way is its own reward. And every time I have violated it, I have felt like I missed a great opportunity—the opportunity to be myself.

Realizing what I was about to give up, I stopped the car. I went into a restaurant—Bobby Van's, a popular Bridge-hampton hangout—and got a table. I ordered a brimming glass of red wine and asked for two dinner rolls. I whispered kiddush to myself and made the blessing over the bread. That night over my improvised and solitary Sabbath table at Bobby Van's, I realized that the challenge to my Orthodoxy was not my job—*The Times* had been remarkably accommodating—but myself. I couldn't continue to blame my wayward tendencies on the demands of the paper. I had to decide on the kind of life I wanted to live and live it.

Judaism, I knew, thrives in community. Soon after my Friday-night dinner at Bobby Van's, I moved from the isolated estate to an apartment in Roslyn, just walking distance from a small synagogue run by Robert Block, an offbeat and creative rabbi who had been a classmate of mine at Yeshiva University. His synagogue was Orthodox, with men on one side and women on the other, but it was open minded and open armed: Jews of all persuasions were welcomed, and the rabbi never demanded more from people religiously than they were ready to take on. The synagogue, in a converted Roslyn bar, stood in the shadow of Roslyn's large Conservative and Reform congregations. With Orthodoxy the less popular option, Rabbi Block often had trouble mustering the necessary quorum of ten men to begin prayers. And so, on Saturday mornings I came to expect a visit from the young rabbi, who good-naturedly roused me from my bed for prayer.

I continued reporting for the "Long Island Weekly," working out of the pressroom of the county courthouse in Mineola, the Nassau county seat, but I realized that I had to do more for the daily paper if I was ever going to get back to the main office in Times Square. I found that I was well known on the island but virtually forgotten by the people who made the decisions in New York.

A year later, after two years on Long Island, a new metropolitan editor, Sydney Schanberg, summoned me back to Manhattan to cover education. Sydney had just returned from Cambodia and was the closest thing I had ever known to a real live newspaper hero. After the Americans had pulled out in 1975, Sydney had remained in Phnom Penh against the wishes of the American government and *The New York Times*. For two weeks nobody—not his family, *The Times* or the American government—knew if he was alive or dead. But he eventually emerged on the Thai border and wrote a brilliant account of the fall of Phnom Penh. The story of his escape and the ordeal of his office assistant, Dith Pran, were told in the movie *The Killing Fields*.

What a privilege to work for this man! He was mercurial, to be sure, sometimes totally obnoxious and rude. But at other times—times when there was a big story—working for Sydney was heaven. When I came across a story about a Queens school district that was defying the Carter administration over the issue of racial quotas, Sydney instilled in me an enthusiasm that I thought only happened in the movies. "Day after day, give me everything you've got on this story," he told me. "And I promise you, I will get every story on Page 1." And he kept his promise. He went in to the Page 1 meeting in the executive editor's office each afternoon and fought for the story as if it were his own.

Sydney assembled great people around him: William E. Farrell was his deputy, and James Clarity was his assignment editor. They were a fun-loving, hardworking, dynamic team. I would do anything for them. Well, almost anything. One summer, Sydney asked me to work Fridays on night rewrite. "But, Sydney, that's Shabbat," I told him. Sydney never brought up the subject again.

As an education reporter, my assignment centered on the Board of Education at 110 Livingston Street in Brooklyn, an address that had come to be synonymous with bureaucracy. I did my best to spend less time at the board and more time at the schools, where I found much better fodder for stories. I also followed New York State education issues and made a monthly trip to the state capital, Albany, to cover the meetings of the Board of Regents. In those days, *The Times* maintained a four-person bureau at the Capitol to cover the governor and the legislature. I got to know the people there well on my trips upstate.

One day while I was in the Times Square office, I got a call from Steve Weisman, then the Albany bureau chief, inviting me to the annual dinner of the Legislative Correspondents Association, which was to be held on a Friday night in the early spring. "You're an honorary member of the bureau," Steve said. "We'll rent you a tuxedo and get you a hotel room for the night." The annual dinner is a gala affair where the press roasts the politicians in elaborate skits and the politicians respond with barbed speeches. Of course the governor, Hugh Carey, would be there, as would Mario Cuomo, the lieutenant governor. It was a great opportunity to meet people, make contacts and have a good time. I told Weisman I would let him know.

I got off the phone and sighed. It was tempting. In those days, the education writers sat right next to the religion writers. Ken Briggs, who was religion editor at the time, saw the look on my face and asked, "Ari, is everything all right?"

I told Ken my dilemma. Friday night is Shabbat, of course, but a ticket to the Legislative Correspondents Association Dinner is a great opportunity. Ken, an ordained Methodist minister, said just six words, "How can you compare the two?" I called Weisman back and told him I couldn't make it.

As fate would have it, my next assignment was Albany. Albany, 150 miles up the New York State Thruway from Manhattan, might sound like some form of journalistic Siberia, but in reality it was one of the best beats on *The Times* for a young reporter. For many, a session or two in Albany was a springboard to a job as a foreign correspondent. Steve Weisman, Francis X. Clines, Sydney Schanberg, William E. Farrell, Linda Greenhouse had all worked in the Albany Bureau. And all of my colleagues in my first year there—1979—went on to foreign posts: Richard Meislin to Mexico City, E. J. Dionne to Rome and Sheila Rule to Nairobi and later London.

I was pleased. Albany had certain advantages. The legislative session lasted only six months of the year (January to June), so I didn't have to move upstate permanently. Since moving back to New York from Long Island, I was getting involved once again in a synagogue and was again sharing an apartment with my brother Dov. Although I was dating frequently, there was nobody I would miss by living upstate. In fact, Dov and I had set up a pretty comfortable life for ourselves. We shared a modern two-bedroom apartment on West End Avenue, had a housekeeper in once a week to clean and do the laundry and maintained pretty separate lives. Once a week—on Friday nights—we would eat together, gathering around our Sabbath table a regular club of aging Orthodox bachelors, all of us in our late twenties. I know that doesn't sound old, but in the Orthodox world people marry young. Many of our married friends were on their second or third children and a few were on their second wives. But we were holdouts and proud of it.

When Dov and I got our new apartment together in 1978 (I was twenty-eight, he was twenty-four) we threw a housewarming party. My aunt Mindella looked at our well-equipped kitchen and our unpainted wood furniture from Conran's and couldn't restrain herself. "Where are your wives?" she wanted to know. "You boys should really be

starting families." Traumatized by divorce at a young age
and enjoying our freedom, we dated often but never thought
too seriously about getting married.

Our tight bachelor group lived in a dual world of sexual
liberation and Orthodox tradition. We saw little inconsistent
with spending the night with a girlfriend and then rushing
off to synagogue for the morning prayers. And we took both
parts of our lives seriously. Just as the religious life was
pursued with integrity, so were relationships. Relationships
were monogamous and lasted for months or even a year at
a time. Only rarely, in our circle at least, did they resolve
themselves in marriage. More often, there would be a
breakup—some of them like minidivorces, with friends taking sides and alienation—and then, after a decent interval,
another relationship.

We lived in the late 1970s and early eighties in a rare
window of sexual opportunity, between the waning days of
the sexual revolution and the onset of AIDS. For many of
the modern Orthodox, sex is not a major area of conflict.
Rationalizations abound, including the Jewish teaching that
sex is a positive and healthy gift from God. That is, as long
as the sex is heterosexual and not adulterous.

Each of us rationalized it in his own way. I was confident
that my sexual relationships with my girlfriends were
healthier and more positive than the homosexual experiences of the frustrated boys I had gone to yeshiva high
school with. I also knew that I was happier than many of
my friends who went into early marriages without any sexual or emotional experience with women.

There was another group of friends that I could compare
myself with in this calculation. There were many who like
me had been raised in Orthodox homes, gone through the
yeshiva system but rejected the whole package as soon as
they were on their own. My final justification for succumb-
ing to my sexual drive came right from the pages of the
Talmud. Even the Talmud acknowledges that sometimes the
male sex drive is overwhelming. If a man cannot banish

sexual thoughts from his mind, he should put on dark clothes, go to another town, find a woman and satisfy his lust, the Talmud advises. Just be discreet.

There was only one Orthodox rabbi who was willing to acknowledge this new sexual ethic and, in so doing, challenge it. His name was Shlomo Riskin, and he was the driving force behind a remarkable institution on the West Side of Manhattan called Lincoln Square Synagogue. Orthodoxy, which has a tendency to be closed, cliquish and a mystery to outsiders, was transformed by Riskin into something warm, inviting and attractive. Most Orthodox rabbis talk to "the religious," but Riskin spoke to the religious and, as he liked to put it, "the not yet religious." Even the separate seating of men and women in his synagogue did not seem archaic. It was a shul-in-the-round, with women occupying the rear half of the sphere and men the front half and everyone facing inward. When men looked up from their prayer books they saw women; when women looked up they saw men.

Once you knew the system, it was easy to figure out who was available. In Orthodox synagogues, married men wear the white prayer shawl known as the talith and married women cover their hair with a hat or a scarf. It's Saturday morning, the service is boring and you have no plans for the night? Just gaze across to the women's section. Who is that cute one with the short black hair (no hat) and red dress? Keep an eye on her. Does she seem familiar with the service? Is she singing along? Reading the Hebrew with mumbling lips or following along silently in the English? Is she sitting alone or with a friend? Do I know the friend? I wonder what they are talking about? Does she laugh easily? Where does her gaze fall? Can I catch her eye?

After the service, the synagogue pours out onto the street, husbands and wives find each other and seal their reunion with a "Shabbat Shalom" kiss. Dating couples join, careful to demonstrate just the appropriate amount of affection in public. Clusters of single people form. Introductions are made, but they are not even necessary because here the easiest pick-up line in New York is at the tip of your tongue: "Shabbat Shalom. What did you think of the sermon?" No need for the awkward "Haven't I met you somewhere before?" or "You look familiar." Sex comes later, if at all, in this ritual. And when someone invites you home, it is for a Shabbat meal with a group of friends, not for a roll in bed. At least not initially.

For a variety of motives, Jewish New York singles flocked to Lincoln Square. Largely on the strength of its single population, Lincoln Square grew into one of the most active synagogues in Manhattan. And most remarkable for an Orthodox synagogue, with its emphasis on the family, Lincoln Square remains dominated by single people. Of its 1,300 members, over 50 percent are unmarried.

Still, with the great success he achieved in the late 1970s, Riskin was unhappy. He began to talk more and more from the pulpit about Jewish family values, about the centrality of the family in Jewish life. He began with wisecracks about the aging bachelors in the congregation, like myself, and then got serious. "I know about the men who take their tefillin with them when they go out Saturday nights," he said in one sermon.

The line was widely repeated and quoted. It being the Sabbath, I didn't take notes, but the rest of the sermon went something like this: "You have to start getting serious about your lives and about your Judaism and about the women you are dating. Be fair. Be responsible. Judaism is not sustained by a single life-style. Don't be afraid of commitment."

The image he drew was a humorous one, and all too familiar to my crowd. From the time of our bar mitzvahs on, we had been taught to pray each morning with our tefillin, the black leather straps and boxes worn on the head and left arm that contain passages from the Scriptures. The proficient among us knew how to satisfy this ritual in a matter of minutes, quickly taking the boxes out of the velvet bag, binding the straps and reciting an abridged version of the morning prayer. It is a kind of purifying ritual that starts the day and helps remind you who you are.

Tefillin were a snap for an Orthodox teenager, but once women started showing up in bed, what happened? Riskin was saying, find out how the women got there. And ask yourself, do they belong? Is premarital sex compatible with your Orthodoxy, your synagogue, your tefillin? His answer was clearly no.

At the time, the Orthodox girl I was dating and I were struggling with the issue of premarital sex. That is, I was struggling one way and she was struggling the other. I insisted that sex was compatible with our dating relationship and she—I'll call her Wendy—insisted that it must wait until marriage. In his sermon, Riskin clearly took Wendy's side and I, swayed by his argument, decided to take what he said seriously. After all, he had the courage to confront an issue that other Orthodox rabbis pretended didn't exist. I stopped pressuring Wendy on sex and took to heart Riskin's admonitions about "commitment."

Nonetheless, my relationship with Wendy didn't flourish. Even with sex out of the way, another religion-related problem loomed in our relationship. Wendy, a bubbly Hebrew schoolteacher from the Midwest, took her Orthodoxy very seriously. She knew I was steadfast in my religious observance with one big *if*. If I had an emergency assignment from my newspaper, I told her, I would have to work—even on Shabbat. I explained to her that I considered my work more than a job; to me it was a calling. I had a moral responsibility to report the news, and Jewish law might have to bend to accommodate my vocation. She didn't like that, but we both felt that we could put the issue on hold, and we did, until one night just such an emergency arose.

I was home from Albany one weekend, staying at the apartment I shared with my brother. At midnight, after our Friday-night dinner guests had left, the telephone in my room rang. As is my Sabbath custom, I let the answering machine get it. There was a frantic editor on the line. Nelson

Rockefeller, the former vice president and former New York governor, had been found dead in the apartment of a young woman friend. All the political reporters were being called in to help write his obituary and to investigate the circumstances of his death. I quickly got dressed and took a subway downtown.

The next morning, Wendy was concerned when she looked across to the men's section and didn't see me in the synagogue. We had plans to have lunch and spend the day together. She sought out my brother, who told her what had happened. Ari had worked through the night and was sleeping it off, Dov explained. "He will drop by to see you later."

When we did get together, Wendy was furious. She paced around me like a teacher as she spoke. Her pace became a stomp; her speech became a holler. "How could you?" "What kind of Jew are you?" And: "I'm not going to live my life not knowing if you will be home for Shabbat!"

My old conflict was returning to haunt me. It had taken a new form, moving from journalism versus Judaism to journalism versus Wendy, but it was still there. I had not fully resolved my conflicts for myself, how could I expect someone else to accept them?

The problem was that no one I knew in the Orthodox community was willing to struggle with these issues. I had always been close with Rabbi Z, but he had warned me against going into journalism to begin with. I couldn't go to him now to talk about a girlfriend who couldn't accept my compromises. I began to wonder if Rabbi Riskin would understand. After all, he had the courage to struggle with the sexual issues. I decided that I would talk with him.

In the meantime, my Albany assignment was working out well. In some ways, it was the perfect job for me because one member of the bureau had to work Sundays. I happily volunteered and ended up working in Albany from Sunday to Thursday. After the deadline Thursday night, I would hop on a Trailways bus for the trip back to Manhattan, where I would spend Friday night with my bachelor friends and, if we weren't fighting, Saturdays with Wendy. If old governors would just stop dying at inconvenient times, it looked like being Orthodox in Albany was going to be a cinch.

Then came the plans for the Legislative Correspondents Association Dinner. When I had turned down an invitation to the dinner while I was writing on education in New York, I knew that it was a big social and political gathering. But once I was in Albany, I realized that the dinner was more than that: participation in the dinner separated those on the inside and those on the outside. Reporters—there were probably fifty of them in Albany representing different newspapers, wire services and radio stations from around the state—spent two months rehearsing skits and songs for the dinner. There was makeup and costumes and rehearsals virtually every night as the show date drew near. Assembly-men and senators, lobbyists and lawyers, legislative pages and clerks, reporters and newspaper publishers, everybody was going to the LCA, as the dinner came to be known.

But I wasn't going. I planned to leave Albany the night before, just as I did every Thursday night, and be at home for Shabbat dinner on Friday night. "You're not in the LCA show?" asked A. J. Carter, a reporter from *Newsday* who had gone to Columbia Journalism School with me and had a starring role in the show. "No," I told him. "I am a Sabbath observer."

While the LCA mania was building up, so was the session. A few weeks before the weekend of the LCA dinner, the governor, the Democrats in the Assembly and the Republicans in the Senate were deadlocked on some spending bills. Both houses were called into emergency session and were going to work through the weekend to hammer out their differences. Rich Meislin, the bureau chief, told me he would need me in town for the weekend. He said that I probably would not have to write anything; he just wanted somebody sitting in on the debate in the Assembly Chamber.

The New York State Legislature, the Capitol guides tell the tourists, is the only one in the nation where reporters actually sit on the legislative floor. Most other legislatures exile the reporters to a press gallery, but in Albany they get to sit right under the Speaker's podium, looking out on the rows of legislators' desks. Reporters were so much a part of the scene that one old-timer—Gerry Allen of the *Buffalo Evening News*—used to vote regularly on state legislation. He would yell out "yea" or "nay" (and sometimes both) when the Speaker called for voice votes from the floor.

I sat in one of the press seats that Friday afternoon, listening with mild interest to the debate, occasionally writing down quotes in my reporter's notebook. I was also watching the big marble clock over the Assembly door, knowing that Shabbat would start at 6:32. There was a collision in my head when I saw the two hands of the clock brush against each other. Shabbat was coming in two minutes, and here I was sitting in the legislature with a pen in my hand.

My mind leaped back over the years to a painful incident in my childhood. I was twelve years old and watching my mother light the candles on the white tablecloth that covered the kitchen table in our tiny apartment in Jackson Heights. I was wearing a white shirt, red tie and my dark blue "Shabbat suit"—my only suit. On my head was a white knit yarmulke. The house was rich with the smell of her Shabbat chicken. My mother leaned over, and I felt her kiss on my cheek as she said, "Shabbat Shalom, dear." I left the apartment and was walking by myself through the darkening streets to the synagogue for the evening service when I saw a small, bent-over woman standing helplessly on the corner, two big shopping bags at her side. "Are you okay?" I stopped to ask her. "I'm so tired," she told me. She put her hand into her purse and fished out a shiny new dime. "Here," she said, "this is for you. You are so kind. Just come with me and carry my bags to my house. I live on the next block."

The woman of course didn't know it, but she had presented me—a twelve-year-old yeshiva boy—with a terrible religious quandary. It is a great mitzvah to help old people, I knew. But I was also acutely aware that it was Shabbat. On Shabbat one could not handle money and, even if I were to forgo the tip, I knew that it was not permissible to carry her bags. It is a sin to carry packages in the street on Shabbat. I stood immobilized for a moment, not knowing what to do. "Sorry, I am late, late for synagogue," I told her. I ran the rest of the way to shul, not looking back to see this frail woman whom I had abandoned.

On that Friday night in the state legislature I could still picture the scene so vividly: the woman standing there helplessly on the street corner and the young boy running away from his conflict, only to take refuge in the synagogue. It is a searing, haunting montage, one that raises many questions. How could Jewish law be so cruel? Did I do the right thing when I was twelve? Was I doing the right thing now, sitting in the Assembly Chamber at the age of twenty-nine? Why did I persist in my faith? Was it the magic of those candles? Was it my mother's kiss on the cheek? Why couldn't I grow up? Why couldn't the law grow up? Couldn't the law be reasonable? Couldn't it be flexible? Couldn't I?

And then I thought of a way out, an obscure teaching of my rebbe, Rabbi Siegel, came back to me in a flash. We were gathered around his desk in the yeshiva, and he was teaching us the thirty-nine categories of work that are prohibited on Shabbat. We discussed writing. "What is writing?" he asked us in his singsong pedagogical manner and then went on to sing the answer himself: "You have violated the prohibition of writing on Shabbat if you write two letters—two letters that cannot be erased. That is writing."

My reverie over, I looked up at the clock. 6:32. Just them, I heard a legislator on the floor say something quotable. I put away my pen and took out a pencil and captured the quote in my notebook. "You're not going to like this, Rabbi Siegel," I muttered to myself, "but you've given me a way out."

To my mind, I made it through the weekend following the letter, if not the spirit, of the law. I felt good that I had avoided my conflict by writing in pencil, knowing full well that Rabbi Siegel and others would certainly object to my interpretation. But I wasn't prepared for the reaction of my colleagues.

A. J. Carter sauntered by. "Well, I thought you were a Sabbath observer," he said.

"It's hard to explain," I told him.

"I can still get you a part in the LCA," he replied gloating.

"Fuck you," I wanted to say. But I just said, "No thanks."

On one of my weekends back in Manhattan, I arranged to talk with Rabbi Riskin.

Shlomo Riskin is a bright, intense man with a remarkable amount of energy. He was brought up in a nonobservant household but fell under the sway of an Orthodox grandmother. He resolved to follow the old traditions and, the story goes, passed up Harvard, where he had been admitted, to study Judaism at Yeshiva University. His speaking style was full of emotion. While giving sermons, he would bounce up and down on the balls of his feet, waving his hands this way and that. Like most rabbis, he was always "on," shaking hands, smiling, dispensing advice, condolences, best wishes. The first time I saw him relaxed was when I arranged to meet with him in his cramped office above the sanctuary. He moved a pile of correspondence and a stack of books to clear two chairs for us, then he fell into his seat and loosened his tie. I told him about the clashes that had occurred between my profession and my faith and how my inability to resolve these conflicts had become a terrible strain on my relationship with Wendy.

Riskin listened with great interest. He told me that he thought my work was very important, not only for my own well-being but for the sake of the Jewish community. "There has never been an observant person at *The New York*

*Times* before," he said. "You have a tremendous, tremendous opportunity to do good."

At the same time, he said, as a Jew I had an obligation to follow halacha, or Jewish law. He said that I should be careful about taking too many liberties with the law; my pencil-on-Shabbat logic had gone too far, he said. I was not a rabbi, he reminded me, and I had no halachic right to rule on matters of Jewish law. The proper way to proceed when I had a conflict, he said, was to consult a rabbi. He said he stood ready to give me guidance.

Okay, I said. Let's get practical. After all, that is just what the Talmud would do at a time like this, give a *haycha timzah*—a theoretical example. It is Saturday and I have just been assigned to the Chicago Bureau and there is a terrible plane crash. Bodies are strewn around the city. Can I go cover it?

He thought a moment and then began to ask questions. Can someone else drive you? Can someone help you take notes? Can you dictate your story instead of write it?

Yes. Yes. Yes. I told him. So, can I cover it?

He said that he could not give me a blanket approval but that if things had to be done in an emergency there were proper, halachic ways to do them. Orthodox doctors, he said, were given wide latitude to treat the sick on the Sabbath even when a patient's life was not hanging in the balance. My situation as a journalist was, to be sure, somewhat different, but still allowances could be made—if a rabbi were consulted on a case-by-case basis. Again, Riskin said, he stood ready to guide me.

I left his office feeling triumphant. I knew it could be done. I rushed to see Wendy and told her everything Riskin had said. But she was not swayed. "Impossible!" she said. "He doesn't know what he's talking about. He's wrong."

I threw up my hands. I realized that there could be no future to this relationship. I wasn't your typical Orthodox guy, and she, unfortunately, was your typical Orthodox girl. Wendy and I broke up.

So there I was, pushing thirty, having to explain myself
to everyone, from my Orthodox girlfriend to my rabbi to
my secular newspaper colleagues. No one seemed to understand.

Riskin tried, but ultimately, his solution was impractical.
As with sex, he could see the problems created by Orthodoxy's clash with the modern world, but his answers fell
back on old, tired ways. I couldn't live my life tethered to a
rabbi who would make judgments on my every move. He
wanted me to call him as each situation arose, but both he
and I knew that he wouldn't even answer the telephone on
the Sabbath to respond to my questions.

No, I decided, I cannot rely on others. I must be suffi-
ciently educated in Jewish law to know what can and cannot
be done. The law, I was certain, is far more flexible and
compassionate than the rabbis had told us. This, I knew, was
treading on dangerous ground since, as a basic principle of
Jewish law, the laws were given to the rabbis to decide and
not to laymen. In a sense, I had to begin to become my own
rabbi.

# African
# Religions

Rabbi Noah related the following tale: "An old woman visited the cemetery, and gazing at the peaceful graves, she commented: 'Holy souls! Pure souls! How happy is your lot! How soothing is your sleep! And yet I have no wish to be with you!' "

My friend Fran and I sat next to each other the second semester in a course called "Introduction to African Religions," which was taught by a wonderful associate professor, Lamin Sanneh. Born in the West African nation of Gambia, Sanneh had inherited Islam from his father, African tribal religion from his mother and Christian faith by choice. His father was a strict Muslim who railed against native superstition and reliance on amulets for good luck or magic. But his mother snuck her native good-luck charms into the house, sometimes burying them in the earthen floor of their kitchen. As a young man, Sanneh converted to Christianity, was baptized in the Methodist Church and left Africa for an education in England. What resulted was a worldview and a mellifluous accent that took the best of the different cultures he had encountered. I used to think it was worth going to his class just to hear the gentle sound of his voice, his vocabulary and his rich imagery.

"In Africa," he told us in the first class, "people talk about philosophy and theology like Bostonians talk about the Patriots." He told of being at the airport in Ghana and getting theological questions from clerks who were reading the Old Testament under their desks. "The religious spirit permeates the African world. People are always saying prayers; when they meet, when they part."

Sanneh drew a distinction between two kinds of religious experience. The "natural religions" of Africa stem out of the primitive experiences of man: seeing one's shadow, having a dream, watching the death of a loved one. All these make man come to the conclusion that there is a power beyond, a power greater than man. Primitive man creates stories and myths to explain natural phenomena, like the story of a cock crowing at the sun to get back its flying wings. Then there are the "revealed religions" of the West, all of which begin with stories: God created the earth, Moses got the Law on Sinai, Jesus was born of a Virgin. These stories help man cope with the dreams, the setting sun and death.

If revealed religion is a rock, a series of fundamentals on which to build faith, natural religion is like a river, a dynamic, ever-changing faith that can even pick up a few rocks along the way. Take Christianity in Africa. Dating back to the influx of missionaries from Europe beginning in the late 1800s, Africans for the most part opened their arms to Christianity, all the while remaining distinctly African. In Malawi, for example, there had long been a mighty ancestral figure of adoration known as Mbona. When the missionaries came, the Africans continued their devotion to Mbona, they just portrayed him differently—instead of a warrior figure they made him a black man on a cross. Soon, people began adding another myth to the ancestral figure. They said that Mbona was born of a virgin. "Missionaries did not disrupt" African religions, Sanneh told us. "They added another layer."

While there was some resistance to the Christian missionaries, the history of the missionaries in Africa is not as bitter as that of the missionaries in India. Gandhi writes passionately against the efforts to proselytize Hindus, accusing the missionaries of robbing the native beliefs and culture. The African readiness to accept Christianity might have had something to do with a concept of God that was, to begin with, closer to the Western image. One day Sanneh drew a triangle on the blackboard. At the pinnacle was God, the line to the right represented ancestors, the line to the left represented intermediary forces known as *orisha*. From that tripartite African representation of God, it is but a short leap —a mere step—to the Christian concept of a Trinity. The Indians, with their constellation of Hindu Gods, had a much greater leap to Christianity.

Sometimes the assimilation of Christianity into African religious culture had humorous turns. The missionaries read the Africans Bible stories, much to the natives' delight, especially when they heard, "And the Lord God made for Adam and for his wife garments of skins, and clothed them." Why, the natives wanted to know, weren't the missionaries also wearing leather clothes? The Africans also read of the celebrations at the Temple in Jerusalem and asked the missionaries why they didn't have drums and dances. "Hallelujah," they quoted from Psalm 150.

> Praise God in His Sanctuary. . .
> Praise Him with drum and dance,
> With flute and strings praise Him.
> Praise Him with cymbals clashing
> With resounding cymbals praise Him.

Sometimes the combination of the two cultures proved deadly. Sanneh told of an African woman, revered as a prophet by the members of her village, who in the mid-1800s had a vision that if all the local cattle were slaughtered they would be brought back to life tenfold. The natives followed her vision, complete with the Christological notion of resurrection, and waited anxiously for a miracle as the carcasses rotted. Hundreds of villagers died of starvation.

Despite the malleability of the African faith, the early missionaries met with only limited success in winning converts. It wasn't until the 1950s, when the Bible became widely available in native African languages, that Christianity swept the continent. With the Bible in their own hands, the natives could create a distinctly African church. That is just what Matthew Ajuoga, a Luo tribesman, did in 1956 when, with a Luo translation of the Bible in hand, he created the Church of Christ in Africa. Over the next thirty years, Africans converted to Christianity at phenomenal rates; sometimes there were as many as six thousand conversions a day, Sanneh told us. The flourishing of Christianity in Africa, taken with the growing number of Christians in Latin America, brought about the shift to more Christians in the Southern Hemisphere than in the Northern. Remarkably, the American and European missionaries who had gone South to convert the heathen were now outnumbered by them.

Despite the broad swath that Christianity cut across Africa, there were many who did not come under its influence. One of these was the Nuer, an isolated tribe of the southern Sudan that were the subject of a monumental study by the anthropologist E. E. Evans-Pritchard in 1953. Evans-Pritchard broke the convention of the aloof academics of the day by studying the Nuer people from within. He lived with them and recorded his findings in a book called *Nuer Religion*. Sanneh used the book to introduce us to African religions.

The more I read about and heard about this "primitive" tribe and their beliefs and values, the more I saw of myself. There were so many parallels—good parallels, parallels that I am proud of—that I decided to do my final paper on Judaism and the Nuer. The most striking similarity perhaps was the concept of animal sacrifice, something that I had never been totally comfortable with in Judaism. After all, Orthodox Jews pray for the restoration of animal sacrifice in the Temple that will be rebuilt when the Messiah is revealed. As an "enlightened," modern person, I sometimes had to ask myself if I really wanted to see animal sacrifice restored. In fact, Conservative Judaism, the branch just to the left of Orthodoxy, deleted the prayers for the restoration of sacrifice in their new prayer book. Reform Judaism dropped those references long ago. How could I, as a modern person, keep praying for sacrifices?

The Nuer helped me understand. By learning about their sacrificial rites, I was better able to understand sacrifice in the Jewish tradition. For the Nuer, sacrifice is a way of substituting one life for another—the life of the animal for the life of a man who is in danger of death because of either illness or mortal sin. In the ritual, the animal is killed, the blood is poured and some prime portions of meat are given to the priest. Then the family that brought the offering sits down for a festive meal. Put in those terms, it is not all that different from the ancient Paschal sacrifice. And, once you separate out the blood and slaughter, is it really all that different from the modern Passover seder or, for that matter, from Thanksgiving? In our civilized society, we kill to eat. In ancient Israel and among the Nuer, they kill for forgiveness—and then they eat. Are we really so much more refined?

On an academic level, I also learned from my experience the first semester about how to craft a good final paper. Rather than report different facts, I tried to build an argument. And I was sure to save my conclusions for the end. Emulating Sanneh's use of the personal in class, I also included some first-person reflections in my paper. And it paid off. I got an A. Here is how my paper began:

When I was a boy, I spent a good deal of time in the Orthodox Jewish home of my grandparents in Hartford, Conn. My grandparents always seemed to be visiting the cemetery, either for the burial of friends or to pray at the graves of their parents or siblings. When they returned home, they would never enter through the front door. They would come to the rear of the house, where there would be a cup and a basin waiting for them. One by one, they would pour water on each hand three times before entering the house through the back door.

I was too young to go to the cemetery and, unlike the adults, I had no one to visit there. But I do remember thinking, "How persistent the spirits of the dead are. We trick them by entering through the back, wash them from our hands, but still they linger with us.'''

Memories like this one kept occurring to me as I was reading E. E. Evans-Pritchard's *Nuer Religion*. The traditional African religious rites are performed in villages a world away from my own and yet they are familiar.

My interest in the links between Africa and Judaism was not solely academic. Eighteen months before I had enrolled in the Div School, in fact, *The Times* had sent me to Africa for a reporting assignment that was a tryout for a position as a foreign correspondent. After spending two legislative sessions in Albany, 1979 and 1980, I was brought back to Times Square to write about transportation. For the next four years I woke up each morning to 1010 WINS News Radio to prepare myself for my daily encounter with the nation's largest and most antiquated subway system. Every day there was a story: a derailment, a sniper, a fare increase, a service cutback. I even did a story about "token suckers," young men who would stuff up turnstile slots and then vacuum the tokens out with their mouths. I never lacked for ideas, had a great time and again used my schedule—Fridays and Saturdays off—to my advantage. What was often a mediocre story on a Tuesday or a Wednesday could be squirreled away for the weekend. I would come in on Sunday, the slowest news day of the week, and (with my journalistic integrity still intact) turn a so-so story into a Page 1 story.

I was thriving at *The Times* and, when you're thriving and unattached (as I was), there is always talk about a foreign job. In fact, when Shira and I began to date seriously in 1983, we talked a lot about the possibility of going abroad. Shira was excited at the prospect; if she was going to be a free-lance journalist in the States, she reasoned, it could even be better abroad. At the time, the East Africa Bureau in Nairobi was opening up, and my name was being kicked around. After our wedding, I told the foreign editor that marriage was not going to eliminate me from the competition. In fact, most people saw being married as a distinct advantage in Nairobi, a job that was often described as a lonely outpost. The editors, of course, took their time in deciding how to fill the job. In fact, they waited until Shira was five months pregnant with Adam to give me a tryout. In April 1984, on two days' notice, I was sent to the southern African nation of Zimbabwe to investigate allegations that zealots from one tribe, the Entelbele, had killed five hundred members of another tribe, the Matabele.

Zimbabwe, my first foreign assignment, was a remarkable personal experience but a professional disaster. I couldn't confirm the story I had been sent for and, even if I had been able to, I couldn't figure out how to use the telex. I couldn't even manage to write one of those pithy "journal" stories, in which you tell what people are talking about on the streets of Harare. Government officials, so accommodating to *New York Times* reporters in the United States, wouldn't even see me. (One minister said he might be able to fit me in two months down the road. "But I'm only here for four weeks," I pleaded.) I finally figured out how to use the telex, but the foreign desk in New York didn't use my stories. I didn't really blame them; there was nothing happening in Zimbabwe. The whole situation was so ironic. My great Judaism-journalism conflict had centered on the question What if you are abroad on Shabbat and there is a war. Aren't you going to cover it? Here I was abroad, and there was no war. Not on Saturday or any day. Saturdays, like most of the days of the week, I was off. I spent my free time lolling around the rooftop pool of the Meikels Hotel in

downtown Harare, Zimbabwe's capital. I looked up at the
sky and wanted to cry: "Lord! Test me! Just give me a good
war to cover!"

I was getting so bored that I left Harare and went on
safari. I spent a weekend on a game farm, where the lions
and impala grazed outside my motel window, then took a
trip to Victoria Falls, a wonder of the world on the Zambezi
River that makes Niagara Falls look like an amusement park
ride. Nobody at *The Times* seemed to miss me. Nor did they
question my phone bill, which ran to $900 for the month
with my daily conversations with my wife in New York.

Finally, after five weeks, Warren Hoge, the foreign editor,
said that it was time for me to come back to New York. He
didn't even sound angry. I mentioned to him that I was
planning to return via Nairobi so that I could take a look at
the bureau and living arrangements there. I asked if he
thought, given my performance, that I should still go.
"Sure," he said. "Definitely go to Nairobi."

A bit confused—and wondering if, unbeknownst to me, I
had done a good job—I flew to Nairobi. I stayed in a downtown hotel and, as is my wont, spent some time on the
telephone checking out the Jewish life in Kenya. On the off
chance that I would be sent there, I wanted to be prepared.
A synagogue and a part-time rabbi serve the small community made up mostly of Israelis working in East Africa. Kosher chicken is flown in regularly, and a mohel will come by
special request from Israel to circumcise a newborn boy (a
good thing to know if your wife is pregnant).

The one hardship I had in Africa as an observant Jew was
food. Zimbabwe is a landlocked country and, although there
are a few rivers, there isn't much fish. Fish is the savior of
kosher people who travel. With no fish, I lived on the alternatives: eggs, cheese and bread. Fruits and vegetables, a
healthier kosher staple, were risky because of bacteria; local
produce could really mess up your stomach if you weren't
accustomed to it. I lost some weight, but it was a worthwhile
trade-off for the experience. I would go abroad for the paper
again. But since Zimbabwe nobody's asked me.

# CHAPTER 16

# Islam

As for Ishmael, I have heeded you. I hereby
bless him. I will make him fertile and
exceedingly numerous. He shall be the father of
twelve chieftains, and I will make of him a great
nation. But my covenant I will maintain with
Isaac.

— Genesis 17:20–21

Another faith I studied at the Div School
that shed light on my own was Islam. I
got a good basic introduction to Islam in my world religions
class with Diana Eck the first semester and decided to delve
deeper by taking a course in the spring called "Muslim Religious Life." It was taught by Annemarie Schimmel, a di-
minutive German woman who had been teaching at Harvard
for two decades.

Schimmel had a most unusual style. She would shuffle
into the classroom at the last minute, after everyone was
seated, then ceremoniously plant her purse directly in front
of her on her desk. She would stare straight ahead and smile,
all the while making no eye contact. Then she would take
three steps backward until she hit the blackboard and sit on
her hands on the little shelf used for chalk and erasers. She
would be silent for a moment and, as if in a trancelike state,
close her eyes and lecture for the next fifty minutes. The
first day of classes I was convinced that she was blind. I

checked under her desk looking for a sleeping Seeing-Eye dog. Then I figured that maybe someone would come to class when it was over and escort her back home. But nobody came. We knew the lecture was over when she opened her eyes, picked up her pocketbook by its stiff arched handles and walked, unassisted, out the door. She never consulted an outline or a note as she lectured. It was all in her head. Only on rare occasions would she open her eyes, usually to write something on the blackboard or to pass a piece of Islamic art around the classroom.

Once the lights went off in the classroom, but Schimmel kept lecturing. We were, after all, a class of graduate students, so nobody was going to snicker or yell "Who turned off the lights?" After a few seconds in the dark, one student got up and fixed the timer on the light switch so that the lights went back on. Schimmel never missed a beat.

Behind this odd style, however, there was a deeply spiritual, even mystical woman, who was full of knowledge, anecdotes and flashes of humor. When we were learning about the Muslim concept of heaven, she told us about the houris, the women in heaven charged with taking care of those men who had lived righteous lives on earth. The phenomenon of the houris, she told us, raises the question, What do righteous women get? She told of a Hadith—a sacred writing—in which an elderly woman asks Muhammad whether old women would be in heaven. " 'No,' he told the woman. 'Only young women will. The old women will be transformed into young beauties.' " Schimmel opened her eyes, looked right at us and added: "That, I think, is an authentic Hadith."

Like a modern-day Scheherazade, Schimmel spun tales of Islamic life gathered in a lifetime of world travel. She told of a truck driver in Turkey who engaged her in a debate on the New Testament, of a tour guide in Saudi Arabia who told her he was "actually looking forward to Ramadan" and of the difficulty of looking up a person in a phone book in Pakistan because "everybody has five names." She told how, as a woman, she was not allowed to enter a mosque in India where Muhammad's hair was reputedly on display as an object of veneration. "Even Indira Gandhi cannot come in here," the guard told her. But beyond the wonderful stories, Schimmel put flesh on a culture and a religion that I, like most Jews, approach with considerable apprehension.

Islam is the youngest of the world's major faiths. The Prophet Muhammad was born in the year 570 in Mecca. Today, with 750 million followers, Islam is second only to Christianity in its number of adherents. Although we have come to associate Islam with the Middle East, it is a worldwide faith. There are 60 million Muslims in the Soviet Union, 90 million in Africa and 130 million in Indonesia, the largest Muslim country in the world.

Literally, Islam is not a religion but an act. It means "to surrender"; an adherent is a Muslim or "one who surrenders." As Jane I. Smith, another Div School instructor, put it, "Islam is the act; Muslim is the actor." The name of the Koran, the sacred book of Islam, literally means "recitation."

Muslims respect the Old and New Testaments but believe that the Koran supersedes the teachings of Moses and Jesus. In Islam, the Koran is more than just another record of revelation; it is revelation itself. The text is to Muslims what Jesus is to Christianity—God's revelation on earth. Muhammad, an illiterate camel driver, was neither a deity (like Jesus) nor a teacher (like Moses). He is the vehicle for the Koran, a work revealed to him through prophecy over a twenty-three-year period.

Muhammad's illiteracy has tremendous theological significance. One Muslim scholar, Seyyed Hossein Nasr, compares it with Mary's virginity. Just as Jesus was conceived without human interference, so the Koran was revealed through Muhammad without human intervention. In Islam, the very sounds and words are part of the revelation, playing a role similar to that of Jesus in Christianity. Wilfred Cantwell Smith, a retired Harvard professor who remains a guru for many on the Div School faculty, compares Christian communion—the sharing of the blood and body of Christ—to the practice in Islam of memorizing the Koran in Arabic. In fact, the Koran cannot be translated; it retains its full impact and holiness only in Arabic.

Islam is based on "five pillars," religious principles that have parallels especially in Judaism and also in Christianity. There is (1) the confession of faith ("There is no God but Allah and Muhammad is His Prophet); (2) prayer; (3) alms-giving; (4) fasting and (5) pilgrimage. Like Judaism, Islam stresses religious practice over theology. Its system of law —*sharia*—is similar to the Jewish legal system of halacha.

In class, Schimmel brought the legal system to life by talking about its mystical powers. For example, in discussing the religious power of the Koran, she told us of a wonderful ceremony that takes place when a boy reaches the age of four years, four months and four days. On this day, the boy is dressed up like a little bridegroom and sent to school to recite his first verse of the Koran. The verse is written in honey on a slate and, after the boy masters it, the honey is dissolved in water. The boy drinks the sweet holy words as a spiritual and physical nourishment.

The words of the Koran have such power that they are written on daggers and shields and over the beds of the sick. Prayers have enormous power for good and, if abused, for bad. Schimmel told of a woman she knew whose arms swelled even as she recited the ninety-nine names of Allah for healing. It turned out that she had mixed up the order of the names, and when she put them right, the swelling went down. In Islam, everything praises God. One legend has it that the buzzes of bees are the words of the Koran. Why else would honey be so sweet?

Like other faiths, Islam struggles with the question of human suffering and why some prayers are answered and some are not. One teaching says that man is like the night-ingale. God keeps man in cages because He loves the music of his prayers. If He is slow to answer, it is only because He loves the song and does not want it to end.

The Koran emphasizes that Muhammad was a man and not a god, yet a tradition of veneration of the Prophet has come about. Why? Schimmel quoted from the Koran, which calls Muhammad "the most beautiful example." Instead of Imitatio Dei, she told us, Muslims believe in Imitatio Muhammad; an imitation not in suffering, as with some Christians, but in action. Thus, Muslims name their children Muhammad and emulate the Prophet's actions as described in the Koran and in sacred literature. There are traditions that say that Muhammad ate with three fingers of his right hand; that he liked lamb, squash, dates and honey and that his clothes were green and white. "From these stories," Schimmel said, "we get a whole mosaic of Muhammad's life. For the Muslim, this is the way to remain close to the Prophet."

Schimmel also told us how Muslims turned the religious ban against graven images (faces in pictures are often veiled) into an obsession with calligraphy; about the architecture of mosques and the Muslim influence on music and fashion. "Islam," she told us one day, "introduced wide baggy pants for women." This came about because there is so much genuflecting in Muslim worship that women had to find ways to maintain their modest dress. "Saris would not do," Schimmel said. "They were modest enough, but they would slip off with all the movement required in prayer."

Among my classmates in the course on Islam was Mark, twenty-four years old and one of the only Muslims in the Div School.

Mark was one of a growing number of American blacks around the nation who have rejected Christianity and embraced Islam. As a Muslim, he straddles two of the major currents in Islam in the United States today. He made his profession of faith—the *shahadah*—at an orthodox Sunni mosque, one that embraces Muslims of different colors and nationalities from around the world, and he is also loyal to the separatist Nation of Islam led by Louis Farrakhan. Farrakhan, who is widely known for making anti-Semitic statements—calling Judaism a "gutter religion" and praising Hitler—believes in a culture of black supremacy in which blacks and whites do not mix.

Mark's road to the Div School was unusual. He grew up in what he called "a nominally Christian home" in Delaware. "My folks attended a Methodist church when I was a boy," he said. The church, however, did not satisfy Mark's religious yearnings, and he got involved with an evangelical church in neighboring Maryland. "They had a strong youth outreach and sent a fleet of buses into three states to round up teenagers," he recalled. "I became pretty zealous, and by the time I was in high school, I signed up as an assistant preacher in the church."

As time went on, however, Mark found that he had doubts about Christian theology that were not being addressed by the church. While he enjoyed the warmth and spirit that the church provided, he still could not fully accept basic concepts like the Virgin Birth, Original Sin, the notion of the Trinity. "I also came to question their commitment to social justice issues," he said of the church he attended. "They did not confront racism, for example. In time, I began to see them for what they were—an offshoot of a white southern evangelical tradition."

The church continued to have a strong hold on him, however, a hold that was not broken until he was accepted to Harvard as an undergraduate. " 'Godless Harvard,' is what they called it. I think they were hoping I'd go to Bob Jones University."

Once at Harvard College, Mark continued to feel a religious yearning. "As an undergraduate, I majored in comparative religion. For me it was as much a personal quest as an academic endeavor. I would learn about different traditions in class—Christianity, Islam, Judaism—and then I would visit different religious communities in the Boston area. I tried three different Islamic communities, visited the Jewish services at Hillel, tried the Unitarians and the African Methodists."

After graduating from college in 1983, Mark went back to Delaware, where he continued his religious quest. A year later he made a decision. He was going to be a Unitarian minister and applied to the Div School's M.Div. program, the degree for ministers. Upon his return to Cambridge to attend the Div School, however, he stopped by the Sunni mosque he had visited when he was an undergraduate. Unexpectedly, he declared himself a Muslim. Already accepted at the Div School, Mark decided to stay and pursue his degree, substituting his new interest in Islam for his abandoned Christianity.

My career path at *The Times* also took some unexpected twists and turns after I returned from Africa in 1984. Realizing that it would be a long time—if ever—before I would get another shot at a foreign assignment, I began casting about for something new to do at the paper. The answer to what I should do next came, of all places, at a funeral. Rabbi Mordecai Kaplan, the founder of Reconstructionist Judaism, died at the age of 101, and his funeral was held at the synagogue he founded, the Society for the Advancement of Judaism, not far from our apartment on the West Side of Manhattan. The funeral was on a Friday—the first day of my weekend—so Shira and I decided to go. I had always been fascinated with Kaplan. He had been ordained as an Orthodox rabbi and served for several years as the spiritual leader of the Jewish Center, a prominent Orthodox synagogue on West Eighty-sixth Street that I knew well.

After my mother moved with my brothers and me to Manhattan when I was thirteen, we became active members of the Jewish Center. Kaplan was already long gone, forced out by the Orthodox congregation because he had tried reforms, such as eliminating the separate seating for men and women. Kaplan, who is famous for developing the notion of "Judaism as a civilization," moved down the block and opened his own synagogue. One of the stories I heard in childhood that stayed with me—because it is so impressive

—was that even as he had sought to change Judaism, Kaplan was himself an observant Jew. Every day, the story went, he put on tefillin in the manner of all devout Jews.

The funeral was quite touching, as family members and colleagues of Kaplan eulogized the man before his plain pine coffin. Ken Briggs, the religion editor of *The Times*, was there to do a story about the funeral. Afterwards, Shira, Ken and I walked over to Broadway for coffee. Ken told us that there would soon be an opening on the two-man religion desk, and he asked if I was interested. I guess he figured that anyone who spent his day off at a funeral was a prime candidate. He was right. Back at the paper, I let my editors know of my interest; within days (and without much preparation) I was a religion writer on the nation's best newspaper.

Working alongside Ken, a Methodist minister in his early forties, was wonderful. He was a good newspaperman, fast and comprehensive on deadline, and had an admirable style on a feature and a news analysis. He also had a broad range of knowledge about different faiths; he was able to write about Orthodox Judaism one day and Zen Buddhism the next. But more important than his journalism was Ken's presence. In a newsroom renowned for its coldness, Ken's remarkably cluttered desk in the back of the room was an oasis of warmth. While most reporters on deadline would bark at others who came by, Ken would make time for just about anyone at any time. He'd be there to give advice, talk about the Red Sox, tell a joke or just listen. If there was a pastor in the newsroom of *The New York Times*, it was Ken Briggs.

The year that I worked with him had its rough spots for me. Shira gave birth to Adam seven weeks before her due date. Since he was under five pounds, Adam spent the first month of his life in an incubator at the Neonatal Intensive Care Unit of Lenox Hill Hospital attached to a half dozen monitors that beeped and thumped and occasionally sounded alarms when his heartbeat or breathing momentarily stopped. Shira and I spent our days shuttling between home, work and the hospital, afraid to fully articulate our fears about our tiny son. But Adam bounced back quickly, shedding monitors as the weeks went by and gaining the eleven ounces that made him a candidate for discharge. One night when he tipped five pounds on the nursery scale, we bundled our little treasure up in a cloth carrier on Shira's chest and brought him home. Once he was there, I didn't want to leave. The job that for so many years had been my obsession had little pull on me. More than anything, I wanted to stay home and learn to be a father.

In that sense, as in many others, the year at Harvard, coming so soon after Adam's birth, was a godsend. As a graduate student, I had time to spend with my son that I never had as a daily journalist. It was the second year of Adam's life, the year he learned to walk and began to talk. Something remarkable happened between us that year. Adam began to see me as a primary caregiver rather than the remote father figure who is only around after a long day at work.

The change in our relationship struck me at 3:00 one morning when Shira and I were fast asleep. Adam stood up in his crib and began calling, "Daddy! Daddy!" His bottle was empty and he wanted *me* to fill it. Until that time, it had always been "Mommy! Mommy!" but with Mommy working that year and Daddy going to school, Daddy was around a lot more often. I, of course, didn't relish getting out of bed at 3:00 A.M., but I did welcome being able to learn how to become a nurturing father in the best sense of the word. Lessons like that stay with you.

# CHAPTER 17

# Women in Religion

The Sifre wrote: "When the daughters of
Zelophehad heard that the land was being
divided among men to the exclusion of women,
they assembled together to take counsel. They
said, 'The compassion of God is not as the
compassion of men. The compassion of men
extends to men more than to women, but the
compassion of God extends equally to men and
women.' "

The year I spent at Harvard was something
of a milestone for the Div School. It was
the year the school tipped from having a mostly male student body to having a mostly female student body. Of the
497 students that year, 53 percent were women. The fact of
a female majority was all the more remarkable because it
wasn't until 1955 that women were first admitted to what
had been an all-male bastion. In just thirty years, women
had come to dominate the most prominent Christian seminary in the United States. This, of course, was a phenomenon bigger than Harvard. The *1985 Fact Book on
Theological Education* showed that 26 percent of the nation's
Protestant theological students were women, as against 10
percent in 1972. The great surge of women entering divinity
schools and seminaries came in the late 1970s, as more and
more Protestant churches opened up their ministries to
women. In 1980, in response to this growth, Harvard Divin-

ity set up a Women's Studies in Religion Program, which, according to the school catalog, helps prepare women for ministry, brings in special lecturers on women's issues and examines the "male-centeredness and sexism in the religious traditions of the world."

Women-centered courses abounded. Among them were "Roman Catholic Bishops: A Feminist Perspective," which I took in the fall, and "Women in Religion: Image and Practice," which I took in the spring. Other offerings included "Women in Islamic Tradition," "Feminist Perspectives on Ministry," "Black Women in Religion: The Autobiographical Voice," "Women, Femininity and 19th Century Religious Heresy" and "Women and the New Testament."

Despite their numerical strength, women operated at the Div School as if under siege. There was a popular women's martial arts course offered in a formal main-floor reception room. The course, given in the fall, was geared to warding off attackers. All kinds of grunts, kicks and screams could be heard from the room. I peered in through a window in the door one day, and the instructor gave me a look that said, "You are the enemy. Get lost." Inside, several women were pummeling an imaginary man into submission on the floor.

Men were clearly the enemy. Here is a listing from an issue of the *Nave*, the weekly calendar of events put out by the Div School: "8 A.M. Women's Caucus. Mary Segers, Research Associate, will be discussing her current research on abortion and public policy. All women welcome." The message, of course, was "no men allowed."

Still, I was one of ten men in a class of eighty who took "Women in Religion: Image and Practice." Geared as I was to investigating contemporary issues in religion, I could not think of a better issue to explore than feminism in the church. The class met two times a week for lectures and films and once a week in smaller discussion groups. While I had generally become an active participant in my classes, I largely kept quiet in this one. As in my first days at the Div

School, I returned to the role of observer. Again I was the reporter, the outsider looking in.

"Women in Religion" was an ambitious course that looked at the role of women in Hinduism, Christianity and Islam and was taught by three feminist faculty members who were experts in the respective faiths. In addition, there were four guest lecturers and four films: *Devi*, which means "The Goddess"; *Dadi and Her Family*, about the matriarch of a poor Hindu family; *Behind the Veil*, a film about Islamic fundamentalism, and *The Veiled Revolution*, which is about feminism in Christian religious orders. Readings for the course, which came from a wide variety of sources, were distributed in booklets of photocopies from the original works.

When we studied Hinduism, we read a harrowing eyewitness account of childbirth in India written in 1926 by the anthropologist Katherine Mayo. Her book, *Mother India*, describes a dark, unventilated room with a dirt floor in which a smoky fire burned (to ward off the evil eye) while a young woman in labor moaned. The midwives or *dhai* came from the lowest class of "untouchables" and appeared to have trained with Charles Manson.

If the delivery is at all delayed, the dhai is expected to explore the reason for the delay. She thrusts her long, unwashed hand, loaded with dirty rings and bracelets and encrusted with untold living contaminations, into the patient's body, pulling and twisting at what she finds there. If the delivery is long delayed and difficult . . . the dhai resorts to all her traditions. She kneads the patient with her fists; stands her against the wall and butts her with her head; props her upright on the bare ground, seizes her hands and shoves against her thighs with gruesome bare feet. . . . Also, she makes balls of strange substances, such as hollyhock roots, or dirty string, or rags full of quince-seeds; or earth or earth mixed with cloves, butter and marigold flowers; or nuts, or spices—any irritant—and thrusts them into the uterus, to hasten the event. In some parts of the country, goats' hair, scorpions' stings, monkey-skulls, and snake-skins are considered valuable applications.

While most of my classmates grimaced, one woman in the group rushed to the defense of her sisters in the East. "It is wrong to view this from our Western eyes," she said. "It might sound disgusting to us, but it has validity for the Hindus; it even makes the experience holy for them. I bet they would find our antiseptic, high-tech delivery rooms ludicrous. How can we judge?"

I can't say that I fully agreed with her, but my mind did go back to the birth of our son in one of those antiseptic, high-tech delivery rooms. It was terribly impersonal and intrusive, especially all the wires and monitors, both internal and external. The obstetrician gave Shira an episiotomy, an incision to help the baby come out quickly, and then thrust his hand into her to hasten the removal of the placenta. I wondered if there is not a middle ground between the ancient Hindu way and the modern American hospital, maybe natural childbirth.

If there was one unifying theme to "Women in Religion," it was that women have always had a central religious role in the home even as they were being denied full participation by men in communal worship and ritual. The argument was also made again and again that women had once played a greater role but that men had taken it away from them. The time had come, everyone seemed to agree, for the women to take it back.

For example, we saw slides of a medieval painting that appeared to show women in vestments performing the Eucharist, an act denied to them by the modern Roman Catholic church. We even heard the fairy tale–like story of "Pope Joan," who had been mistaken for years as "Pope John" until one day she had a baby. And we met Biblical and Koranic scholars who showed how passages from Scripture had been misinterpreted to subjugate women. "The Bible is both the source of our wounds and the source of power," one feminist theologian told us. In one class, we explored one of the wounding passages, Ephesians 5:22–26:

> Wives, be subject to your husbands, as to the Lord. For the husband is the head of the wife as Christ is the head of the church, his body, and is himself its Savior. As the church is subject to Christ, so let wives also be subject in everything to their husbands. Husbands, love your wives, as Christ loved the church and gave himself up for her.

A review of the literature on this passage—conducted in class by a Harvard faculty member, Bernadette Brooten—was instructive. Fundamentalist Christians, of course, take it literally. In *The Total Woman*, Marabel Morgan writes that she had an unhappy marriage until she turned to the Bible. Once she purged any notions of independence and learned who was boss, she was happy. Her goal, as ordained by God, was to make her man happy. However, another conservative Christian writer, Patricia Grundy, had some problems with the role of women as described in the New Testament. So she turned to the Greek original and found that the word *head* in the phrase "the husband is the head of the wife" is from the Greek *kephale*, which can also mean "source." Grundy accepts the authority of the text but quarrels with the modern translation.

And then we were told about Susan Brooks Thistlethwaite, a feminist who runs a shelter for battered women. Women call her and say, "I am a Christian woman, but . . ." The Bible has made them so fearful of their husbands that they are afraid to complain about their abuse. For Thistlethwaite, the key is showing women other Bible passages that can empower them, including the less frequently quoted lines that follow the Ephesians passage just quoted: "Even so husbands should love their wives as their own bodies. He who loves his wife loves himself." Thistlethwaite leads Bible study groups for battered women.

Then we turned to the works of Elisabeth Schüssler Fiorenza, who deals with the Ephesians passage in her book *In Memory of Her*. The Biblical passage cannot be seen as the revelation of God, she writes, because God does not oppress. She looks at the background of the passage and sees that it is the continuation of the Aristotelian model of family and not the model of Jesus, who, she maintains, had a discipleship of men and women. Schüssler Fiorenza then distinguishes between what she considers revealed Bible passages and those that she considers perversions of the revealed word.

And then comes Mary Daly, a professor of theology at Boston College and a self-described "post-Christian." Daly, who was brought up a Roman Catholic, rejects the authority of the Bible. In the beginning, she said, she looked to the Bible, but later she realized that that meant that she was looking to a man. Among her other quips: "If God is a man, man must be a God." Once an advocate of women's ordination into the Catholic priesthood, she later rejected the notion, saying, "That would be like black people wanting to be members of the KKK."

Islam's attitude toward women was also treated in the course, although with kid gloves. Here a whole different set of rules seemed to apply. While fundamentalism was bad in Hinduism and even worse in Christianity, it was somehow made virtuous in Islam. Jane Smith, a Div School faculty member who taught the Islam section of "Women in Religion," told how Muslim women are threatened by feminism "as we know it" in the West. "Feminism is seen as a plot to overthrow Islam," she explained. "The fear of Muslim women is that they will be liberated from their religion."

To Muslim women, the threat comes not from men but from Western values, Smith said. "Muslim men are not the enemy." On hearing this, I saw the women in class lean forward as if to better understand how it could be that there are feminists who do not hate men. Smith continued: "Women are seen as the repository of fundamental values. That doesn't mean that they stay at home—they go to university, they study the Koran, but they also enable the men to be the breadwinners by making sure the children are being educated and seeing to it that the home is properly run." Smith showed slides of women in the *chador*, or veil, at the university, carrying guns in battle, leading women's services in the mosque and caring for the extended family in the home.

Everyone in the class sat and listened respectfully. Nobody dared to impose Western values on Muslim women, even though they were quick to impose liberal values on Christian Fundamentalists. Everybody seemed to hiss when we read Marabel Morgan on taking care of her husband, but everyone listened with respect when we heard tales of Muslim women doing precisely the same thing.

The crowning example of this double standard was an Islamic "fashion show" that the three main lecturers for "Women in Religion" put on for the class at the end of the semester. One donned the hat with a short veil favored by university students, the second a cream-colored cloak that covered the head and shoulders and the third a black full-dress veil worn by devout older women. "Evening wear," one of the lecturers joked. I watched these American feminists wearing the veil of their Eastern sisters with surprise. In my wildest dreams I could not imagine any of them putting on—even in jest—the black habits of Catholic nuns or the wigs of ultra-Orthodox Jewish women or even the heavy makeup and high heels of Tammy Bakker or Marabel Morgan.

Despite my cynicism, the women at the Div School did have an impact on my thinking. While I was aware of their inconsistencies, I was also becoming increasingly aware of my own.

I was not an early feminist. I came late to feminism, I believe, because of the matriarchal nature of my family. For the most part, I was raised by my mother and her three sisters and their mother; and by my father and his two sisters and their mother. I grew up in the homes of these aunts and grandmothers and ate at their kitchen tables. The women who probably had the greatest influence on me were my great-aunts, Minnie, a widow, and Paulie, who never married. Lavishing on me love and, its extension, rich cholesterol-laden food, Minnie and Paulie have always treated me like their own child. Women ran the world of my childhood, they were strong-willed, decisive and independent. It was men who needed the liberation.

All this had fit conveniently into my religious worldview. Women seemed to be in charge everywhere, except in the synagogue. That was the domain of the men. It takes ten men to constitute a *minyan*, a quorum for public prayer. Women cannot be counted in their number. And only men can lead the service or read from the Torah. Women sit separately, behind a low wall or on the other side of a curtain.

When I was a young boy, I asked my father why men and women couldn't sit together. "Men and women like each other," he explained gently. "And if they were to sit together they would talk instead of pray." Never mind that the men talked incessantly in the synagogues of my youth and still could sit together. The logic of separate seating was not something I was going to challenge, and besides, as I grew up, I came to enjoy the male camaraderie of the synagogue. After all, if it didn't make sense that women should be separated, it was not my battle.

It was not my battle, that is, until our daughter was born two years after I left the Div School. We named her Emma, after the fiery Emma Goldman, the writer, lecturer and passionate advocate of individual freedom over that of the state. We dreamed of raising a Jewish daughter who would have every opportunity and who could pursue any goal. She could be a businesswomen, a mother, a writer, a scholar, a lawyer or any combination she chose. No holds barred. Could I really imagine raising her with anything but full equality as a Jew?

# CHAPTER 18

# New Testament

The Pulnoer Rabbi related this parable: "A Christian king once invited the ambassadors of several countries to a banquet. Among the guests was a Jew. In the theological debate that ensued, the king invited a Mohammedan guest to state his opinion regarding Jesus. The Moslem asserted that Jesus was not the Son of God, but merely a distinguished Prophet.

"The Jew, when called upon, stated his belief that Jesus was merely a Jew. 'Jesus was one of us,' he said, 'Who, therefore, knows better than ourselves his true nature?' "

There was probably no course that I looked forward to more than "New Testament." The Div School sometimes seemed so devoid of Christian spirituality that I thought the only place I was sure to find it was in the Christian Scripture. "Introduction to the New Testament" was taught by Bernadette Brooten, who began her first class with a tribute to the late Dean George MacRae, who had been scheduled to teach the course. Brooten, an assistant professor, had been recruited to fill his shoes. With emotion, she said that she hoped the course would be "conducted according to George's ideals: rigorous scholarship, intellectual honesty and attention to detail."

What a nice beginning, I thought, a class that opens with a prayer. I was hopeful. Brooten, a Roman Catholic and a feminist, gave well-researched, if somewhat pedantic, lectures, providing a solid academic base for New Testament study. She was tall and sturdy-looking, with short brown hair; she flashed a warm smile when she made a good point.

Unlike Moses and Muhammad, who were, according to tradition, involved in the writing of the Old Testament and the Koran, Jesus wrote none of the Christian Scripture himself; the Gospels, based on the accounts of the Apostles, were written down some seventy or eighty years after Jesus's death. The Gospels were a new form of literature, quite different from what follows in the New Testament, the letters and the apocalyptic literature. The Gospels—literally "the Good News"—are not biographies in that they do not tell us the full story of Jesus's life but tell only of his birth and the brief period—some three years—of his public ministry.

Through textual analysis, Brooten showed why scholars believe that Mark was the first of the Gospels and why it is obvious that Matthew was written with a Jewish audience in mind while the others were written for Gentiles. Matthew is the most Jewish of the Gospels, complete with a reluctance to utter unnecessarily the name of God. For example, while Mark and Luke speak of "the Kingdom of *God*," Matthew speaks of "the Kingdom of *Heaven*." Maybe the most valuable thing Brooten taught me was that the New Testament was written to be read out loud rather than silently as we today might read a book. Reading out loud was the practice of the day, she reminded us, bringing the point home with a wonderful quotation from Cicero, who apologized to a friend for being tardy in responding to a letter with these words: "Please excuse me but I have been unable to read your letter because my throat is sore."

I was enjoying Brooten's class until I realized that I was still not learning how Christians *feel*. In her course the Bible was being presented as literature, great literature to be sure, but we were spending too much time on literary criticism and no time on theology.

My friend Edward told me about another New Testament course that was a joint venture of the Div School and two neighboring theological schools—Episcopal Divinity School and the Weston School of Theology, the Jesuit seminary. After five Brooten lectures, I walked across the Cambridge Common, past the old Radcliffe campus to the Weston classroom where the alternative course was being held. Class was already in session, and I quickly found a seat. I listened for a moment and then wondered if I had walked into the right room. Was I in church or in school, I wondered. The lecturer, Jerome Neyrey, a gaunt Jesuit in a Roman collar, was speaking animatedly, building his case verse by verse with an evangelical fervor.

Neyrey's lecture was on the Gospel of Luke, and when I entered the room he was dealing with the teaching of Jesus in Luke 14:13. "When you give a feast, invite the poor, the maimed, the lame, the blind," Neyrey read out loud from the Bible he held open in the palm of his hand. Neyrey contrasted Jesus's "teaching of compassion" with Leviticus 21:18. As he mentioned the citation, a hundred Bibles in the classroom were noisily shuffled back to the Old Testament. Again, Neyrey read out loud: "For no one who has a blemish shall draw near, a man blind or lame, or one who has a mutilated face or a limb too long."

The teaching of Jesus, Neyrey told us with enthusiasm, was designed to undo the uncharitable and exclusionary rules of the Old Testament. I was aghast at Neyrey's misreading of the text. You see, Neyrey had picked not just any Old Testament passage, but one of my favorites. When we were youngsters, my cousin Michael and I used to look it up in the synagogue and laugh at the end of that very same passage, which concludes the list of those excluded with: "a hunchback, or a dwarf, or a man with a defect in his sight or an itching disease or scabs or crushed testicles." To our preadolescent minds, the "crushed testicle" line was one of the funniest in the Bible. But I also knew the beginning of the chapter: "Say to Aaron." The passage clearly refers to those in the priestly family who are excluded from temple service because of disability. It was unfair and just plain ignorant of Neyrey to compare these exclusions with those in Luke, which refer to a man who gives a feast in his house!

I got so angry at his misinterpretation that I felt the blood rise to my face. It is not my nature to stand up and object, especially on my first day in a new class, so I held my peace until the lecture was over. As soon as Neyrey finished, I approached the lectern and made my point. No, he said flatly. He was right and I was wrong. "I've been doing a great deal of research into this period," he assured me. "There were no Florence Nightingales among the Jews in those days." I protested and began to say, "Just look at the text. It says 'Say to Aaron.' " But Neyrey cut me off. He said that he couldn't discuss the matter any further and turned to greet an older gentleman who was visiting the class.

I was furious and excited as I left the classroom. Finally I had found a dose of Christian triumphalism, maybe even a touch of anti-Semitism. Finally I had found what I had been looking for all year. On the spot, I decided to drop the literary criticism approach of Brooten and sign up for this alternative.

Neyrey, representing the Jesuit-run Weston School of Theology, was one of three instructors for the New Testament course. The others were Dieter Georgi, a Lutheran minister on the faculty of Harvard Divinity, and Eugene Goetchius, an Episcopal priest who was on the staff of Episcopal Divinity. The three divided the twenty-seven books of the New Testament and took turns lecturing in class.

Going to class was like going to a different church each week. All the preachers were good, but each had his own perspective and style. Goetchius, heavyset and the eldest of the three, was an avuncular type who gave the lightest and often most welcome lectures. When we were studying about speaking in tongues in I Corinthians, he brought in a tape recording of people babbling unintelligibly from an actual church service. He once apologized for always quoting the King James Version (published in 1611) by explaining, "That's when I was born."

Neyrey, by contrast, had no time for jokes. He was intent on covering as much of the text as possible, giving a summary of each book from his perspective, a perspective that often belittled the Old Testament and Judaism.

Georgi was the perfect foil for Neyrey. He was a German Bible scholar who spent half the year teaching at the University of Frankfurt and the other half at Harvard. He was a proud preacher of the Gospel but one who did not believe it should be advanced to the detriment of Jews and Judaism. Georgi sat through Neyrey's class on Luke in which the faulty analogy to Leviticus was made and said nothing. But the following week, when Georgi rose to lecture on the Book of Acts, he responded, indirectly but forcefully. Misinterpretations of Luke, he said, have long been used to flame the fires of anti-Semitism. "Without Luke, there would have been no Auschwitz," he stated. It was an extraordinary statement coming from the German Bible scholar.

And so I became a student of the New Testament. My whole life I have eyed with suspicion those who read Bibles in public; I always thought they were a little odd. But I soon found myself carrying my bright red *Oxford Annotated Bible* in my shoulder bag and pulling it out on the bus and subway. When Shira, Adam and I went to Florida to spend Passover with Shira's parents, I read the New Testament on the plane.

I was, of course, reading it for school, but I couldn't help but be deeply touched by what I was reading. I discovered two powerful things about the New Testament. First, parts of it are beautiful, astoundingly so. It was hard to beat the Sermon on the Mount for sheer poetry. The second thing I discovered was that the New Testament does not speak to me. In the Sermon on the Mount, for example, Jesus has lyrical words of solace ("Blessed are those who mourn, for they shall be comforted") as well as an attack on the "hypocrites" in the synagogue. While his attack might have been warranted, Jesus gave no credit to the consoling and empowering powers of Judaism, which were also going on in the synagogues of his day. After all, Jesus lived in the time of the Tanaim, the Jewish sages who wrote the Mishna, a code that includes laws *and* ethics. It was, after all, Rabbi Akiba, a contemporary of Jesus, who said, "The greatest principle of the Torah is this: 'Love thy neighbor as thyself.' "

In an odd way, my familiarity with the New Testament gave me greater insights into Judaism. I had always wondered why Christians, who say that they revere the Old Testament, do not follow the laws spelled out therein. In the New Testament, I found the Christian justification for abandoning the laws of Moses, largely that a new covenant through Jesus superseded the Mosaic covenant. But since I did not accept Jesus, I could not accept the dismantling of the Mosaic code, a code I still believe exists. Nor could I accept the vision of the Apostle Peter in Acts 10:9–16. It is not one of the most popular New Testament stories (I had never heard of it before reading Acts), so I think it is worth repeating here:

> The next day, as they were on their journey and coming near the city, Peter went up on the housetop to pray, about the sixth hour. And he became hungry and desired something to eat; but while they were preparing it, he fell into a trance and saw the heaven opened, and something descending, like a great sheet, let down by four corners upon the earth. In it were all kinds of animals and reptiles and birds of the air. And there came a voice to him, "Rise, Peter: kill and eat." But Peter said, "No, Lord; for I have never eaten anything that is common or unclean." And the voice came to him again a second time, "What God has cleansed, you must not call common." This happened three times, and the thing was taken up at once to heaven.

With that, Peter had his first *traif* meal. My reaction to his vision, however, was quite different. "Yet another reason to keep kosher!" I scrawled in the margin of my Bible.

For me, keeping kosher is more than a Jewish observance, it is a daily, tangible declaration that the Mosaic covenant was *not* superseded by Jesus. Keeping kosher is my way of saying no to Christianity.

Georgi, tall, balding and athletic-looking, showed me how Christians feel about the New Testament in the loving way he approached the text and in the umbrage he took at those who pervert it for anti-Semitic purposes. I was so impressed with him that I finagled a seat in the popular weekly discussion "section" he held for about a dozen students after the New Testament class met as a whole. (This was no small accomplishment since I had joined the class so late in the semester.) In the section, Georgi managed to put me at ease about a word that had frightened me more than any other at the Div School—*exegesis*. First of all, it sounds so Christian, even though I knew the *-gesis* has nothing to do with "Jesus." I knew it had something to do with interpreting the Scripture, but I was baffled by the methodology that went with it. In order to do an exegesis, the experts say, one uses several tools: literary analysis, form criticism, source criticism and redaction criticism. There were whole courses on exegesis, and two exegetical papers were required in my New Testament class.

"Exegesis," Georgi said one day in his section, "is nothing but what you already do when you read a text." We come to the Scripture with our own ideas, our own prejudices, our own impressions, he explained. In addition, when we approach a text we draw on things that we've read, and we might want to do more reading to help us understand the context in which the Scripture was written. Exegesis, then, is what we already know and what we will find out to make the text our own. "The text is dead," Georgi said. "You have exegesis to raise the dead. Don't leave it to Jesus, it is your business as well."

With that introduction, exegesis became as natural to me as reading and writing. I did two exegetical papers—one on

Jesus's entry into Jerusalem as recounted in Matthew and the other on Paul's argument in Galatians that man becomes right with God only by faith in Christ and not by the performance of good works and ritual observances.

My ultra-Orthodox rabbis would be shocked to hear this, but in doing my exegesis I employed the lessons of my yeshiva days. Exegesis, after all, is nothing more than a Jewish *d'var Torah,* a kind of sermonette on the text. Under my rebbe's tutelage, I gave my first public d'var Torah on a passage in Genesis at a school assembly in fifth grade. Boy, was I nervous, but I had prepared my argument well, and everyone seemed pleased when I was finished.

Likewise, I was nervous some twenty-five years later when I was about to take my New Testament exam, an "open-book" test that included an on-the-spot exegesis. I studied hard, reviewing the text and my class notes. I joined a study group that met late into the night. The weekend before the exam, however, I panicked. I heard that Neyrey would be marking the tests of Georgi's students, and I was sure I was finished. I scoured the bookstores in Harvard Square for study aids, and I found one that I would have been ashamed to use in college, let alone grad school at Harvard. It was called *Cliffs Notes on the New Testament.* I furtively looked around the bookstore to make sure there was nobody there that I knew and took the book to the cash register. My heart did not stop pounding until the cashier put my Cliffs Notes in a brown paper bag. I felt like an adolescent buying his first box of condoms.

As it turned out, the Cliffs Notes were a useful summary of the course. It's hard to say if they had anything to do with my success, but I did get an A on the exam. In the process, thanks to Dieter Georgi and Jerome Neyrey, I finally got a deeper sense of how Christians believe.

# CHAPTER 19

# Graduation

An ignorant farmer and his son came to the Yom Kippur services at the synagogue of the Baal Shem Tov. The son, who could not read a word of Hebrew, brought with him the whistle that he ordinarily used when watching the cattle. During the Ne'ila prayer, the boy, moved by the spirit of the day, took out the whistle and blew it. The Baal Shem Tov rose and declared: "God has opened the gates! The rabbis, with all their prayers and learning, could not prevail with God; only the young herdsman in his ignorance, by his simple desire to serve God."

I didn't wear a cap and gown on Thursday, June 5, 1986, but Shira and Adam played along with my fantasy of graduating that day from Harvard Divinity School. Shira brought her camera, and Adam beamed proudly as I walked among the five thousand graduates gathered in Harvard Yard. A brass band played the school song, "Fair Harvard," cocktails were served under crimson-trimmed tents and valedictory addresses were given in English and Latin. The three of us stood on the sidelines and waited as Derek Bok, Harvard's president, worked his way through the different schools until he got to "the women and men of Harvard Divinity School." When he conferred degrees on my class, I tossed an imaginary mortarboard into the air.

Despite my diligent schoolwork, I was only halfway toward a master of theological studies degree by the end of the school year. I had been well aware that it was a two-year program when I'd enrolled in the fall, so I knew I would not graduate. But I didn't realize how disappointed I would be, and how instantly nostalgic I would feel about the Div School. There were moments when I said, What the hell, I'll quit *The Times* and stay at Harvard another year and finish my theological education. But I knew that was impractical, for now at least. My newspaper had sent me, and to my newspaper I would return. Finish my degree? Maybe someday, I thought . . .

Leaving was hard. I made the rounds of all my professors to say good-bye. I thanked Lamin Sanneh for teaching me that African religions aren't primitive, Bill Hutchison for unraveling American Protestantism, Louis Jacobs for giving me a new perspective on Judaism and Annemarie Schimmel for doing the same with Islam. I decided to steer clear of Jerome Neyrey, but I warmly embraced Dieter Georgi for opening my eyes to the New Testament. And, most of all, I stopped by to thank Diane Eck for the best line from my year at Div School: "If you know one religion . . . you don't know any." So here I was, with not one religion under my belt but a whole interfaith convocation. I emerged with greater confidence, both as a religion writer and as a Jew.

I thought back to the fears that had plagued me when I began at the Div School. Four went down to the orchard, the Talmud said. One fell gravely ill and died, one became a heretic, one went mad and one, Rabbi Akiba, emerged whole. In the right-wing Orthodox yeshivas of my youth, I was taught the story as a parable about the dangers of the non-Jewish world.

After my year at the Div School, however, I see the story of the rabbis and the orchard in a whole new light. Rather than dwell on the failure of the three rabbis who ventured and were lost, I prefer to focus on the success of Rabbi Akiba. He was unafraid to open himself up to the Christian and Greek cultures of his time. Yet he remained steadfast in his Jewish convictions.

Jews don't have saints, but if we did, Rabbi Akiba would be mine. His courage in the face of religious challenge sustained me in my faith through Div School. And I believe Rabbi Akiba also stands by me in my work. He even stays with me when I cover a story in church or have a vegetarian meal in a nonkosher restaurant. "Go for it," Rabbi Akiba whispers in my ear. "Go into the orchard. Judaism is meant to be challenged. That is where it gets its life."

With Div School over, Shira, Adam and I returned to our apartment on the West Side of Manhattan and went back to our favorite synagogue. It was officially called Congregation Kehilath Jacob, but everybody knew it as the Carlebach Shul, after the two rabbinical brothers who ran it, Shlomo and Eli Chaim Carlebach. They were identical twins and, although well into their sixties, still bore a striking resemblance to each other. Shlomo had achieved some fame as a popular Jewish singer-songwriter, a kind of Hasidic Pete Seeger, while Eli Chaim, the father of five daughters, was more of a teacher and scholar. Both had an incredible ability to share the warmth of Judaism. The Orthodox congregation, which took up the first floor of a small brownstone on West Seventy-ninth Street, became a haven for Jews of all stripes as well as non-Jews who were seeking a religious experience.

The glue that held the small synagogue together was Hadassah Carlebach, a wise and talented woman from a Hasidic family in France who was married to Eli Chaim. Every Sabbath after services, Hadassah laid out a lavish vegetarian kiddush that put other congregations to shame. While sponge cake and wine are the normal kiddush fare, the Carlebach kiddush only began there. In the winters, they served hot *cholent*—a traditional Jewish stew made of beans and vegetables—and in the summers, a variety of salads. And everyone was welcome. Homeless men and women, sometimes with their children in tow, would join us at the Carlebach table.

In accordance with Orthodox tradition, men led the prayers and read the Torah, but there was an openness to women not found in most Orthodox congregations. Women were often called upon to give an exegesis, a d'var Torah, and every Saturday Rabbi Eli Chaim would wade into the women's section during the Torah reading and bless every woman by her Hebrew name. Once a month, a special "women's service"—in which women led the prayers and read the Torah—was held in a room separate from the main service. And on one Saturday morning in the main shul, Rabbi Eli Chaim asked Shira to lead the congregation in the early-morning blessings. One worshiper was so indignant at this show of egalitarianism that he stormed out in protest. (It was a sore loss to the congregation, since we were still assembling a minyan, but Rabbi Eli Chaim only smiled when he heard of the man's departure.)

Shira, the daughter of a Conservative rabbi, is not Orthodox. She is also not Conservative or Reform. She eschews denominationalism in favor of, as she puts it, "taking the best from each." And the Carlebachs represented what is best in Orthodoxy. If we missed a Shabbat in shul, Eli Chaim would call during the week to see if we were all right. After Shira gave birth to Adam one hot day in August, Eli Chaim arrived in his shirtsleeves, his sidelocks curled up around his ears, to deliver two shopping bags full of food freshly cooked by Hadassah. No one ever questioned our religious observance; the Carlebachs didn't care what we ate or how we slept. They accepted us. And we learned by their example, showing kindness to the strangers who came to the synagogue, helping set up the meals in shul and volunteering to prepare the Torah readings. Once, when Eli Chaim had tired while leading the service on Yom Kippur, he asked me to take over as the cantor for Shacharit, the morning prayer. I assumed the role with pride.

But maybe the one happiest at Carlebach's was Adam. He

was almost two years old when we returned to New York from Harvard, where he apparently took an advanced course in the terrible twos. He was a lively, rambunctious, mischievous toddler who rarely stood still or kept quiet—until he saw Reb Eli Chaim. Eli Chaim was a man of physical beauty and spiritual nobility. He had a mane of thick, wavy white hair and a long beard of the same color and texture. When Eli Chaim prayed the silent prayer, he would unravel the long, curly sidelocks he kept tucked behind his ears and finger them gently. On the Sabbath, he wore silk gowns with fine paisley designs in red and blue over his robust frame.

When I brought Adam to shul, he would go right for Eli Chaim, who would gather the little boy up in his arms. The rabbi would press his soft, bearded face against the pudgy cheeks of Adam and rock back and forth in silence. Adam would be quiet as long as the rabbi held him. Once, during the closing N'ilah prayer on Yom Kippur—when the gates of heaven are said to be open to Jewish supplications—Adam fell asleep in Eli Chaim's arms and stayed asleep until the stars came out.

As happy as we were at the Carlebach shul, however, our apartment in Manhattan was a constant source of frustration. We had only one bedroom, and Adam, who slept in a makeshift nursery in the living room, was fast taking over the house. Diapers, toys and children's books and record covers were everywhere. Taking Adam outdoors to play meant a nineteen-floor elevator ride and then a walk through dirty, congested streets, past panhandlers and drug sellers, to the park.

When our rental apartment building was converted into a cooperative one year after we returned from Harvard, we bought the apartment and, taking advantage of the 1980s boom in real estate prices, sold it a few days later for twice the amount. With our considerable profit, we bought a lovely three-bedroom Tudor in Westchester County.

The hardest part of saying good-bye to Manhattan was

parting with the Carlebach shul. It represented an Orthodox Judaism we could love. We did our best to cover ourselves, however, by choosing a Westchester community that was within walking distance of two vibrant synagogues—one Orthodox and the other Conservative. With excitement, we moved into our new suburban home right before the High Holy Days. We had to decide quickly where we would pray, so I preempted Shira, who wanted to check out both congregations before making up our minds, and joined the Orthodox shul.

The rabbi of the Orthodox congregation had been a classmate of mine at Crown Heights Mesifta and, although we had not seen each other in twenty years, we recognized each other immediately the first time I walked into the synagogue. He said that he had been following my career at *The Times*.

The second Shabbat I was there, he approached me after the service and said that he recalled that I had been a fine student cantor when we were together in high school. "We have trouble finding the right kind of people to *daven* here," he said, using the Yiddish word for prayer. He asked if I would from time to time lead the service. The congregation had no regular cantor, so laymen alternated in filling the role, known as *sh'liach t'zibur*.

I told the rabbi that I was new in the community and didn't feel that comfortable in leading the services. After all, sh'liach t'zibur means "the public messenger."

"Well, think about it, Ari," the rabbi said, shaking my hand with all the warmth he could muster. "We are very, very happy to have you in our community."

The next Shabbat, at the wine-and-sponge-cake kiddush, one of the officers of the congregation approached me and asked if I would lead the Mincha, or afternoon service, on Yom Kippur. "I already told the rabbi that I did not feel right about davening here just yet," I explained. But the man, a psychiatrist who fancied himself among those of the liberal wing of the congregation persisted. No, I said.

Meanwhile, my little family was being treated like visiting royalty. The big Orthodox suburban form of social entertainment is Shabbat meals and, in our first few weekends there, we never had to cook. It was all rather flattering, until we began to notice that the neighborhood had some of the flavor of an upper-middle-class European shtetl. Gossip was a major activity of the community, we knew, because we heard gossip about everyone; we could only imagine what was being said about us. As we were invited out, our hosts extracted a payment: they grilled us about our jobs, our families, our education and, more subtly, about our religious observance and income.

At one such gathering, at the home of a doctor, the conversation turned to the rabbi's salary, which was under review by the synagogue board. "I don't know how anyone earning what he makes a year could afford to live in this community," the doctor said, naming the rabbi's salary. Shira and I gave each other a smile. Our income barely approached the rabbi's. Our host, whose house was expensively decorated and whose land stretched over a running brook, went on to say that he would never want his son to be a rabbi or a schoolteacher. "How would he live on that kind of salary?"

His best friend, an accountant, told how his son came home from school one day and announced that he wanted to be a forest ranger. "I told him, 'You like our house? Well, if you're a forest ranger you could never afford a house like this.' And besides, how could he possibly be religious? I told him, there are no shuls in the forest."

Everybody had a good laugh. But I mulled the story over in my head. Imagine a child, a sensitive child, a child who loves plants and flowers and maybe fancies animals and the great outdoors. The child tells his father that it would be nice to live a life devoted to these things. But the father reminds the child of the two great icons of Jewish suburbia: Money and Community. What would I tell my kid?

The psychiatrist who had been trying to recruit me to lead the synagogue service was also there. "How can you be Orthodox and be a reporter?" he asked me. Exasperated by his persistence, I told him: "I'm not like you doctors who get all sorts of rabbinical dispensations for working on Shabbat. If an emergency arises, I consult the law and make my own dispensations. That, frankly, is why I've been trying to tell you that I don't want to lead the davening on Yom Kippur. I don't think most of the people would accept my interpretations of the law."

Over in another corner, I heard Shira engaged in a tense and lively conversation with the accountant's wife. They were talking about social dancing. The accountant's wife said that she did not allow her teenage son to go to parties where boys and girls danced together. "Why not?" Shira said. "It's the healthiest thing in the world." It turned out that the community, in a recent swing to the religious right, was on a campaign against social dancing. For years it had been part of the festivities at the annual synagogue dinner, but the rabbi—my classmate—had recently outlawed it.

The accountant's wife admitted that her resistance to dancing was only in part religious. "I remember going to dances as a teenager and feeling so uncomfortable," she told Shira. "My son doesn't need that."

"Social interaction can of course be awkward," Shira responded. "But it's a necessary part of adolescence. Besides, do you live your life avoiding situations that are awkward?"

Yes, the woman responded. She said that she hated going to business meetings where the food was not kosher and the people not Orthodox.

Shira told her how she and I look forward to just such situations, how we consider them broadening and, in terms of the food, a challenge. She told her of our meal with Cardinal O'Connor and how we'd named our son Adam Joachim, in honor of my music teacher. And, relishing the woman's increasingly perplexed reaction, Shira added: "Every Christmas, we go to the *Messiah* Sing-in at Avery Fisher Hall. Can you imagine the experience? Four thousand voices in one gigantic choir. It's magnificent."

As Shira and I left, we resolved not to accept any more

Sabbath invitations; clearly we were not on the same wavelength as these people, not financially, Jewishly or philosophically. At the same time, I was sure that the idea of my leading the Yom Kippur service had been dropped. But the psychiatrist was at it again a few days later. "I've spoken with the rabbi, and he says, 'Everyone starts with a clean slate on Yom Kippur.' We want you to lead the service."

I finally relented. I said, All right, I'm as vain as the next guy, I will lead the Mincha service on Yom Kippur. And, I have to admit, I became excited at the prospect. I began to practice the special holiday melodies, singing at the top of my lungs as I drove down the highway. I made arrangements to visit the mikveh, the ritual bath, that would render me religiously ready to represent the congregation. And I acquired a *kittle*, the white shroud in which Jews are buried. It is worn on Yom Kippur by those who lead the services and others as a stark reminder of human mortality. Every morning I got up and put on my tefillin in the hope that God would find me worthy.

There was another reason why I was happy. When I had taken up the cello ten years earlier, I'd all but stopped singing the music of the synagogue, substituting the instrument for my voice and, in some ways, my teacher, Mr. J, for my father. Here was a chance to get back to the synagogue. With pride, I told my father, my first and primary music teacher, that I would be leading the service.

But that was not the end of the matter. The synagogue gossip mill was already in high gear. As soon as I accepted the call to lead the prayer, protests were raised. The objections came back to me like the counts in an indictment: I wrote on the Sabbath, I ate in nonkosher restaurants, my son was named after a non-Jew, I sang "Christmas carols," I read the New Testament, I danced with my wife.

The battles I had fought throughout my adult life to remain Orthodox were not seen as battles at all by my coreligionists of the 1980s but as compromises, compromises that diminished me in their eyes and somehow threatened the cozy world of the Orthodox.

When Yom Kippur came, I did not lead the service in the synagogue. I stayed home and prayed by myself.

The Yom Kippur incident taught me a great deal about the state of contemporary Orthodoxy. Much like Fundamentalist Christianity and Islam, Orthodox Judaism took a sharp turn to the right in the 1980s. Intolerance and witchhunting—whether in Iran, in Israel, in Vatican City or in Lynchburg, Virginia—have become standard religious practice. Diversity, tolerance and pluralism seem to have been banished from the religious vocabulary. Even the rabbis of my college years, who had preached the outward-looking Modern Orthodoxy, have moved one large step to the right. Instead of looking *out* to see how traditional Jewish practice could coexist and synthesize with the modern world, they increasingly look *inward*, mostly for validation from the right-wing elements of Orthodoxy.

Examples abound. Orthodox synagogues around the country have banned social dancing. More and more married women are covering their hair. The list of forbidden foods has grown to include M & M's and certain suspect brands of ice cream. Tuna fish sandwiches in nonkosher restaurants, once a staple of the Modern Orthodox, have been outlawed from the pulpit. A rumor even swept the Orthodox community that Coca-Cola is unkosher; someone, the story went, discovered Coke's closely guarded "secret ingredient" and determined it is traif. One rabbi even outlawed salad bars—where the diner can carefully choose the fare—because there may be tiny worms in the lettuce. (In Orthodox homes, supposedly, the lettuce is more carefully washed to eliminate the tiny unkosher creatures.)

Orthodoxy has become more and more narrow. On the surface, it seems that my old rebbe, Rabbi Siegel, has triumphed.

The aftermath of the Yom Kippur incident, however, suggested another reality. The day after I withdrew in the face of questions about my worthiness to lead the congregation in prayer, I got a call from an officer of the synagogue. "We're terribly embarrassed," he said. "This never should have come up. This is a modern shul. Most everyone here 'eats out.' We just don't talk about it." *Eats out* is a term used among the Orthodox to describe how some observant Jews eat vegetarian foods in nonkosher restaurants. Some only eat cold salads and sandwiches—tuna fish sandwiches are a good example—others eat hot foods, such as broiled fish.

A few days later, a synagogue member who has also led congregational worship approached me meekly with a confession. "Sometimes I come home after sundown on Friday nights," he said. "What I do is I just slump down in the backseat of the taxi." Someone else told me point-blank: "It's all your fault. If you had just kept your big mouth shut, all this would never have happened."

My response is, in effect, my credo. I don't keep my mouth shut because I make no apologies for the way I have melded Jewish practice with the other aspects of my life, be they at *The Times* or at the Div School. To my mind, Judaism is diminished if it is painted too narrowly. From my life journey, I believe that traditional Judaism is large enough, compassionate enough, forgiving enough and tolerant enough to encompass the world.

# Postgraduate

The Rozdoler Rabbi was asked: "Wherein does
the desire to become a Rabbi differ from other
desires?" He answered: "Before one attains the
desire to become a Rabbi, he must break himself
of every other desire."

Three months after I finished my year at
the Div School, a new dean took over with
ambitious plans for improving the school. He was Ronald
Thiemann, a Lutheran minister who had spent ten years at
Haverford College in Pennsylvania, a Quaker school, where
he had served as chairman of the Religion Department and,
later, as acting president. On a visit to Boston my first year
back at *The Times*, I stopped by to have lunch with Thiemann. A burly, balding man with a thick, black beard, the
new dean acknowledged that the Div School "was at a low
point" the year I attended. He said he planned to turn things
around.

In his first years, Thiemann has put the school on sound
financial footing, filled several important teaching posts that
had long been vacant and established joint programs with
other parts of the university in the hope of ending the Divinity School's isolation. His most important achievement,
several students told me, was bringing back Krister Sten-

dahl, the former Div School dean, to be the school's first chaplain. Stendahl, a retired bishop of the Lutheran church, has put his energies into fostering a sense of spirituality and a tradition of Christian worship at the Div School. While other religions are still respected, there is a growing reverence for the school's Christian roots.

While Dean Thiemann deserves a lot of the credit for improvements at the Div School, national trends have been on his side. In the early 1990s, the mainline Protestant churches have begun to recover from their 1980s slump. The darlings of the 1980s, the Evangelicals and Roman Catholics, appear to be losing ground. Evangelicals stumbled badly with the scandals of the television ministries of Jim and Tammy Bakker and Jimmy Swaggart. And in 1989, Jerry Falwell's faltering Moral Majority closed its doors. Meanwhile, Roman Catholics have become so mired in internecine struggles over authority with Rome and the antiabortion cause that they have lost much of the moral influence they once had over those outside their church.

The stage is set in the 1990s for a resurgence of a more powerful Protestant church in the United States. Divinity Schools like Harvard stand ready to lead and to benefit.

The students of the 1980s, my classmates, should, by all logic, be coming into their full careers in the nineties. As the new decade dawned, I decided to check up on some of them.

Of my friends, only one—Diane—is a minister in a church, and she works at it only part-time. In school, Diane was the head of the Gay and Lesbian Caucus and was leaning toward a career in ministry, although she was concerned about the public nature of the job. She wasn't sure she wanted to "live in a fishbowl."

After getting her degree, Diane was interviewed by regional officials of her denomination, the United Church of Christ, and took a series of psychological tests. Her name was put on an "approved" list, and she was soon "called" as an associate pastor by a New England church with fewer than one hundred members, most of them elderly.

As is the practice in her denomination, Diane was ordained in her first pulpit. Congregants, friends and denominational officials participated. "It was like a wedding," Diane said. The most powerful moment in the ceremony, she recalled, was when the members of the church came up one by one to symbolically lay their hands on their new minister.

The congregation that called her does not know Diane is a lesbian. "I never raised the issue with them," Diane said. "If I did, I would never have gotten the job. Sure, there is a degree to which I am leading a dual life, but that doesn't seem like a problem right now. My lover comes to church, she's joined us in pot-luck dinners and at other functions. My congregation knows that we live together; how we live together is just something that hasn't been named. We're all sort of family. They accept all sorts of odd combinations in our family, so why not this one?"

Diane works only ten hours a week at the church. The rest of the week she serves as a chaplain at a medical clinic for low-income people. "I work very hard and make way too little money," she said in a telephone conversation late one night. "I'm sure I could do temporary word processing and make more. But I would not choose something else. Most other kinds of work sound quite boring to me."

The way she has structured her life works for now, Diane said, but someday she may want to make some changes. For one thing, she hopes to "adopt and raise a child." But, she said, "I'm not sure I could do that on the salary I'm making now." For another, someday she may feel it necessary to publicly declare her homosexuality, as she did in Div School.

But, for now, she's happy. "I love what I'm doing and I feel comfortable with the compromises I make to be where I am."

Ann, my Unitarian friend who finds God in language, had also hoped to be working as a minister after receiving her M.Div. degree. Soon after graduation she was ordained in the church where she grew up and then, at the request of denominational officials, took an internship before being fully accepted into the Fellowship of Unitarian Ministers.

She went off to the West Coast to assist in a big-city church but immediately ran into conflicts with the senior minister. "It was a disaster. He was a terrible person to work with, on his fifth marriage and a suspected alcoholic." But it was Ann who got the bad report. "He said that I did not have a personality suited to the ministry, that I lacked the emotional well-being and that I was defensive and self-centered."

The denomination's Fellowship Committee, which makes the final judgment on candidates, asked Ann to undergo a psychological evaluation. After reviewing the results, the committee asked Ann to wait two years before applying again for a church assignment. "They didn't turn me down," Ann said anxiously. "They said apply again in two years. They told me that I have 'abundant gifts' for the ministry. I hope they're still there in two years."

In the meantime, Ann is doing secretarial work in an office that serves Harvard undergraduates. The job enables her to take Harvard courses, and she is continuing her study of German. She is thinking of studying for a doctorate in theology as she awaits the time she can reapply to the Fellowship Committee. "I feel very strongly that the ministry is what I'm supposed to do," she said. "It is the career that most fully uses the gifts I have. Sure, what happened is frustrating, but I'll wait."

Like Ann, my businessman-friend Robert was also turned down for the pulpit ministry. "The Episcopal church told me that, with the gifts I have, my ministry is in finance."

Since graduation, Robert has reorganized his bankrupt company, "paying back every single creditor 100 cents to the dollar," he said with pride. He has gone back into financing human service projects, such as hospitals, schools and low-income housing. But instead of using federal dollars, which are no longer available, he is now using tax-exempt bonds. Business is good, even better than before the bankruptcy. His company is currently financing some $75 million worth of projects.

Robert said that he was disappointed that he cannot serve as an Episcopal priest, "but not bitter." The experience of the Div School has changed him and his family forever. He has remarried and brought his children back into the church. His daughter is an altar girl, and his son sings in the local church choir. "And no meal is taken in this house without there being grace and thanks offered.

"I was once a tough, hard-nosed, competitive banker," he said. "But no more." Quoting Henri Nouwen, a former Div School faculty member, Robert expressed his new mission in life: "We have to make ourselves a window through which others can see God in themselves."

Justin, who entered Div School with the hope of someday teaching religion in a Catholic high school, is working for a bank in Minneapolis. "I handle customers whose assets are in excess of $10 million," Justin told me. It was not his first choice. Thoughts of joining a religious order have also been banished. Soon after graduation, he married his girlfriend, Chris, and they now live in a three-bedroom ranch house in a Minneapolis suburb. "When I left Harvard, I went through a very painful birthing process," he said. "I have a strong moral sense, a strong religious foundation. However, in terms of the practical world, all that wasn't worth anything."

Justin graduated with a master of theological studies but found that there was little demand for a high school religion teacher with no experience. Then he applied to work in management in several nonprofit charitable organizations but found, "I couldn't break into the network." A friend told him that Norwest, a large Midwest bank, had a program to hire and train liberal arts types. Just as he had had little hope three years earlier when he applied to Harvard Divinity

School, Justin didn't think that a Classics major who had studied religion in graduate school would be of much interest to a bank. To his surprise, he got the job.

Although he has tried to make it clear to his colleagues that he is a graduate of Harvard Divinity School, some people still hear what they want to hear. "So how *was* the Business School?" one friend keeps asking.

My Muslim classmate Mark has become more involved in his faith since graduating from the Div School. He increasingly uses his Muslim name, Abdul, although he has not legally changed his name, as some converts have, out of deference to his parents. Mark has taken a leave of absence from his doctoral studies in African-American history at Temple University to work as a lobbyist on consumer rights and environmental issues. As for the future, he said, "I'm open. I still have a sense of pursuing a religious vocation, but as a Muslim just how to do that is a big problem and puzzle now. A lot of key issues will have to be addressed in the next decade. We will have to define the political, social and religious agenda."

Since graduation my friend Fran has been working full time for what she calls "the Mother Church," the headquarters of Christian Science in Boston. For a time, she worked as an assistant to the editor of the *Christian Science Monitor*, now she answers press inquiries in the church's media office. Christian Science has no professional ministers, but Fran serves as a lay minister with the title First Reader in her church in Waltham.

When I called her recently, she told me that she and her boyfriend, Glenn, hope to get married "within a year." Glenn is not a Christian Scientist, but that poses no problem for either of them. He owns a comic-book store called the Magic Dragon in Medford, Massachusetts.

"We don't live together—yet," she said. "Be sure to get that right. It could ruin my reputation in the church!" With a laugh, Fran agreed that the same fact—her *not* living with her boyfriend—could ruin her reputation at the Div School, where no one ever spoke of delaying gratification. But Fran didn't seem to care.

My friend Gary now lives on Nantucket with "my lover, Robert." They settled there because Robert, an architect, has a successful practice on the island. Gary has picked up odd jobs, working as a florist for a time and now selling appliances. His experience at the Div School—what he saw as the competitiveness and the dearth of good jobs for graduates—has soured Gary on the notion of pursuing further graduate studies in religion. He does, however, miss the academic atmosphere and spoke to me about the possibility of getting a job in a theology library, "in order to keep a foot in the door. In the library I could be surrounded by intelligent people in the field—and still have a job!"

My Anglican friend Lynda is contemplating the priesthood but has yet to make a formal application. One disappointment since graduating the Div School was her rejection when she applied for Harvard's doctoral program in ethics. After Lynda got her master's, she and her husband and three sons have moved back to Canada, where Lynda is working toward a doctorate in pastoral counseling at the University of Toronto. She also drives back and forth once a week to Montreal, where she is taking courses in ethics at McGill.
Lynda, who had warned me at the Div School against seeing God as the "great puppeteer," couldn't help but use the same imagery when I asked her about the future. "I don't know where I want to be, but I'm enjoying my courses," she said. As for the next step, "I think God will let me know one of these days."

As for me, five years after leaving the Div School, I still feel its imprint. The foundation that I received there in Scripture and World Religions has made it possible for me to explore a wide variety of faiths and help explain them—teach them, if you will—to my readers. I have written articles about the popularity of Islam among American blacks; the growing number of celibate priests who leave the priesthood to marry; the simple, communal life of the Anabaptists; Catholic opposition to AIDS education that mentions condoms; the roadblocks for women in the black pulpit; the divisions among the branches of Judaism; the struggle over ordaining gays; and a host of breaking news stories, including the assassination of Rabbi Meir Kahane and the religious response to the war in the Persian Gulf.

But something far more important than a list of news articles has resulted from my Div School experience. Today, when I go on assignment to a church, synagogue, mosque or temple, I no longer go as a stranger, an outsider. The ideas preached and the rituals practiced are familiar, unthreatening and, ultimately, enriching to me. The amazing dialogue that began at Harvard between the Judaism within me and other faiths I encountered continues at St. Paul Community Baptist Church in a black section of Brooklyn, at St. Patrick's Cathedral on Fifth Avenue, at a Reform temple in Cincinnati, at a Zen retreat center in Los Angeles, at a Sunni mosque in Detroit.

Rabbi Siegel still catches up with me sometimes, waving his finger and warning of the dangers of interfaith encounters. But I have other visions as well. Sometimes, I see Bill Doe, my Catholic neighbor who inspired me to be my own rabbi. At other times, I see my Div School classmates, whose lives show me that deep and abiding spirituality can express itself through many paths. Or, in my mind's eye, I see Diana Eck, who taught me that one can take a look at a religion from within without being part of that faith.

I am sitting in a black Baptist church and feel swept away by the incredible combination of pain, joy and music ricocheting through the building. I am sitting in a Russian Orthodox church, surrounded by statues and icons, and feel a sense of mystery and transcendence. I am sitting among

Quakers at a Friends' meeting and feel a serenity I have never before known.

In each case I leave as a Jew, rooted in the richness of my own faith but nourished by the faith of others.

I also leave as a journalist, and not as a rabbi or a theologian. Journalism continues to be my craft, although the allure of ministry remains. Not long ago, I preached my first sermon; I was invited to speak at an interfaith Thanksgiving service in the Westchester town where I live. And on my desk at home I have catalogs and applications from several rabbinical seminaries. I leaf through them, I toy with the notion, but I hold back. Ultimately, I know that I still feel more comfortable writing than preaching, more comfortable observing than delving. And so, for now, a journalist I remain.

"Look," a mortarboarded classmate told me when he saw the disappointment in my eyes at not getting a degree during the Harvard graduation exercises. "Each one of us serves God in a different way. Perhaps your ministry is through journalism."

I've been thinking about that a lot lately. Maybe I did find God at Harvard.

# PHOTO ACKNOWLEDGMENTS